WJEC
CBAC

MATHEMATICS

Pure Mathematics
Unit P1

Dr H Thomas

AS/A LEVEL

WJEC AS/A Level Mathematics
Pure Mathematics Unit P1

Published by the Welsh Joint Education Committee
245 Western Avenue, Cardiff, CF5 2YX

First published 2001

Printed by Hackman Printers Ltd
Clydach Vale, Tonypandy, Rhondda, CF40 2XX

ISBN: 1 86085 460 5

PREFACE

This text is the first of three volumes which will cover between them most of the mathematical methods required for a modular A level course in mathematics. Specifically, the text is based on the P1 Syllabus of the Welsh Joint Education Committee which is being introduced in September 2000.

It is assumed that the reader will have successfully completed a GCSE course in mathematics and will have access to a calculator possessing mathematical functions.

The text concludes with six revision papers. It is believed that these tests should be completed in approximately one hour by students who are ready to sit their A level examinations.

Readers may wish to omit Sections 2.2, 2.5 as the material should have been covered in GCSE. The material covered in Section 3.2 may be omitted without causing difficulty in Chapter 3.

CONTENTS

Chapter 1

Indices, Surds and Polynomials

1.1 Indices

Let b represent any number. Consider the following examples.

Example 1.1

$$b^4 \times b^3 = (b \times b \times b \times b) \times (b \times b \times b)$$
$$= b \times b \times b \times b \times b \times b \times b$$
$$= b^7 = b^{4+3}.$$

> The factors can be associated by removal of brackets.

Example 1.2

$$b^8 \div b^3 = \frac{b^8}{b^3}$$
$$= \frac{b \times b \times b \times b \times b \times b \times b \times b}{b \times b \times b}$$
$$= b \times b \times b \times b \times b = b^5$$

so $$b^8 \div b^3 = b^{8-3}.$$

> 3 bs can be cancelled leaving 5 bs on top.

Example 1.3

$$b^3 \div b^5 = \frac{b^3}{b^5} = \frac{b \times b \times b}{b \times b \times b \times b \times b}$$
$$= \frac{1}{b \times b} = \frac{1}{b^2}.$$

If we say $\dfrac{1}{b^2}$ is b^{-2} then

$$b^3 \div b^5 = b^{3-5}.$$

Example 1.4

$$(b^2)^3 = (b^2) \times (b^2) \times (b^2)$$
$$= b^2 \times b^2 \times b^2$$
$$= b^{2+2+2} = b^6 = b^{3\times2}.$$

> b^2 factor 3 times

These exercises illustrate the following rules of indices when m and n are positive integers m and n :-

$$b^m \times b^n = b^{m+n}$$
$$b^m \div b^n = b^{m-n}$$
$$(b^m)^n = b^{mn}$$

Rules I

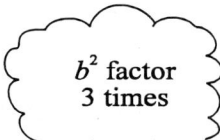

> m, n positive integers

We can use these laws even when letters and numbers are both involved.

Example 1.5

(a) $\quad 3a^2b^2 \times 4a^3b^6 \times 2a^4b^3 \; = \; 3 \times 4 \times 2 \times a^{2+3+4} \, b^{2+6+3}$
$$= \; 24a^9b^{11}.$$

(b) $\quad (3b^2a^3)^2 \times 6b^3a^2 \times 4b^2a = 3^{1\times2} \, b^{2\times2}a^{3\times2} \times 6b^3a^2 \times 4b^2a$
$$= \; 3^2 \times 6 \times 4 \times b^{4+3+2} \, a^{6+2+1}$$
$$= \; 216b^9a^9.$$

We can use the second of Rules I to give a meaning to b^0.

Example 1.6

$$\frac{b^6}{b^6} \; = \; b^{6-6} \; = \; b^0.$$

But $\qquad \dfrac{b^6}{b^6} \; = \; 1.$

> Anything divided by itself gives one, except 0/0

Thus $\qquad \boxed{b^0 \; = \; 1, \quad \text{whatever } b \text{ is.}} \qquad$ Rule II

Rules I can be extended to cases where the indices are rational numbers, both positive and negative.

Example 1.7

Let $\qquad\qquad b^x \; = \; \sqrt{b}$.

Then $\qquad b^x \times b^x \; = \; b.$

Assuming the first of rules I applies, we have

$$b^{2x} \; = \; b^1$$

so $\qquad\qquad 2x \; = \; 1 \text{ and } x \; = \; \tfrac{1}{2}.$

> A rational number is a number of the form p/q where p and q are integers.

Thus $\qquad \boxed{\sqrt{b} \; = \; b^{\frac{1}{2}}.} \qquad$ Rule III

Similarly for any <u>positive</u> integer n,

$$\boxed{\sqrt[n]{b} \; = \; b^{\frac{1}{n}}.} \qquad \text{Rule III'}$$

More generally, for any positive or negative integer m and any positive integer n, since

$$\underbrace{b^{\frac{m}{n}} \times b^{\frac{m}{n}} \times \ldots \times b^{\frac{m}{n}}}_{(n \text{ factors})} \; = \; b^{\frac{m}{n}+\frac{m}{n}+\cdots+\frac{m}{n}} \; = \; b^{\frac{m}{n}.n} \; = \; b^m,$$

we may write $\qquad \sqrt[n]{b^m} \; = \; b^{\frac{m}{n}}. \qquad \text{(i)}$

We can find an alternative form for $b^{\frac{m}{n}}$, because

$$\left(\sqrt[n]{b}\right)^m \; = \; (b^{\frac{1}{n}})^m \; = \; \underbrace{b^{\frac{1}{n}} \times b^{\frac{1}{n}} \times \ldots \times b^{\frac{1}{n}}}_{(m \text{ factors})}$$

$$= \; b^{\frac{1}{n}+\frac{1}{n}+\cdots+\frac{1}{n}}$$

$$= \; b^{\frac{m}{n}}.$$

> assuming Rule I applies

Thus $\qquad b^{\frac{m}{n}} \; = \; \left(\sqrt[n]{b}\right)^m. \qquad \text{(ii)}$

(i) and (ii) can be combined to give

$$b^{\frac{m}{n}} = \left(\sqrt[n]{b}\right)^m \quad \text{or} \quad \sqrt[n]{b^m} \qquad \text{Rule IV}$$

Negative indices can easily be interpreted as appropriate reciprocals.

Example 1.8

Assuming b^{-4} satisfies

$$b^{-4} \times b^4 = b^{-4+4} = b^0 = 1,$$

we are able to interpret b^{-4} as $\dfrac{1}{b^4}$.

Similarly, $\qquad b^{-\frac{1}{2}} = \dfrac{1}{b^{\frac{1}{2}}} = \dfrac{1}{\sqrt{b}}$.

More generally for any rational numbers $\dfrac{k}{l}$,

$$b^{-\frac{k}{l}} = \frac{1}{b^{\frac{k}{l}}} \qquad \text{Rule V}$$

The rules may be summarised as follows.

Rules I'
$$\begin{aligned} b^k \times b^l &= b^{k+l} \\ b^k \div b^l &= b^{k-l} \\ (b^k)^l &= b^{kl} \end{aligned}$$

k and *l* integers or rational, both positive and negative

with Rule II

Rule III

Rule IV

Rule V

$$b^0 = 1$$
$$\sqrt[n]{b} = b^{\frac{1}{n}}$$
$$\begin{cases} b^{\frac{m}{n}} = \sqrt[n]{b^m} \\ b^{\frac{m}{n}} = \left(\sqrt[n]{b}\right)^m \end{cases}$$
$$b^{-\frac{k}{l}} = \frac{1}{b^{\frac{k}{l}}}$$

m positive or negative integer, *n* positive integer

Exercises 1.1

1. Write with positive indices :-

(i) a^{-2} (ii) $x^{-\frac{1}{2}}$ (iii) $(b^{-3})^2$ (iv) $\left(\dfrac{1}{a}\right)^{-1}$ (v) $\left(\dfrac{1}{b}\right)^{-2}$.

2. Simplify (i) $a^3 \div a^2$ (ii) $b^6 \div b^{-2}$ (iii) $x^3 \div (-x)^4$ (iv) $(16a^4b^6)^{\frac{1}{2}}$

(v) $(4x^2y^5)^{\frac{3}{2}} \div 16xy^{\frac{1}{2}}$ (vi) $(64)^{\frac{1}{3}}$ (vii) $(8)^{-\frac{1}{3}}$ (viii) $\left(\dfrac{27}{125}\right)^{\frac{2}{3}}$ (ix) $\left(\dfrac{36}{64}\right)^{-\frac{3}{2}}$.

3. Write down in their simplest forms :-
   (i) the positive square root of $49a^2b^6$ (ii) the cube root of $64x^9y^6$.

4. If $x = 64^{\frac{3}{2}}$ and $y = 4^{-4}$ find, without using a calculator, the value of xy^2.

It is often necessary to use the rules to simplify more complicated expressions.

Example 1.9

Simplify $\dfrac{(x+2)^{\frac{1}{2}} - 2(x+2)^{-\frac{1}{2}}}{(x+2)^{\frac{1}{2}}}$.

Now $\dfrac{(x+2)^{\frac{1}{2}} - 2(x+2)^{-\frac{1}{2}}}{(x+2)^{\frac{1}{2}}} \times \dfrac{(x+2)^{\frac{1}{2}}}{(x+2)^{\frac{1}{2}}}$

Multiplying by $\dfrac{(x+2)^{1/2}}{(x+2)^{1/2}} = 1$ doesn't change the value of the expression but removes the negative index.

$= \dfrac{(x+2)^{\frac{1}{2}+\frac{1}{2}} - 2(x+2)^{-\frac{1}{2}+\frac{1}{2}}}{(x+2)^{\frac{1}{2}+\frac{1}{2}}}$

$= \dfrac{(x+2)^1 - 2(x+2)^0}{(x+2)^1}$

$= \dfrac{x+2-2}{x+2} = \dfrac{x}{x+2}$.

Exercises 1.2
Simplify the following :-

(i) $\dfrac{(x^2+1)^{\frac{1}{2}} - x^2(x^2+1)^{-\frac{1}{2}}}{x^2+1}$ (ii) $\dfrac{3(a+1)^{\frac{1}{3}} - a(a+1)^{-\frac{2}{3}}}{(a+1)^{\frac{1}{3}}}$

(iii) $\dfrac{b^{-\frac{1}{2}}(b^2+2)^{\frac{1}{2}} - b^{\frac{1}{2}}(b^2+2)^{-\frac{1}{2}}}{b^{\frac{1}{2}}(b^2+2)^{\frac{3}{2}}}$ (iv) $\dfrac{(x+y)^{\frac{1}{2}} - (x-y)^{-\frac{1}{2}}}{x^2-y^2-1}$

(v) $\dfrac{x^{\frac{1}{2}}x^{-\frac{3}{4}}}{x^{\frac{3}{4}}}$ (vi) $\dfrac{(2x^2+3)^{\frac{4}{5}} - 2x^2(2x^2+3)^{-\frac{1}{5}}}{(2x^2+3)^{\frac{4}{5}}}$.

1.2 Surds

We introduce surds by means of some exercises.

Exercises 1.3
Find the following square roots, using the $\sqrt{\ }$ key on your calculator where necessary.
(a) $\sqrt{4}$,   (b) $\sqrt{36}$,   (c) $\sqrt{12.25}$,   (d) $\sqrt{3}$,   (e) $\sqrt{13}$.

There is a difference between exercises (a), (b), (c) and exercises (d), (e).

The first cases have exact answers :- 2, 6, 3.5; whilst cases (d), (e) do not have exact answers : 1.732050808 . . . and 3.605551275 . . .
The calculator has given the answers to (d), (e) to 10 figures but these answers are not exact. Numbers such as $\sqrt{3}$, $\sqrt{13}$, which cannot be calculated exactly, are said to be surds. Surds often occur in calculations and some facility in their manipulation is often helpful.

Example 1.10
(a) Express $\sqrt{54}$ as the simplest possible surd.
$$\sqrt{54} = \sqrt{9 \times 6} = \sqrt{9} \times \sqrt{6} = 3\sqrt{6}.$$
(b) Express as the square root of a single number:
  (i) $4\sqrt{5}$ (ii) $3\sqrt{3}$ (iii) $6\sqrt{2}$

(i) $4\sqrt{5} = \sqrt{16} \times \sqrt{5} = \sqrt{16 \times 5} = \sqrt{80}.$

(ii) $3\sqrt{3} = \sqrt{9} \times \sqrt{3} = \sqrt{9 \times 3} = \sqrt{27}.$

(iii) $6\sqrt{2} = \sqrt{36} \times \sqrt{2} = \sqrt{72}.$

(c) Expand and simplify $\left(2\sqrt{3} + \sqrt{6}\right)\left(\sqrt{3} - \sqrt{6}\right)$.
$$\left(2\sqrt{3} + \sqrt{6}\right)\left(\sqrt{3} - \sqrt{6}\right) = 2 \times 3 - 2\sqrt{3} \times \sqrt{6} + \sqrt{6} \times \sqrt{3} - 6$$
$$= 6 - 2\sqrt{18} + \sqrt{18} - 6$$
$$= -\sqrt{18} = -3\sqrt{2}.$$

Note that
$\sqrt{3} \times \sqrt{3} = 3$

(d) Simplify the following by removing all surds from the denominator:
$$\frac{5 - \sqrt{3}}{9 + 2\sqrt{3}}.$$

$$\frac{5 - \sqrt{3}}{9 + 2\sqrt{3}} = \frac{(5 - \sqrt{3})(9 - 2\sqrt{3})}{(9 + 2\sqrt{3})(9 - 2\sqrt{3})}$$
$$= \frac{45 - 10\sqrt{3} - 9\sqrt{3} + 6}{81 - 18\sqrt{3} + 18\sqrt{3} - 12}$$
$$= \frac{51 - 19\sqrt{3}}{69} = \frac{17}{23} - \frac{19\sqrt{3}}{69}.$$

Again multiplication by 1 doesn't affect the value of the expression

More generally, we can remove $\sqrt{a} + \sqrt{b}$ from any denominator by multiplying the original expression by
$$\frac{\sqrt{a} - \sqrt{b}}{\sqrt{a} - \sqrt{b}}.$$

Removal of a surd from a denominator is known as **rationalising.**

Example 1.11

Rationalise (i) $\dfrac{3}{\sqrt{5}-\sqrt{2}}$ (ii) $\dfrac{5}{\sqrt{8}}$

(i) $\dfrac{3}{\sqrt{5}-\sqrt{2}} = \dfrac{3(\sqrt{5}+\sqrt{2})}{(\sqrt{5}-\sqrt{2})(\sqrt{5}+\sqrt{2})} = \dfrac{3(\sqrt{5}+\sqrt{2})}{5+\sqrt{10}-\sqrt{10}-2}$

$\qquad = \dfrac{3(\sqrt{5}+\sqrt{2})}{3} = \sqrt{5}+\sqrt{2}$.

(ii) $\qquad \dfrac{5}{\sqrt{8}} = \dfrac{5}{\sqrt{8}}\dfrac{\sqrt{8}}{\sqrt{8}} = \dfrac{5\sqrt{8}}{8}$.

Exercises 1.4

1. Express in terms of the simplest possible surds :-

(i) $\sqrt{20}$ (ii) $\sqrt{18}$ (iii) $\sqrt{72}$ (iv) $\sqrt{180}$ (v) $\sqrt{250}$.

2. Simplify

(i) $\sqrt{3}(2-\sqrt{3})$ (ii) $\sqrt{2}(5-2\sqrt{2})$ (iii) $(\sqrt{3}-\sqrt{2})(\sqrt{3}+\sqrt{2})$

(iv) $(2\sqrt{3}+2)(3\sqrt{3}-2)$ (v) $(3\sqrt{6}-2)^2$ (iv) $(\sqrt{x}-x)(\sqrt{x}+x)$.

3. Simplify the following by rationalising the denominator :-

(i) $\dfrac{1}{\sqrt{5}}$ (ii) $\dfrac{1}{\sqrt{18}}$ (iii) $\dfrac{3}{\sqrt{54}}$ (iv) $\dfrac{1}{\sqrt{3}+1}$ (v) $\dfrac{1}{\sqrt{2}-1}$

(vi) $\dfrac{5}{\sqrt{5}-2}$ (vii) $\dfrac{1}{\sqrt{5}-\sqrt{3}}$ (viii) $\dfrac{1}{\sqrt{3}+1}+\dfrac{1}{\sqrt{3}-1}$.

1.3 Polynomial functions

Given expressions like (i) x^2+2x-3, (ii) $\sqrt{x^2+2}$, (iii) $\dfrac{1}{x+3}$, we can find values of these expressions if we replace x by a number.

Example 1.12

Find the values in (i), (ii) and (iii) when $x = -1$:-

(i) $(-1)^2+2(-1)-3 = 1-2-3 = -4.$

(ii) $\qquad \sqrt{(-1)^2+2} = \sqrt{1+2} = \sqrt{3}$

$\qquad$ or 1.7321 to 4 dec. places.

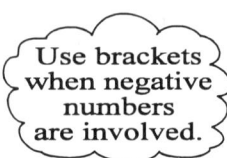

Use brackets when negative numbers are involved.

(iii) $\qquad \dfrac{1}{(-1)+3} = \dfrac{1}{-1+3} = \dfrac{1}{2} = 0.5.$

Expressions such as these which take values in response to the allocation of values to x are called **functions**. Later we shall meet many more examples of functions. However, at present we confine our discussion to functions such as x^2+2x-3.

We write $f(x) = x^2+2x-3$.

Then the result of example (i) above can be summarised as $f(-1) = -4$.

Again, $f(2) = 2^2+2(2)-3 = 4+4-3 = 5.$

The particular functions to be considered here contain terms that involve positive powers of x and / or numbers. These functions are known as **polynomials**. The highest positive power of x defines the degree of the polynomial.

Example 1.13

$x^3 - 3x^2 + 4$, $x^7 - 6x + 4$, and x^5 are polynomials of degrees 3, 7, 5 respectively,

but $\sqrt{x + 2}$, $\dfrac{1}{2x^2 + 4x + 5}$, $x^2 + \dfrac{1}{x} - 3$

and 4 are not polynomials.

> Some workers consider $4 = 4x^0$ to be a polynomial, but we require positive powers here.

1.4 Addition and subtraction of polynomials

When polynomials containing the same letter are added (subtracted) the result is obtained by adding (subtracting) corresponding terms. The answer is often a polynomial but not always so (it could be a pure number).

Example 1.14

Add $f(x) = x^4 + 3x^3 + 2x^2 + 9x - 7$

and $g(x) = x^3 - 7x^2 - 9x + 2.$

$$f(x) + g(x) = x^4 + (3+1)x^3 + (-7+2)x^2 + (9-9)x - 7 + 2$$
$$= x^4 + 4x^3 - 5x^2 - 5,$$

a polynomial of degree 4.

Example 1.15

Subtract $f(x) = x^3 + 3x^2 - 7x + 9$

from $g(x) = x^3 + 3x^2 - 7x + 4.$

$$g(x) - f(x) = x^3 + 3x^2 - 7x + 4$$
$$- (x^3 + 3x^2 - 7x + 9)$$
$$= (1-1)x^3 + (3-3)x^2 + (-7+7)x + 4 - 9$$
$$= -5 \text{ , which is not a polynomial.}$$

> Useful to use brackets when subtracting.

1.5 Multiplication of polynomials

Two polynomials can be multiplied together by multiplying every term in the first with every term in the second.

Example 1.16

Multiply $3x^2 - 2x + 5$ and $2x^3 - 6x^2 + 4x - 9$.

It is convenient to introduce brackets when multiplying polynomials.

$$(3x^2 - 2x + 5)(2x^3 - 6x^2 + 4x - 9)$$
$$= 6x^5 - 18x^4 + 12x^3 - 27x^2 - 4x^4 + 12x^3$$
$$- 8x^2 + 18x + 10x^3 - 30x^2 + 20x - 45$$
$$= 6x^5 - 22x^4 + 34x^3 - 65x^2 + 38x - 45.$$

> Multiply terms in second bracket by (i) $3x^2$ (ii) $-2x$ (iii) 5.

Example 1.17

Multiply $2x + 1$, $3x + 2$, $x - 3$.

$$(2x + 1)(3x + 2)(x - 3) = (6x^2 + 4x + 3x + 2)(x - 3)$$
$$= (6x^2 + 7x + 2)(x - 3)$$
$$= 6x^3 - 18x^2 + 7x^2 - 21x + 2x - 6$$
$$= 6x^3 - 11x^2 - 19x - 6.$$

> Multiply the first two first.

Exercises 1.5

Multiply out the following :-

(i) $(x + 4)(x - 4)$ (ii) $(2x + 1)(x + 2)$ (iii) $(x + 1)(x + 2)(2x - 3)$

(iv) $(x^2 + 4x + 9)(x^2 - 3x - 2)$ (v) $(3x - 4y)(3x + 5y)$

(vi) $(x + 2)^2$ (vii) $(3x - 2)^2$ (viii) $(x + 3)^3$ (ix) $(x - 1)^2(x + 2)$.

1.6   Factors

Previously we combined a number of polynomials by multiplication to obtain a resulting polynomial. The problem to be considered now is the converse : which polynomials must be multiplied together to obtain a given polynomial? The answer, of course, may not be unique.

Example 1.18

$$6x^3 - 11x^2 - 19x - 6$$

can be written as $(2x + 1)(3x^2 - 7x - 6)$

or $(2x + 1)(3x + 2)(x - 3)$ amongst others, for instance.

The decomposition of a polynomial into polynomials of lower degree is called **factorisation**; and the component polynomials are called **factors**.

We restrict our consideration to factorising first degree (linear) and second degree (quadratic) polynomials. **Second degree (quadratic) polynomials are sometimes called quadratic functions.**

Example 1.19

Factorise $3x - 9$.

In this case 3 is a common factor of the two terms and so

$$3x - 9 = 3(x - 3).$$

Example 1.20

Factorise $4x^2 - 16x$.

Here both terms have a common factor $4x$.

Then $4x^2 - 16x = 4x(x - 4)$.

> Take **all** common factors into account.

In the last two examples, the factorisation was achieved by observing that the two terms possessed common factors. When the quadratic expression contains 3 terms, factorisation using common factors is not possible.

Example 1.21

Factorise $x^2 + 8x + 12$.

In this case no factors exist which are common to all terms. If the factors are $x + a$, $x + b$, the product is

$$(x + a)(x + b) = x^2 + (a + b)x + ab.$$

The product is $x^2 + 8x + 12$

if
$$a + b = 8,$$
$$ab = 12.$$

We require two numbers a, b whose product (ab) is 12 and sum ($a + b$) is 8.
It is easy to see that the numbers are 2 and 6 so

$$x^2 + 8x + 12 = (x + 2)(x + 6).$$

Example 1.22

Factorise $x^2 - 8x - 48$.

Here $ab = -48$ and $a + b = -8$.

We require two factors of -48 which when added give -8.
Since the product of the two numbers is negative we require
one positive and one negative factor of -48.

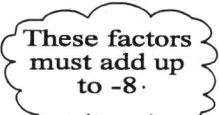
These factors must add up to -8.

Write out the factors of -48.

	1	−1	2	−2	3	−3	4	−4
	−48	48	−24	24	−16	16	−12	12
Add	−47	47	−22	22	−13	13	−8	8

The factors 4 and -12 will do the trick.
So $\quad x^2 - 8x - 48 = (x + 4)(x - 12)$.

The procedure can be streamlined.

Example 1.23

Factorise $x^2 - 19x + 48$.

We require two factors of $+48$ which add up to -19. Both factors are negative.
As before, we write down factors of $+48$.

	−1	−2	−3
	−48	−24	−16
Add	−49	−26	−19
			Stop here

Then $\quad x^2 - 19x + 48 = (x - 3)(x - 16)$.

The procedure is more complicated when the coefficient of x^2 in the quadratic is not equal to 1.

Example 1.24

Factorise $6x^2 + 7x + 2$.

Now if $6x^2 + 7x + 2 = (ax + b)(cx + d)$

then $6x^2 + 7x + 2 \equiv acx^2 + (ad + bc)x + bd$.

To match the two expressions, we then require

$$ac = 6, \quad bd = 2 \text{ and } ad + bc = 7.$$

We note that $12 = 6 \times 2$.

$$\left(\begin{array}{c}\text{coefficient}\\ \text{of } x^2\end{array}\right)\left(\begin{array}{c}\text{constant}\\ \text{term}\end{array}\right)$$

> *a, b, c, d* to be found

> *abcd* = 12

Now ad, bc are factors of $abcd$ (12) and they add up to 7.

Initially, we attempt to find two factors of 12 which add up to 7, in other words to find ad and bc. It is easy to see that the factors are $+3$ and $+4$.

Then $6x^2 + 7x + 2 = 6x^2 + 3x + 4x + 2$

$$= 3x(2x + 1) + 2(2x + 1)$$

$$\underbrace{\qquad\qquad}_{\text{common factor}}$$

$$= (3x + 2)(2x + 1)$$

> Split the $7x$ into $3x + 4x$

Summarising, we see that the procedure is essentially as follows :-

Procedure

To factorise a quadratic in x :-

(i) Multiply coefficient of x^2 (6) by constant term (2).

(ii) Find two factors of the result of (i) which add to the coefficient of the term in x ($3 + 4 = 7$).

(iii) Split the term in x into two terms giving four terms in all.

(iv) Factorise the four terms initally in pairs, then group factors.

> The quadratic may involve another letter, of course

Example 1.25

Factorise $5y^2 - 8y - 4$.

The expression is a quadratic in y.

Now $5 \times -4 = -20$.

$$\left(\begin{array}{c}\text{coefficient}\\ \text{of } y^2\end{array}\right)\left(\begin{array}{c}\text{constant}\\ \text{term}\end{array}\right)$$

> Step (i)

We require two factors of -20 which add to -8. One factor is positive, the other negative.

Factors of -20 are

	1	-1	2	
	-20	20	-10	
Add	-19	19	-8	etc

> Step (ii)

$\therefore$ Factors are 2 and -10.

Then $5y^2 - 8y - 4 = 5y^2 + 2y - 10y - 4$

$$= y(5y + 2) - 2(5y + 2)$$

$$= (y - 2)(5y + 2).$$

> Step (iii)

> Step (iv)

Example 1.26

Factorise $6x^2 - 16x + 10$.

Now $6 \times 10 = 60$ and we require two factors of 60 which add to -16. Both factors of 60 are therefore negative. Factors are :-

$$
\begin{array}{cccccc}
-1 & -2 & -3 & -4 & -5 & -6 \\
-60 & -30 & -20 & -15 & -12 & -10 \\
\hline
\text{Add} \quad -61 & -32 & -23 & -19 & -17 & -16
\end{array}
$$

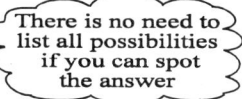

There is no need to list all possibilities if you can spot the answer

Then
$$
\begin{aligned}
6x^2 - 16x + 10 &= 6x^2 - 6x - 10x + 10 \\
&= 6x(x - 1) - 10(x - 1) \\
&= (6x - 10)(x - 1) \text{ or } 2(3x - 5)(x - 1).
\end{aligned}
$$

The essence of the method used in examples 1.25 – 1.26 is that the middle term may be split into two terms. It should be noted that the order of splitting is not important. Thus, referring to example 1.25 for instance, we may write alternatively
$$
\begin{aligned}
5y^2 - 8y - 4 &= 5y^2 - 10y + 2y - 4 \\
&= 5y(y - 2) + 2(y - 2) = (5y + 2)(y - 2)
\end{aligned}
$$
which is the answer given previously with the factors reversed.

Exercises 1.6

1. Factorise (i) $x^2 + 5x + 4$ (ii) $x^2 - 5x + 4$ (iii) $x^2 - 3x - 4$
   (iv) $x^2 + 23x + 90$ (v) $x^2 - 23x + 90$ (vi) $x^2 + 13x - 90$ (vii) $l^2 + l - 6$
   (viii) $l^2 - l - 6$ (ix) $p^2 + 2p - 63$ (x) $x^2 - 3x - 28$.

2. Factorise (i) $2x^2 + 3x + 1$ (ii) $3t^2 + 7t + 4$ (iii) $4x^2 - 15x - 4$
   (iv) $4x^2 - 7x - 2$ (v) $4x^2 - 15x - 25$ (vi) $6x^2 - x - 2$ (vii) $3y^2 - 5y - 2$
   (viii) $8y^2 - 30y + 7$ (ix) $10x^2 - 9x - 9$ (x) $7x^2 + 17x - 12$.

Chapter 2

Solution of Equations

A good deal of mathematical activity is concerned with the solution of equations.

2.1 Equations and identities

From our knowledge of multiplication of brackets it is easy to see that
$$(x + 3)(x + 5) = x^2 + 8x + 15.$$
The result is true for all values of x.
To underline this, we write
$$(x + 3)(x + 5) \equiv x^2 + 8x + 15,$$
the additional line in $\equiv$ indicating the given relationship is an identity.
Other identities are
$$3(x + 5) \equiv 3x^2 + 15$$
and $\qquad x(x - 3) \equiv x^2 - 3x.$

Definition

An **identity** is a relationship involving a letter which is valid whatever number is substituted for the letter.
The relationship $x^2 + 8x + 15 = 2x + 7$ is not an identity : it is only valid if certain values are susbstituted for x. Thus if $x = -2$, both sides are equal to 3 and if $x = -4$, both sides are equal to -1. In other words, the relationship is valid when $x = -2$ or -4.
However, if $x = 1$, the left hand side has value 24 and the right hand side has value 9. Thus the relationship doesn't hold when $x = 1$ and so cannot be an identity. (Remember an identity holds for <u>all</u> values of x).
Again the relationship
$$x + 9 = 2x + 5$$
is only valid when $x = 4$, both sides then having value 13.
These last relationships are examples of **equations**.

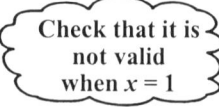

Check that it is
not valid
when $x = 1$

Definition

An **equation** is a relationship involving letter(s) which is valid only when certain values are assigned to the letter(s).

Exercises 2.1

Classify the following as identities or equations.

(i) $(x + 3)(x^2 + 3x + 4) = x^3 + 6x^2 + 13x + 12$

(ii) $2x - 7 = x + 3$

(iii) $x^2 = -3x - 2$

(iv) $3x(x + 6) = 3x^2 + 18x$

(v) $(x + y)^2 = x^2 + 2xy + y^2$

(vi) $3x + 2(4y + 5x) = 3(2x + 10y)$

(vii) $(x + 1)^2 = x^2 + 3x + 2$

(viii) $(x - 1)(x + 1) = x^2 - 1.$

Our interest in this chapter relates to equations.
If a number x is such that
$$6x = 54$$
it is not difficult to see that the equation is valid when $x = 9$, and is not valid for any other value of x. We say that the equation is satisfied by $x = 9$ or that the solution of the equation is $x = 9$. When we decide that $x = 9$ satisfies the equation i.e. we have found the value of x, we say we have solved the equation.

Definition

Finding the value(s) to be assigned to the letter(s) so that a relationship is valid is known as solving the equation.

We shall solve some different types of equations in this chapter. It is useful before doing so to state some of the algebraic rules which may assist us.

Manipulation Rules for use with equations

In the following, a, b, c, d are real numbers.

(i) If $ba = bc$ then $a = c$, i.e. both sides may be divided by the same number; similarly for multiplication.

> $2a = 6$
> $a = 6/2 = 3$
> $c/3 = 4$ so
> $c = 4 \times 3 = 12$

(ii) If $a + c = a + d$ then $c = d$
i.e. the same number may be subtracted from both sides.
A similar rule applies for addition.

> $a + 3 = 6$
> $a = 6 - 3 = 3$
> $b - 4 = 5$
> $b = 5 + 4 = 9$

(iii) If $ab = 0$ then either $a = 0$ or $b = 0$ or both are zero.

> However, if $ab = 6$, it does not follow that $a = 6$ or $b = 6$.

(iv) $a(b + c) = ab + ac$ and $-d(a - b) = -da + db.$

2.2 Linear equations

The simplest type of equation is the **linear** equation where letters occur singly and to the first power. We illustrate the method of solution by two examples.

Example 2.1

Solve $2(x - 1) = 6(x - 5) - 2(x - 3)$

Remove brackets and note any changes of sign (Rule iv)

$$2x - 2 = 6x - 30 - 2x + 6$$

so $2x - 2 = 4x - 24.$

Collect all terms involving x to one side, all other terms to the other side. Rule (ii) enables us to do this by adding $- 2x$ and $+24$ to both sides :

$\therefore \quad - 2 + 24 = 4x - 2x.$

$\therefore \qquad 22 = 2x.$

$\therefore \qquad x = \dfrac{22}{2} = 11 \quad$ rule (i).

Example 2.2

At a club dinner there were 10 more members than non-members. The members paid £7.00, the non-members paid £5.00 and the total receipts were £310. How many members and non-members were at the dinner?

Let the number of members be x so that the number of non-members is $x - 10$. Then the members pay £$7x$ and the non-members pay £$5(x - 10)$, and the total amount is £310.

Then $7x + 5(x - 10) = 310.$

$\therefore \quad 7x + 5x - 50 = 310 \qquad$ (Rule (iv))

$\qquad 12x - 50 = 310.$

$\qquad 12x = 310 + 50 = 360 \quad$ (Rule (ii), add 50 to both sides)

$\therefore \qquad x = \dfrac{360}{12} = 30. \qquad$ (Rule (i))

$\therefore$ Number of members is 30, number of non-members is 20.

(check $7 \times 30 + 5 \times 20 = 310$).

Exercises 2.2

1 Solve the following equations :-

(i) $4(2y - 5) = 3(2y + 8)$

(ii) $\dfrac{2a - 5}{3} - \dfrac{3a - 1}{4} = \dfrac{3}{2}$

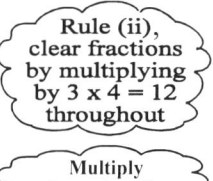
Rule (ii), clear fractions by multiplying by 3 x 4 = 12 throughout

(iii) $\dfrac{x}{7} + \dfrac{(1 - x)}{5} = x - 22.$

Multiply throughout by 7 x 5 = 35

2. The perimeter of a rectangular field is 500 m. If one of the adjacent sides is 20m longer than the other, find the area of the field.

3. At present, I am three times as old as my son. Five years ago I was four times as old as my son. How old is my son now?

4. A bookseller buys 120 copies of a certain paperback. He sells some at the published price of £5.50 and the remainder in the sales season at £2.50 each. If the total receipts for the paperbacks are £510, find the number of paper backs at each price.

5. A man walks from one village to another at an average speed of 4 km an hour. On the return journey he walks at an average speed of 5 km an hour. The time taken for the double journey was 2 hours 15 mins. Find the distance between the villages.

6. The weekly wage of two people working in a factory are £180 and £244 respectively. It was agreed to increase the two wages by the same amount so that the higher wage was 4/3 of the lower wage. What was the increase given?

7. A bus carries 28 passengers, some with 80 p tickets and the remainder with 95 p tickets. If the total receipts are £25.85, find the number of 95 p tickets.

2.3   Quadratic equations

An equation of the form
$$ax^2 + bx + c = 0, \ (a \neq 0)$$
where a, b and c are real numbers is called a **quadratic** equation.

Thus $2x^2 + 3x + 5 = 0$ and $4x^2 - 9x + 7 = 0$ are quadratic equations but $2x + 9 = 0$ is not (the latter is a linear equation, of course).

Being equations, quadratic equations are only valid if particular numerical values are assigned to x. In fact, quadratic equations hold for at most two values of x.

Before working through some examples, we note rule (iii) given earlier in a different notation :-

If $\alpha\beta = 0$ then either $\alpha = 0$ or $\beta = 0$ or both α and β equal zero.

Example 2.3

Solve $2x^2 - 11x + 12 = 0$.

The left hand side factorises into
$$(2x - 3)(x - 4) = 0 \quad \text{(check)}.$$
Then from rule (iii), $2x - 3 = 0$ or $x - 4 = 0$.

(Note that both brackets cannot be equal to zero simultaneously).

> If $\alpha\beta = 0$ then $\alpha = 0$ or $\beta = 0$

Then $2x = 3$ so $x = \dfrac{3}{2}$,

or $x - 4 = 0$ so $x = 4$.

$\therefore$ Solution is $x = \dfrac{3}{2}$ or 4.

15

Example 2.4

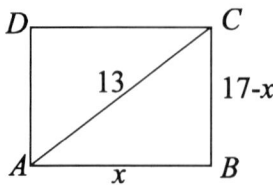

A consequence of Pythagoras' Theorem is that the square on the diagonal of a rectangle is equal to the sum of the squares on two adjacent sides. The diagonal of a particular rectangle is 13 cm and the sum of the lengths of two adjacent sides is 17 cm. Find the possible values of x, the length of AB in cm, as shown in the diagram.

Then by Pythagoras' Theorem,

$$x^2 + (17 - x)^2 = 13^2.$$

$$\therefore \quad x^2 + (17 - x)(17 - x) = 169$$

so $\quad x^2 + 289 - 34x + x^2 = 169.$

Grouping terms, we obtain by means of rule (i)

$$2x^2 - 34x + 120 = 0$$

or $\quad x^2 - 17x + 60 = 0.$

> Remember to divide <u>throughout</u> by a number.

After factorisation, this becomes

$$(x - 5)(x - 12) = 0 \quad \text{(check)}.$$

$$\therefore \quad x - 5 = 0 \text{ or } x - 12 = 0$$

so $\quad x = 5 \text{ or } x = 12.$

> $\alpha\beta = 0$ gives
> $\alpha = 0$ or $\beta = 0$

When the quadratic doesn't factorise, we first **complete the square** to solve the equation.

Example 2.5

Solve the equation $x^2 + 3x + 1 = 0$.

The expression doesn't factorise. However we note that

$$x^2 + 3x + 1 = \left(x + \frac{3}{2}\right)^2 + 1 - \left(\frac{3}{2}\right)^2$$

$$= \left(x + \frac{3}{2}\right)^2 - \frac{5}{4},$$

as can easily be verified by multiplying out the bracket. This particular method of rewriting is called **completing the square**. Then the equation becomes

$$\left(x + \frac{3}{2}\right)^2 - \frac{5}{4} = 0,$$

$$\therefore \quad \left(x + \frac{3}{2}\right)^2 = \frac{5}{4}$$

> Remember any positive number has two square roots, + and −.

so that $\quad x + \frac{3}{2} = \pm\sqrt{\frac{5}{4}},$

$$x = -\frac{3}{2} \pm \sqrt{\frac{5}{4}}.$$

$$\therefore \quad x = -\frac{3}{2} + \sqrt{\frac{5}{4}} \text{ or } -\frac{3}{2} - \sqrt{\frac{5}{4}} \text{ in surd form,}$$

or $\quad x = -0.382 \text{ or } -2.618,$ correct to 3 decimal places.

We explore completion of the square in more detail. Now

$$ax^2 + bx + c = a\left(x^2 + \frac{b}{a}x + \frac{c}{a}\right)$$

$$= a\left[\left(x + \frac{b}{2a}\right)^2 + \frac{c}{a} - \frac{b^2}{4a^2}\right].$$

Note that $\frac{b}{2a}$ in the bracket $\left(x + \frac{b}{2a}\right)^2$ is one half the coefficient of x in the bracket,

and $\frac{b^2}{4a^2}$ must be subtracted because $\left(x + \frac{b}{2a}\right)^2$ introduces a term $\frac{b^2}{4a^2}$ on expansion,

which must be cancelled out.

Example 2.6

Solve the quadratic equation
$$ax^2 + bx + c = 0,$$
giving the answer in terms of a, b and c.

$$ax^2 + bx + c = 0$$

or $$x^2 + \frac{b}{a}x + \frac{c}{a} = 0.$$

> You may divide by the number a since $a \neq 0$.

Complete the square to obtain

$$\left(x + \frac{b}{2a}\right)^2 + \frac{c}{a} - \frac{b^2}{4a^2} = 0.$$

$$\therefore \left(x + \frac{b}{2a}\right)^2 = \frac{b^2}{4a^2} - \frac{c}{a} = \frac{b^2 - 4ac}{4a^2}.$$

$$\therefore x + \frac{b}{2a} = \pm\sqrt{\frac{b^2 - 4ac}{4a^2}} = \frac{\pm\sqrt{b^2 - 4ac}}{2a}.$$

$$\therefore x = -\frac{b}{2a} \pm \frac{\sqrt{b^2 - 4ac}}{2a}$$

so the two solutions are

$$x = \frac{-b \pm \sqrt{b^2 - 4ac}}{2a}.$$

Summary

The two solutions of
$$ax^2 + bx + c = 0 \quad (a \neq 0)$$
are given by $x = \dfrac{-b \pm \sqrt{b^2 - 4ac}}{2a}.$

This result is known as the quadratic formula and may be used directly to solve quadratic equations.

The solutions of an equation are called the <u>roots</u> of the equation.

Example 2.7

Solve the following quadratic equations by using the formula.

(i) $x^2 + 3x - 2 = 0$

(ii) $x^2 + 4.5x + 5.0625 = 0$

(iii) $2x^2 + 3x + 2 = 0.$

(i) $x^2 + 3x - 2 = 0$

$$x = \frac{-3 \pm \sqrt{3^2 - 4(1)(-2)}}{2}$$

$$= \frac{-3 \pm \sqrt{9+8}}{2} = \frac{-3 \pm \sqrt{17}}{2}$$

$$\left(x = \frac{-b \pm \sqrt{b^2 - 4ac}}{2a} \right.$$
$$\left. a=1,\ b=3,\ c=-2 \right)$$

so the two roots are

$$x = \frac{-3 + \sqrt{17}}{2} \quad \text{and} \quad \frac{-3 - \sqrt{17}}{2} \quad \text{in surd form.}$$

'roots' means 'solutions'

(ii) $x^2 + 4.5x + 5.0625 = 0.$

$a = 1,\ b = 4.5$
$c = 5.0625$

$$x = \frac{-4.5 \pm \sqrt{4.5^2 - 4(1)(5.0625)}}{2}$$

$$= \frac{-4.5 \pm \sqrt{0}}{2} = -2.25 \quad \text{(twice)}.$$

The two roots are equal.

(iii) $2x^2 + 3x + 2 = 0.$

$$x = \frac{-3 \pm \sqrt{3^2 - 4(2)(2)}}{4} \qquad (a = 2, b = 3, c = 2)$$

so $x = \dfrac{-3 \pm \sqrt{-7}}{4}.$

No answers exist in our usual ('real') number system because we can't find $\sqrt{-7}$ in that number system. In fact, we can't find the square root of any – number in that system. To convince yourself, try to find $\sqrt{-7}$ on your calculator.

Square any real number, + or -, and the result is +.

Cases (i), (ii), (iii) indicate there are at least three possibilities (in fact, there are only three) when we attempt to solve quadratic equations, namely

(i) two different real answers exist, $\dfrac{-3 \pm \sqrt{17}}{2}.$

(ii) one real answer exists, i.e. the two answers coincide (-2.25).

(iii) real answers do not exist, $\dfrac{-3 \pm \sqrt{-7}}{4}.$

A look back shows that the various cases arise when

(i) the number under the square root is +,

(ii) the number under the square root is 0,

(iii) the number under the square root is –.

Nature of the roots of a quadratic equation

For the general quadratic equation
$$ax^2 + bx + c = 0$$
we have $\quad x = \dfrac{-b \pm \sqrt{b^2 - 4ac}}{2a} \quad$ and

either (i) real unequal roots $(b^2 - 4ac > 0)$
or   (ii) equal roots $(b^2 - 4ac = 0)$
or   (iii) no real roots $(b^2 - 4ac < 0)$

exist according as $\sqrt{b^2 - 4ac}$ is greater than, equal to, or less than 0.

The quantity $b^2 - 4ac$ is known as the <u>discriminant</u> of the quadratic function given by $f(x) = ax^2 + bx + c$.

Example 2.8

Show that if $4x^2 + (k + 3)x + 5 = 0$ has two unequal roots, then $k^2 + 6k - 71$ is positive.

In this case $a = 4$, $b = k + 3$, $c = 5$.
Then case (i) applies if $(k + 3)^2 - 4(4)(5)$ is positive   discriminant > 0
or $(k + 3)^2 - 80$ is positive.
$\therefore$ $k^2 + 6k + 9 - 80$ is positive
so $k^2 + 6k - 71$ is positive.

Example 2.9

Find the values of k if the equation $x^2 + kx + k + 3 = 0$ has equal roots. Find the values of x for those values of k.

The condition for equal (coincident) roots is   discriminant $= 0$
$$k^2 - 4(1)(k + 3) = 0 \quad (a = 1, b = k, c = k + 3)$$
or $k^2 - 4k - 12 = 0.$

This is a quadratic equation for k which can be solved by factorising or by using the formula. Then either
$$k^2 - 4k - 12 = 0$$
gives $(k + 2)(k - 6) = 0$
so $k = -2, 6.$

or $k = \dfrac{-(-4) \pm \sqrt{(-4)^2 - 4(1)(-12)}}{2}$

$$= \dfrac{4 \pm \sqrt{64}}{2} = \dfrac{4 \pm 8}{2}$$

and $k = \dfrac{4 + 8}{2}$ or $\dfrac{4 - 8}{2}.$

$\therefore$ $k = 6$ or -2 as before.

We substitute the values of k in turn into the original quadratic equation.
When $k = 6$, the quadratic equation becomes
$$x^2 + 6x + 9 = 0$$

which factorises into
$$(x + 3)^2 = 0$$
and $x = -3$ (twice) (or use the formula).
When $k = -2$ the quadratic equation becomes
$$x^2 - 2x + 1 = 0$$
so $(x - 1)^2 = 0$
and $x = 1$ (twice) (or use the formula).

Exercises 2.3

1 Solve the following quadratic equations by first factorising :-
(i) $x^2 - 6x - 7 = 0$ (ii) $x^2 - 13x + 12 = 0$
(iii) $2x^2 - 17x + 8 = 0$ (iv) $x^2 + 9x + 20 = 0$
(v) $3x^2 - 7x - 20 = 0$ (vi) $5x^2 + 32x + 12 = 0$.

2. Use the quadratic formula to solve the following, giving your answers correct to two decimal places :-
(i) $x^2 - 3x - 2 = 0$ (ii) $x^2 + 5x + 2 = 0$
(iii) $2x^2 - 5x = 2$ (iv) $9x^2 - 12x + 4 = 0$
(v) $17.64x^2 - 21x + 6.25 = 0$ (vi) $x^2 - 4x + 5 = 0$.

3. Determine for which of the following equations there are (i) two unequal 'real' roots (ii) equal roots (iii) no 'real' roots.
(a) $3x^2 + 3x - 4 = 0$ (b) $6x^2 + 3x + 4 = 0$
(c) $2x^2 - 3x - 1 = 0$ (d) $2.5x^2 + 4x + 1 = 0$
(e) $3.5x^2 + 7.5x + 4 = 0$ (f) $4\alpha^2 x^2 + 4\alpha\beta x + \beta^2 = 0$.

4. Find the value of a if the equation $(2a - 1)x^2 - 2ax + 1 = 0$ has equal roots. Solve the equation for that single value of x.

5. Show that if there are no real roots of the quadratic equation
$$(2b + 1)x^2 - 3bx + b = 0$$
then $b^2 - 4b$ is negative.

6. The formula for the sum of the first n positive numbers is $\dfrac{1}{2}n(n + 1)$. Find n, the number of numbers, if the sum is 528.

7. The area of a rectangle is A and the sum of two adjacent sides is S. Show that S^2 is greater than or equal to $4A$. <u>Hint</u>: let the sides be x and $S - x$.

We complete our discussion of quadratic equations by considering another use of completing the square.

Solution of Equations

2.4 Maximum and minimum values of quadratic functions

Here we consider <u>quadratic functions</u>,
i.e. those defined by
$$f(x) = ax^2 + bx + c, \quad \text{where } a \neq 0.$$

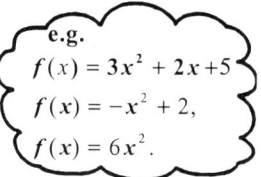

e.g.
$f(x) = 3x^2 + 2x + 5$
$f(x) = -x^2 + 2,$
$f(x) = 6x^2.$

We saw earlier, when discussing completing
the square, that

$$ax^2 + bx + c = a\left[\left(x + \frac{b}{2a}\right)^2 + \frac{c}{a} - \frac{b^2}{4a^2}\right]$$

$$= a\left[\left(x + \frac{b}{2a}\right)^2 + \frac{4ac - b^2}{4a^2}\right]$$

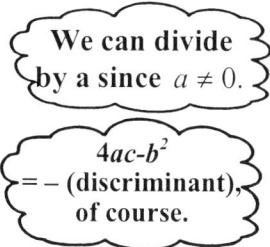

We can divide
by a since $a \neq 0$.

$4ac - b^2$
= − (discriminant),
of course.

Maximum or minimum values of quadratic functions are easily found by completing the square.

Example 2.10
By completing the square in $f(x) = 2x^2 - 3x + 5$,
find its minimum value.

Make coefficient
of x^2 unity.

Now $f(x) = 2x^2 - 3x + 5 = 2\left(x^2 - \frac{3}{2}x + \frac{5}{2}\right)$

Half the coefficient
of x in the squared
bracket.

$$= 2\left[\left(x - \frac{3}{4}\right)^2 + \frac{5}{2} - \frac{9}{16}\right]$$

$$= 2\left[\left(x - \frac{3}{4}\right)^2 + \frac{31}{16}\right]$$

$$= 2\left(x - \frac{3}{4}\right)^2 + \frac{31}{8}.$$

We note that $2\left(x - \frac{3}{4}\right)^2 \geq 0$ and $f(x) = 2\left(x - \frac{3}{4}\right)^2 + \frac{31}{8}$

It can never be < 0
because $2 > 0$

has minimum value when $2\left(x - \frac{3}{4}\right)^2 = 0$, i.e. when $x = \frac{3}{4}$

and $(x - \frac{3}{4})^2 \geq 0.$

The corresponding minimum value is $\frac{31}{8}$.

Example 2.11

By completing the square in $f(x) = -3x^2 - 5x + 7$, find its maximum value.

$$f(x) = -3x^2 - 5x + 7$$
$$= -3\left(x^2 + \frac{5}{3}x - \frac{7}{3} \right)$$
$$= -3\left[\left(x + \frac{5}{6} \right)^2 - \frac{7}{3} - \frac{25}{36} \right]$$
$$= -3\left[\left(x + \frac{5}{6} \right)^2 - \frac{109}{36} \right]$$
$$= -3\left(x + \frac{5}{6} \right)^2 + \frac{109}{12}.$$

> Note that the coefficient of x^2 in bracket must be + 1. Watch your signs!

Since $-3\left(x + \frac{5}{6} \right)^2 < 0$, the <u>maximum</u> value of $f(x)$ occurs when

$$-3\left(x + \frac{5}{6} \right)^2 = 0, \text{ i.e. when } x = -\frac{5}{6}.$$

The corresponding maximum value is $\frac{109}{12}$.

The cases considered in examples 2.10 and 2.11 were special cases of

$$ax^2 + bx + c = a\left[\left(x + \frac{b}{2a} \right)^2 + \frac{4ac - b^2}{4a^2} \right].$$

> Note that we didn't use this formula but worked out each case.

In example 2.10, $a > 0$ and we obtained a <u>minimum</u> value.

> $2x^2 - 3x - 5,$
> $a = 2 > 0$

In example 2.11, $a < 0$ and we obtained a maximum value.

> $-3x^2 - 5x + 7,$
> $a = -3 < 0$

These examples illustrate a general result.

> For the quadratic function
> $$f(x) = ax^2 + bx + c \quad (a \neq 0)$$
> (i) when $a > 0$, $f(x)$ has a minimum value,
> (ii) when $a < 0$, $f(x)$ has a maximum value.

Exercises 2.4

Find for which values of x the following quadratic functions have maximum or minimum values, giving the maximum and minimum values.

(i) $x^2 + 4x + 7$ (ii) $-x^2 + 4x + 7$

(iii) $-x^2 - 3x + 1$ (iv) $4x^2 + 6x - 9$

(v) $2x^2 - x + 7$ (vi) $-4x^2 + 3x + 1$

(vii) $9 + x - x^2$ (viii) $2x - x^2$

(ix) $x^2 + 4$ (x) $9 - x^2$.

2.5   Simultaneous linear equations

The linear and quadratic equations considered earlier contained only one letter, the problem being to find the number(s) to be assigned to the letter so that the equation was satisfied. Often problems involving two or more letters arise, such problems involving two or more equations. It is a fact that to make progress we require as many equations as there are unknown letters e.g. two equations for two letters and so on. In this section we consider two linear equations in two unknowns. Since the equations must both be satisfied by the numerical values to be found, we refer to simultaneous (linear) equations. The method is illustrated by a number of worked examples.

Example 2.12

Solve the equations

$$3x + y = 29, \quad (1)$$

$$4x + 3y = 47. \quad (2)$$

We arrange to have the same coefficient in both equations associated with the same letter, in this case y. Thus multiply (1) by 3 and rewrite the equations to obtain

$$9x + 3y = 87, \quad (1')$$
$$4x + 3y = 47. \quad (2)$$

These are linear equations because x and y occur singly and to the first power.

Coefficients of x could have been made equal by × (1) by 4, (2) by 3. The common coefficient of x is then 12.

When the coefficients of a letter are the same we subtract.

Subtract (2) from (1'), thus eliminating y.

$$\therefore \quad\quad 5x = 40$$

so $$x = \frac{40}{5} = 8. \quad\quad \text{(Rule (i), section 2.1)}$$

Substitute $x = 8$ into one of the above equations, say (1). Then (1) becomes

$$3 \times 8 + y = 29$$

so $$y = 29 - 24 = 5. \quad\quad \text{(Rule (ii), section 2.1)}$$

It is useful to check the values of x and y by substitution in the equation other than the one used to find x. We used (1) so we check in (2).
Then with $x = 8$, $y = 5$, (2) becomes

$$4 \times 8 + 3 \times 5 = 47 \quad \text{(checks)}.$$

Example 2.13

Solve
$$3x + 2y = 8, \quad (1)$$
$$2x - 3y = -3. \quad (2)$$

We could arrange to have the same coefficient of x in (1) and (2). However, here we make the coefficients for y equal in magnitude but opposite in sign. Multiply (1) by 3, (2) by 2 to obtain
$$9x + 6y = 24, \quad (1')$$
$$4x - 6y = -6. \quad (2')$$

Add (1') and (2') to eliminate y.

Then
$$13x = 18.$$
$$\therefore \quad x = \frac{18}{13}.$$

When the coefficients of a letter are equal but opposite in sign we <u>add</u> the equations.

Substitute for x in (1). Then
$$3 \times \frac{18}{13} + 2y = 8.$$
$$\therefore \quad 2y = 8 - 3 \times \frac{18}{13} = \frac{50}{13}.$$
$$\therefore \quad y = \frac{25}{13}.$$

Resist the temptation to express x and y as decimals unless decimal values are asked for.

Substitute in (2).
$$2 \times \frac{18}{13} - 3 \times \frac{25}{13} = \frac{36}{13} - \frac{75}{13} = -3 \quad \text{(checks)}.$$

The method whereby coefficients of letters are made equal (but possibly of different sign) is widely used in the solution of simultaneous linear equations. Another popular method (which we shall also require for the next section) is substitution.

Example 2.14

Solve
$$\frac{a}{2} - \frac{b}{5} = 1, \quad (1)$$
$$a - \frac{b}{3} = 8. \quad (2)$$

We find a in terms of b from equation (2). Then
$$a = 8 + \frac{b}{3}.$$

Find any letter in terms of the other

Substitute this value of a into (1). Thus
$$\frac{1}{2}\left(8 + \frac{b}{3}\right) - \frac{b}{5} = 1.$$
$$\therefore \quad 4 + \frac{b}{6} - \frac{b}{5} = 1.$$
$$\therefore \quad \frac{b}{6} - \frac{b}{5} = -3.$$

Clear the fractions by multiplying throughout by 30 (any number divisible by 5 and 6 will do).

$$\therefore \qquad 5b - 6b = -90$$

so
$$-b = -90$$

and
$$b = \frac{-90}{-1} = 90.$$

Substitution of the value for b in (2) gives

$$a - \frac{90}{3} = 8$$

or
$$a = 8 + 30 = 38.$$

Check in (1): $\dfrac{38}{2} - \dfrac{90}{5} = 19 - 18 = 1$ (checks).

Example 2.15

In the equation $y = mx + c$ it is known that the equation is satisfied by two pairs of x and y, namely $\qquad x = 3, \quad y = 10$

and $\qquad x = -5, \quad y = 2.$

Find the values of m and c.

When $x = 3, y = 10$.

$$\therefore \qquad 10 = 3m + c. \qquad (1)$$

When $x = -5, y = 2$.

$$\therefore \qquad 2 = -5m + c. \qquad (2)$$

The equations are easily solved by both methods considered earlier.

<u>Equal coefficients method</u>

The coefficients of c in (1) and (2) are equal.

Subtract (2) from (1)

Then
$$8 = 3m - (-5m)$$

so
$$8 = 8m.$$

$$\therefore \qquad m = 1.$$

Substitute this value for m in (1)

$$10 = 3 \times 1 + c.$$

$$\therefore \qquad c = 7.$$

Check in (2)

$$-5m + c = -5 \times 1 + 7 = 2 \qquad \text{(checks)}.$$

<u>Substitution</u>

From (1) $\qquad c = 10 - 3m.$

Substitute into (2).

$$2 = -5m + 10 - 3m.$$

$$\therefore \qquad -8 = -8m$$

so
$$m = \frac{-8}{-8} = 1$$

and we find c by substitution as before.

Whilst the equal coefficient method may appear to be the better method in Example 2.15, it is helpful to possess facility in both methods.

Exercises 2.5

1. Solve the following simultaneous linear equations :-

   (i) $3x - 2y = 7$
   $4x + 3y = 15$

   (ii) $5x + 3y = 4$
   $3x + 5y = -4$

   (iii) $a - b = 5$
   $4a - b = 2a + 13$

   (iv) $4(1 - x) = 7x + 8y$
   $6x + y + 18 = 0.$

2. Two numbers a and b are such that the sum of $3a$ and $2b$ is 26, while the sum of a and $2b$ is 14. What are the numbers?

3. The perimeter of a rectangular lawn is 64 m. It is reduced in size so that the length is $\frac{3}{4}$ and the breadth is $\frac{4}{5}$ of the original dimensions. The perimeter is then 50 m. What were the original length and breadth?

4. Find m and c if $y = mx + c$ and $y = 4$ when $x = 3$, and $y = 9$ when $x = 5$.

5. A polynomial function is given by $ax^2 + bx + 2$, where a and b are unknown. Given that the values of the function are 16 and 4 when $x = 2$ and 3 respectively, find the values of a and b.

6. Two polynomials are given by (i) $ax^2 + bx + 4$ and (ii) $2ax^2 - bx + 1$. Given that (i) and (ii) are equal when $x = 2, 3$, find the values of a and b.

7. If $s = ut + \frac{1}{2}at^2$, where u and a are constants and $s = 60$ and 32 when $t = 1$ and 4 respectively, find u and a.

8. If $v = u + at$, where u and a are constants and $v = 13, 29$ when $t = 3, 8$ respectively, find u and a.

2.6 The solution of simultaneous equations: one linear, one quadratic

Terms in the unknowns x and y of the form x^2, xy, y^2 are said to be of second degree. The degree of a term is shown either by its index, (for one letter) or, if it contains two letters, by the sum of the indices.

In this section we consider one linear equation which involves terms of degree one, and a quadratic equation which involves terms of degree 2 and possibly terms of degree one.

Example 2.16

Solve the equations
$$2x + 3y = 1, \quad (1)$$
$$3x^2 + 4y^2 + 6xy = 5. \quad (2)$$

The procedure is to use the first equation (the linear one) to eliminate one of the variables.

Thus from first, $\quad x = \dfrac{1-3y}{2}$.

Substitute in (2).

$$3\left(\frac{1-3y}{2}\right)^2 + 4y^2 + 6\left(\frac{1-3y}{2}\right)y = 5.$$

$$\therefore \quad 3\left(\frac{1-6y+9y^2}{4}\right) + 4y^2 + 3(1-3y)y = 5.$$

Clear the fractions by multiplying throughout by 4.

$$3(1-6y+9y^2) + 4 \times 4y^2 + 4 \times 3(1-3y)y = 4 \times 5.$$

Remove brackets.

$$\therefore \quad 3 - 18y + 27y^2 + 16y^2 + 12y - 36y^2 = 20.$$

So $\quad 7y^2 - 6y - 17 = 0.$

$$\therefore \qquad y = \frac{6 \pm \sqrt{36 + 4 \times 7 \times 17}}{14}$$

$$= \frac{6 \pm \sqrt{512}}{14} = \frac{6 \pm 16\sqrt{2}}{14}$$

$$= \frac{3}{7} \pm \frac{8\sqrt{2}}{7}.$$

When $y = \dfrac{3}{7} + \dfrac{8\sqrt{2}}{7}$,

$$x = \frac{1}{2} - \frac{1}{2} \times 3\left(\frac{3}{7} + \frac{8\sqrt{2}}{7}\right)$$

$$= \frac{1}{2} - \frac{9}{14} - \frac{12\sqrt{2}}{7} = -\frac{1}{7} - \frac{12\sqrt{2}}{7}.$$

When $y = \dfrac{3}{7} - \dfrac{8\sqrt{2}}{7}$,

$$x = \frac{1}{2} - \frac{1}{2} \times 3\left(\frac{3}{7} - \frac{8\sqrt{2}}{7}\right) = -\frac{1}{7} + \frac{12\sqrt{2}}{7}.$$

The solutions are the pairs of numbers

$$x = -\frac{1}{7} - \frac{12\sqrt{2}}{7}, \qquad y = \frac{3}{7} + \frac{8\sqrt{2}}{7},$$

$$x = -\frac{1}{7} + \frac{12\sqrt{2}}{7}, \qquad y = \frac{3}{7} - \frac{8\sqrt{2}}{7}.$$

> There is no need to express the answer in decimal form if you are not asked to do so, although you may wish to do so.

Example 2.17

Find the values of k such that

$$2y - x = 2 \qquad (1)$$

and $\quad x^2 + y^2 + kx - 10y + 29 = 0 \qquad (2)$

are satisfied by only one pair of values of x and y for each value of k. Find the pairs of values of x and y for those values of k.

From (1), $\qquad\qquad x = 2y - 2.$

Substitute in (2).

$\therefore \qquad (2y - 2)^2 + y^2 + k(2y - 2) - 10y + 29 = 0.$

$\therefore \quad 4y^2 - 8y + 4 + y^2 + 2ky - 2k - 10y + 29 = 0.$

$\therefore \qquad\qquad 5y^2 + (2k - 18)y + 33 - 2k = 0. \qquad (2')$

There is only one value of y if

$$(2k - 18)^2 = 4 \times 5(33 - 2k)$$

$b^2 = 4ac$

or $\qquad\qquad (k - 9)^2 = 5(33 - 2k).$

$\therefore \qquad k^2 - 18k + 81 = 165 - 10k$

so $\qquad k^2 - 8k - 84 = 0.$

$\therefore \qquad (k + 6)(k - 14) = 0$

and $\quad k = -6$ or $k = 14.$

When $k = -6$, the equation (2') for y becomes

$$5y^2 + (2 \times -6 - 18)y + 33 - 2(-6) = 0.$$

$\therefore \qquad 5y^2 - 30y + 45 = 0$

or $\qquad y^2 - 6y + 9 = 0.$

$$(y - 3)^2 = 0$$

and $\qquad\qquad y = 3 \quad$ (twice).

From (1), $\qquad x = 2y - 2 = 2 \times 3 - 2 = 4.$

When $k = 14$, the equation (2') for y becomes

$$5y^2 + (2 \times 14 - 18)y + 33 - 2(14) = 0$$

or $\qquad 5y^2 + 10y + 5 = 0.$

$\therefore \qquad y^2 + 2y + 1 = 0$

so $\qquad (y + 1)^2 = 0$

and $\qquad\qquad y = -1 \quad$ (twice).

From (1), $\qquad x = 2y - 2 = 2 \times (-1) - 2 = -4.$

Thus $k = -6$, pair is $(4, 3)$

$\qquad k = 14$, pair is $(-4, -1)$.

Exercises 2.6

1. Solve the following simultaneous equations :-

(i) $\quad x + y = 2$ $\qquad\qquad$ (ii) $\qquad a - b = 7$

$\qquad x^2 - xy = 60$ $\qquad\qquad\qquad 3a^2 - ab - b^2 = 81$

(iii) $2x + y = 30$ $\qquad\qquad$ (iv) $\quad 2a - b = 5$

$\qquad\qquad xy = 52$ $\qquad\qquad\qquad 5a^2 + 3ab = 14$

(v) $2x^2 - 5x - 4xy = 60, \quad 3x + y = 9$

(vi) $x - 2y = 8$, $\dfrac{x^2}{16} + \dfrac{y^2}{9} = 5$

(vii) $\dfrac{1}{x} + \dfrac{1}{y} = -\dfrac{3}{4}$, $x - 3y = 2$ (Hint : multiply the first by xy).

2.   Find the values of k if the following sets of simultaneous equations are satisfied by single pairs of x and y :-

(i) $x + ky = 3$, $x^2 + y^2 + xy - 9 = 0$

(ii) $x + y = 5$, $x^2 + y^2 + 2x + k = 0$

(iii) $2x + y = 4$, $x^2 + y^2 + 4kx + 4 = 0$.

3.   Determine whether the following sets of simultaneous equations possess 'real' solutions:-

(i) $3x + y = 4$, $x^2 + y^2 + xy + 5 = 0$

(ii) $x = 3y + 2$, $x^2 + xy + 9 = 0$

(iii) $2x + 3y + 7 = 0$, $x^2 - 6x + y^2 - 8y - 24 = 0$.

Chapter 3

Sequences and Series

The derivation of mathematical results often involves the summation of series. In this chapter we consider the summation of two particular series. Before considering summation, we first consider sequences.

3.1   Sequences

We consider the following successions of numbers :-

(i) 3, 9, 27, 81

(ii) 1, 3, 5, 7, . . .

(iii) $1\frac{1}{2}, 1\frac{1}{3}, 1\frac{1}{4}, 1\frac{1}{5}, \ldots$

(iv) 1, – 1, 1, – 1, . . .

(v) – 10, 11, – 12, 13, . . .

The succession in (i) differs from the others in that it terminates. In contrast, the dots in (ii) - (v) indicate that those successions never end. Much of our discussion in this chapter relates to infinite successions, i.e. those that are never ending.

All the successions have a common feature: the number at any stage is determined by some definite rule. Thus the fifth value in (ii) is 9, the 6th value in (iii) is $1\frac{1}{7}$, and the 9th value in (iv) is 1.

Exercise 3.1

What is the sixth value in (v)?

Definition

A **sequence** is a succession of numbers whose members are determined by some definite rule. A non-terminating sequence is called an infinite sequence, otherwise it is called a finite sequence.

It is convenient to summarise sequence rules by formulae whenever possible. Such rules enable us to write down the n'th (general) term in a sequence.

Denoting the general sequence as

$$a_1, a_2, a_3, \ldots, a_n, \ldots$$

we see that for (i) $a_1 = 3$, $a_2 = 3^2$, and $a_n = 3^n$ $(n \le 4)$

(ii) $a_1 = 1$, $a_2 = 3$, and $a_n = 2n - 1$

(iii) $a_1 = 1\frac{1}{2}$, $a_2 = 1\frac{1}{3}$, and $a_n = 1 + \dfrac{1}{n+1}$

(iv) $a_1 = 1$, $a_2 = -1$, and $a_n = (-1)^{n+1}$

(v) $a_1 = -10$, $a_2 = 11$, and $a_n = (-1)^n(n+9)$

These sequences demonstrate different types of behaviour as we consider more and more terms.

Example 3.1

In (ii), $a_n = 2n - 1$.

If n increases indefinitely then a_n increases indefinitely.

We write as $n \to \infty$, $a_n \to \infty$, where '$\to \infty$' is short hand for 'increases indefinitely'.

$a_{1000} = 1999,$
$a_{10000} = 19999$

Example 3.2

In (iii), $a_n = 1 + \dfrac{1}{n+1}$.

If n increases indefinitely then $\dfrac{1}{n+1}$ becomes smaller and smaller so that a_n gets closer and closer to 1.

We write as $n \to \infty$, $a_n \to 1$.

$a_{999} = 1.001,$
$a_{9999} = 1.0001$

Example 3.3

In (iv), $a_n = (-1)^{n+1}$.

As n increases indefinitely the terms become alternatively $- 1$ and 1.

Example 3.4

In (v), $a_n = (-1)^n(n + 9)$.

As $n \to \infty$, the terms change sign alternatively but, in contrast to Ex 3.3, increase in magnitude.

These various patterns can be drawn together into definitions.

Definition

(a)　A sequence $a_1, a_2, a_3, \ldots, a_n, \ldots$ is said to be <u>divergent</u> if $a_n \to \infty$ (or $- \infty$) as $n \to \infty$.

(b)　A sequence is said to be <u>convergent</u> if $a_n \to l$ (some unique fixed number) as $n \to \infty$. The number l is said to be the limit of the sequence. In example 3.2, $l = 1$.

(c)　A sequence which is neither convergent or divergent is said to be <u>oscillatory</u>. Example 3.3 concerns an oscillatory sequence whose values $(-1,1)$ recur at fixed intervals. Such a sequence is a <u>periodic</u> oscillatory series.
Example 3.4 gives a sequence whose signs alternate and does not converge (no unique limit) and does not diverge to <u>one</u> of $+ \infty$ or $- \infty$. Such a sequence is a <u>non-periodic</u> oscillatory series.

N.B. Some authors regard all sequences which do not converge to be divergent. Oscillatory sequences as defined here would then be termed divergent.

Summary

Type

1. Convergent : sequence tends to fixed unique limit.

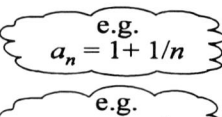

e.g.
$a_n = 1 + 1/n$

2. Divergent : sequence tends to $+\infty$ or $-\infty$.

e.g.
$a_n = 2n-1$
or $a_n = 2-3n$

3. Oscillatory periodic : neither convergent or divergent and some terms recur.

e.g.
$a_n = (-1)^{n+1}$

4. Oscillatory non-periodic : neither convergent or divergent and terms do not recur.

e.g.
$a_n = (-1)^n(n+9)$

Exercises 3.2

In the following questions, the limits of the sequences should be stated where appropriate.

1. Write down the 5th, 8th and nth terms of the following sequences
$$1, 2, 3, 4, \ldots$$
Is this sequence convergent, divergent or oscillatory?

2. Write down the 6th and nth terms of the sequence
$$1, \frac{1}{2}, \frac{1}{4}, \frac{1}{8}, \ldots$$
Is this sequence convergent, divergent or oscillatory?

3. Write down the nth term of the sequence
$$4, 16, 64, 256, \ldots$$
Is this sequence convergent?

4. Is the sequence $\frac{1}{2}, -\frac{1}{4}, \frac{1}{8}, -\frac{1}{16}, \ldots$ oscillatory?

5. Classify the following sequence
$$-1, 0, 1, -1, 0, 1, \ldots$$
as divergent, convergent or oscillatory.

6. Is the oscillatory sequence
$1, \frac{1}{2}, \frac{1}{3}, 1, \frac{1}{2}, \frac{1}{3}, \ldots$ periodic?

7. A sequence is defined in terms of two positive numbers a and d as
$$a, a+d, a+2d, a+3d, \ldots$$
Is the sequence convergent, divergent or oscillatory?

8. Is the conclusion in Q7 changed if one or other (or both) of a and d is negative?

9. The nth term of a sequence is
$$a_n = (-1)^n + \frac{1}{n}.$$
State whether the sequence is convergent, divergent or oscillatory.

10. Write down the nth term of the sequence
$$x, x^2, x^3, \ldots$$
State whether the sequence is convergent, divergent or oscillatory when
(i) $x = \frac{1}{2}$ (ii) $x = -\frac{1}{2}$ (iii) $x = 2$ (iv) $x = -2$ (v) $x = 0$.

11. Write down the nth term of the sequence
$$1, 1, 1, 1, \ldots$$
Is the sequence convergent?

As mentioned earlier, the criterion for convergence of a sequence is the existence of a unique, finite limit. In the next section we consider further the concept of limit.

3.2 Limits and their manipulation

For relatively simple sequences the limits are easily found.

Example 3.5

Write down the unique limits as $n \to \infty$, where they exist, of the sequences :-

(a) $a_n = \dfrac{1}{n^2}$ (b) $b_n = 3n + 1$ (c) $c_n = 1 + \dfrac{(-1)^n}{n}$.

(a) The limit of $\dfrac{1}{n^2}$ is easily seen to be 0 because $\dfrac{1}{n^2}$ can be made as small (i.e. as close to 0) as we please by taking n sufficiently large. Thus

$$\lim_{n\to\infty} \frac{1}{n^2} = 0.$$

> Limit is usually abbreviated as lim

(b) $3n + 1$ increases indefinitely as $n \to \infty$

i.e. $3n + 1 \to \infty$ as $n \to \infty$.

$\therefore$ no unique limit exists.

> ∞ is not a value but denotes the process of increasing indefinitely

(c) The limit of $1 + \dfrac{(-1)^n}{n}$ is 1 because the

term $\dfrac{(-1)^n}{n}$ becomes smaller and smaller as $n \to \infty$.

i.e. $\lim_{n\to\infty} 1 + \dfrac{(-1)^n}{n} = 1$.

To evaluate the limits of more complicated sequence we use (without proof) some standard results and rules.

Standard results for limits

(i) $\lim_{n\to\infty} \dfrac{1}{n^a} = 0$ if $a > 0$.

The limit is 1 if $a = 0$ but doesn't exist if $a < 0$.

(ii) $\lim_{n\to\infty}$ (any constant C) $= C$.

(iii) $\lim_{n\to\infty} (-1)^n$ doesn't exist.

Rules for manipulation of limits

If $\lim_{n\to\infty} a_n = l$, $\lim_{n\to\infty} b_n = m$ and α and β are any constants, then

> Rigorous proofs of these seemingly obvious results are not trivial.

(iv) $\lim_{n\to\infty} (a_n + b_n) = l + m$.

(v) $\lim_{n\to\infty} (a_n - b_n) = l - m$.

(vi) $\lim_{n \to \infty} (\alpha a_n) = \alpha l.$

(vii) $\lim_{n \to \infty} (\alpha a_n + \beta b_n) = \alpha l + \beta m.$

(viii) $\lim_{n \to \infty} a_n b_n = lm.$

(ix) $\lim_{n \to \infty} \dfrac{a_n}{b_n} = \dfrac{l}{m}$ as long as $m \neq 0.$

Example 3.6

Find $\lim_{n \to \infty} \dfrac{n+6}{2n+8}.$

Now $\quad \lim_{n \to \infty} \dfrac{n+6}{2n+8} = \lim_{n \to \infty} \dfrac{1+\frac{6}{n}}{2+\frac{8}{n}} \quad \left(\begin{array}{l} \text{divide top and} \\ \text{bottom by } n \end{array} \right)$

$\qquad\qquad = \dfrac{\lim_{n \to \infty} \left(1+\frac{6}{n}\right)}{\lim_{n \to \infty} \left(2+\frac{8}{n}\right)} \quad \text{(Rule ix)}$

$\qquad\qquad = \dfrac{1}{2}. \qquad\qquad \text{(Rules iv, ii and i twice)}.$

Example 3.7

$\lim_{n \to \infty} \left(\dfrac{3n+4}{4n^2+5n+3} \right) = \lim_{n \to \infty} \left(\dfrac{\frac{3}{n}+\frac{4}{n^2}}{4+\frac{5}{n}+\frac{3}{n^2}} \right)$

> Always divide top and bottom by the largest power of n, n^2 in this case.

$\qquad\qquad = \dfrac{\lim_{n \to \infty} \left(\frac{3}{n}+\frac{4}{n^2} \right)}{\lim_{n \to \infty} \left(4+\frac{5}{n}+\frac{3}{n^2} \right)} \quad \text{(Rule ix)}$

$\qquad\qquad = \dfrac{0}{4} = 0. \qquad \text{(Rules iv and i for top and bottom)}$

Example 3.8

$\lim_{n \to \infty} \dfrac{6}{n} + 3(-1)^n$ doesn't exist, because whilst $\lim_{n \to \infty} \dfrac{6}{n} = 0,$ $\lim_{n \to \infty} (-1)^n$ doesn't exist.

Exercises 3.3

1. Find the limits in the following cases, where they exist:-

(i) $\dfrac{1}{n+1}$ 　　 (ii) $\dfrac{n-1}{n+1}$ 　　 (iii) $\dfrac{n-1}{n^2+1}$ 　　 (iv) $\dfrac{n^2-1}{n^2+1}$

(v) $\dfrac{n^3+3n^2+5}{n^4+4n^2+3n+6}$ 　　　　 (vi) $\dfrac{n^4+3n^2+6}{n^3+2n^2+4n+9}$

(vii) $\dfrac{(-1)^n n}{n^2+1}$ 　　 (viii) $\dfrac{(-1)^n n^2+1}{n^2-1}$ 　　 (ix) $\dfrac{(-1)^n n^2-1}{(-1)^n n^2+1}.$

2. Determine whether the sequences with the given general terms converge:-

(a) $\dfrac{3n+2}{n^2+3n-4}$

(b) $\dfrac{n^2+3n+2}{n^2+3n-4}$

(c) $\dfrac{n^3+3n^2+2}{n^2+3n-4}$

(d) $\dfrac{(-1)^n+n^2}{n^2+n+1}$

(e) $\dfrac{n+1}{(n+2)(n+3)}$

(f) $\dfrac{(n+10)(n+9)}{(n+1)(n+2)}$

(g) $\dfrac{(n^2+10)(n^2+9)}{(n^2+1)(n+2)}$

(h) $\dfrac{(n+1)(n+2)(n+3)}{(n-1)(n-2)(n-3)}$.

3.3 Series

When the terms of a sequence are added or subtracted, the resulting expression is called a series.

For the sequence

$$1, \frac{1}{2}, \frac{1}{3}, \dots, \frac{1}{n}, \dots$$

we can construct a series such as

$$1+\frac{1}{2}+\frac{1}{3}+\dots+\frac{1}{n}+\dots, \quad \text{or} \quad 1-\frac{1}{2}-\frac{1}{3}-\dots-\frac{1}{n}-\dots,$$

or $\quad 1-\dfrac{1}{2}+\dfrac{1}{3}-\dfrac{1}{4}+\dots+(-1)^{n-1}\dfrac{1}{n}+\dots$

The Σ notation

When the general term of a series is known, the series can be represented more concisely. Thus if $a_r = \dfrac{1}{r}$, the series $1+\dfrac{1}{2}+\dfrac{1}{3}+\dots$

can be represented as $\displaystyle\sum_{r=1}^{\infty}\frac{1}{r}$.

> It is convenient to use the letter r instead of n.

The Σ is an elongated S which denotes sum and the $r = 1, \infty$ is interpreted as allowing r to take values $1, 2, 3, \dots$

If the series terminates e.g. $1+\dfrac{1}{2}+\dfrac{1}{3}+\dots+\dfrac{1}{20}$ it may be represented as $\displaystyle\sum_{r=1}^{20}\frac{1}{r}$, the

interpretation being that r takes the values $1, 2, 3, \dots, 20$.

The above representation of a series is known as the **sigma form**.

> Σ is pronounced sigma.

Exercises 3.4

1. Write down $1+\dfrac{1}{2^2}+\dfrac{1}{3^2}+\dots$ in sigma form.

2. Write down $1-\dfrac{1}{2}+\dfrac{1}{3}-\dots$ in sigma form.

   > The rth term is $\dfrac{(-1)^{r+1}}{r}$

3. Write down $1+\dfrac{1}{2}+\dfrac{1}{4}+\dots$ in sigma form.

   > The rth term is $\dfrac{1}{2^{r-1}}$

4. Write down $2+4+8+\dots+128$ in sigma form.

5. Write down $1 + 3 + 5 + 7 + \ldots + 39$ in sigma form.

6. Write down $1\frac{1}{2} + 2\frac{1}{3} + 3\frac{1}{4} + \ldots$ in sigma form.

3.4 Partial sums of series

For an infinite series such as

$$S = \frac{1}{1.2} + \frac{1}{2.3} + \frac{1}{3.4} + \ldots$$

we can construct in turn sums of the first term, the first two terms, the first three terms and so on.

Then

$$S_1 = \frac{1}{1.2} = \frac{1}{2}.$$

$$S_2 = \frac{1}{1.2} + \frac{1}{2.3} = \frac{1}{2} + \frac{1}{6} = \frac{2}{3}.$$

$$S_3 = \frac{1}{1.2} + \frac{1}{2.3} + \frac{1}{3.4} = \frac{2}{3} + \frac{1}{12} = \frac{3}{4}.$$

It turns out that the sum of the first n terms is given by

$$S_n = \frac{n}{n+1}.$$

> You are not expected to derive this.

In effect, we have a sequence formed by the partial sums of the original series:-

$$\frac{1}{2}, \frac{2}{3}, \frac{3}{4}, \ldots, \frac{n}{n+1}, \ldots$$

where, in sigma notation, the nth partial sum is

$$S_n = \sum_{r=1}^{n} \frac{r}{r(r+1)}.$$

Definition

The partial sums of a series is the sequence of sums formed in turn from the first, first two, first three terms and so on.

Example 3.9

Given $S = 1 + 2 + 3 + 4 + \ldots$

we see that the first four partial sums are

$$S_1 = 1, \quad S_2 = 3, \quad S_3 = 6, \quad S_4 = 10.$$

In fact the nth partial sum is

$$S_n = \frac{n(n+1)}{2}.$$

> We shall prove this later.

The sequence of the partial sums is therefore

$$1, 3, 6, \ldots, \frac{n(n+1)}{2}, \ldots$$

Thus from the above, it is clear that, given a series, in principle at least, a sequence of partial sums may be obtained.

In sections 3.1, 3.2 we saw that the sequences can display various types of long term behaviour : convergence, divergence, oscillatory behaviour. Here we apply such considerations to sequences of partial sums.

Example 3.10

Given
$$S = \frac{1}{1.2} + \frac{1}{2.3} + \frac{1}{3.4} + \ldots$$

or
$$S = \sum_{r=1}^{\infty} \frac{1}{r(r+1)},$$

the sequence of associated partial sums was seen to be

$$\frac{1}{2}, \frac{2}{3}, \frac{3}{4}, \ldots, \frac{n}{n+1}, \ldots.$$

Now the nth partial sum $S_n = \dfrac{n}{n+1}$ has limit given by

$$\lim_{n \to \infty} \frac{n}{n+1} = \lim_{n \to \infty} \frac{1}{1 + \frac{1}{n}} = 1.$$

Thus in this case the sequence of partial sums converges.

Example 3.11

The partial sums for

$$S = 1 + 2 + 3 + \ldots \quad \text{form the sequence } 1, 3, 6, \ldots, \frac{n(n+1)}{2}, \ldots$$

As $n \to \infty$, $S_n \to \infty$ so that the sequence of partial sums is divergent.

Examples 3.10 and 3.11 indicate different types of long term behaviour of sequences of partial sums formed from series.

Definition

A series is convergent (divergent, oscillatory) if the sequence of partial sums formed is convergent (divergent, oscillatory).

From the definition, we see that the series in 3.10 and 3.11 are convergent and divergent respectively.

Exercises 3.5

1. The nth partial sum of the series
    $$S = 1 + 3 + 5 + 7 + \ldots 2n + 1 + \ldots$$
    is given by $S_n = n^2$. Is the series convergent?

2. The nth partial sum of the series
    $$S = 1 + \frac{1}{2} + \frac{1}{4} + \frac{1}{8} + \ldots \frac{1}{2^{n-1}} + \ldots$$
    is given by $S_n = 2 - \dfrac{1}{2^{n-1}}$. Is the series convergent?

3.   Given $S = 3 + 9 + 27 + \ldots + 3^n + \ldots$

and the nth partial sum $S_n = \dfrac{3}{2}(3^n - 1)$, state whether the series converges or diverges.

4.   The nth partial sum of the series whose r th term is $\dfrac{4r}{(2r-1)(2r+1)(2r+3)}$

is given by $S_n = \dfrac{1}{2} - \dfrac{4n+3}{2(2n+1)(2n+3)}$.   Is the series convergent?

5.   In this question x denotes some fixed real number. It is known that the nth partial

sum for the series $S = \displaystyle\sum_{r=1}^{\infty} \dfrac{1}{(1+x)[1+(r+1)x]}$

is given by $S_n = \dfrac{n}{(1+x)[1+(n+1)x]}$.

Show that the series is convergent, whatever the value of x,
as long as $x \neq 0$ or -1.

6.   In this question a denotes some fixed real number. Given that for the series

$$S = \sum_{r=1}^{\infty} \dfrac{a^{r-1}}{(1+a^{r-1})(1+a^r)}, \quad \text{the } n\text{th partial sum is given by}$$

$$S_n = \dfrac{1}{1-a}\left[\dfrac{1}{2} - \dfrac{a^n}{1+a^n}\right]$$

show that the series converges for any value of a other than 1.

7.   For the series $S = \dfrac{3}{1.2.4} + \dfrac{4}{2.3.5} + \dfrac{5}{3.4.6} + \ldots$

write down the rth term and the nth partial sum S_n in sigma form.

Given $S_n = \dfrac{29}{30} - \dfrac{1}{n+3} - \dfrac{3}{2(n+2)(n+3)} - \dfrac{4}{3(n+1)(n+2)(n+3)}$

find $\displaystyle\lim_{n\to\infty} S_n$. Is the series convergent?

8.   Given that the nth partial sum S_n of a series is given by $S_n = \dfrac{n}{n+1}$, find the nth

term of the series $a_n = S_n - S_{n-1}$. Find $\displaystyle\lim_{n\to\infty} a_n$.

9.   Given that the nth partial sum of a series is $n^2 + 2n$ find a_n, the nth term of the
series in terms of n. Is $\displaystyle\lim_{n\to\infty} a_n = 0$? Does the series and a_n converge?

10.   Given the nth partial sum $S_n = 1 - \left(\dfrac{1}{3}\right)^n$ of a series, find a_n, the nth term of the

series. Find $\displaystyle\lim_{n\to\infty} a_n$. Does the series and a_n converge?

In the next sections we consider two particular series, namely the arithmetic and geometric series.

3.5   Arithmetic progression (A.P.)

We consider the following sequences :-
(i) 1, 2, 3, 4, . . .
(ii) 2, 5, 8, 11, . . .
(iii) 3, − 1, − 5, − 9, . . .

They all have a common feature: the difference between successive terms is constant. Thus, in (1) the terms increase by 1, in (ii) they increase by 3, and in (iii), terms decrease by 4.

Definition

An arithmetic progression (A.P.) is a sequence in which any term is formed from that immediately preceding it, by adding or subtracting a constant number. That constant number is called the **common difference**.

In general, if an A.P. has first term a and common difference d the terms are then $a, a + d, a + 2d, a + 3d, a + 4d, \ldots$

and the nth term $= a + (n − 1)d$.

> a, d may be positive or negative.

Example 3.12

The 5th term of an A.P. is 8 and the 13th term is 19. Find the common difference, the first term and the nth term.

If the first term is a and common difference is d, the 5th term is $a + 4d$, so

$$a + 4d = 8 \qquad (1)$$

and the 13th term is 19, so

$$a + 12d = 19. \qquad (2).$$

Subtract (1) from (2).

> The coefficients of a in (1) and (2) are equal, so no multiplication of the equations is necessary.

$$8d = 11.$$

$$\therefore \qquad d = \frac{11}{8}.$$

Substitute for d in (1).

$$\therefore \qquad a + 4 \times \frac{11}{8} = 8$$

and

$$a = 8 - \frac{11}{2} = \frac{5}{2}.$$

Check in (2):

$$\frac{5}{2} + 12 \times \frac{11}{8} = \frac{5}{2} + \frac{33}{2} = 19 \quad \text{(checks)}$$

and the nth term is

$$\frac{5}{2} + (n - 1)\frac{11}{8} = \frac{9}{8} + \frac{11n}{8}.$$

Example 3.13

The nth term of an A.P. is $8 − 3n$. Find the first term and the common difference.

The nth term is $8 − 3n$. Putting $n = 1$ we find the first term is $8 − 3 = 5$.

The second term is $8 − (3 \times 2) = 2$.

The common difference is therefore $− 3$.

The sum of *n* terms of an A.P.

Given the sequence of terms of an arithmetic progression, we can find the sum of the first *n* terms, i.e. the *n*th partial sum S_n.

If the *n*th term is *l*, the sum of the series may be written as

$$S_n = a + (a + d) + (a + 2d) + \ldots (l - 2d) + (l - d) + l.$$

so $l = a + (n-1)d$.

Reversing the order,

$$S_n = l + (l - d) + (l - 2d) + \ldots (a + 2d) + (a + d) + a.$$

Add ∴

$$2S_n = (a + l) + (a + l) + (a + l) + \ldots$$
$$+ (a + l) + (a + l) + (a + l)$$

(a + l) n times

and

$$2S_n = n(a + l).$$

∴

$$S_n = \frac{n}{2}(a + l). \qquad (A)$$

The sum may therefore be considered as

(the number of terms) × (average of first and last terms).

Since $l = a + (n - 1)d$ we may also write

$$S_n = \frac{n}{2}[a + a + (n - 1)d]$$

or

$$S_n = \frac{n}{2}[2a + (n - 1)d]. \qquad (B)$$

Either of (A) and (B) may be used in calculations.

Example 3.14

(i) An A.P. of 15 terms whose first term is 1 and whose last term is 9.
We know that $a = 1, l = 9, n = 15$.

∴

$$S_n = \frac{15}{2}(1 + 9) = 75.$$

(ii) $$\sum_{r=1}^{16}(3 + 2r) = 5 + 7 + 9 + \ldots + 35$$

$n = 16, a = 5, l = 35$

$$= \frac{16}{2}(5 + 35) = 320.$$

(iii) In an A.P. the sum of the first twenty terms is 60 and the 8th term is 3 times the 4th term. Find the first term and the sum of the first 54 terms.

Now $$S_n = \frac{n}{2}[2a + (n - 1)d], \quad n = 20 \text{ and } S_{20} = 60.$$

∴

$$\frac{20}{2}[2a + 19d] = 60$$

or

$$2a + 19d = 6. \qquad (1)$$

Also since the 8th term is 3 times the 4th term,

$$a + 7d = 3(a + 3d)$$

so

$$a + d = 0. \qquad (2)$$

Multiply (2) by 2 and subtract from (1)

∴

$$17d = 6$$

so

$$d = \frac{6}{17}, \text{ and } a = -d = -\frac{6}{17}.$$

Then
$$S_{54} = \frac{54}{2}\left[2 \times -\frac{6}{17} + 53 \times \frac{6}{17}\right]$$
$$= 27 \times 51 \times \frac{6}{17} = 486.$$

Exercises 3.6

1. Find the 7th term of the arithmetic progression
   $$4, 7, 10, \ldots$$

2. Find the next three terms of the A.P.
   $$a + 3b, a + b, a - b, \ldots$$

3. The fourth term of an A.P. is 12 and the sixth term is 17. Find the tenth term.

4. Which term of the progression
   $$3.5, 5.4, 7.3, \ldots \quad \text{is } 24.4?$$

5. Find the sum of the first 50 odd integers.

6. The sum of the first n terms of an arithmetic series is $S_n = n^2 - 5n$. Find the fourth term and the nth term.

7. The sum of the first n terms of a series is given by $S_n = 4n^2 - 3n$. Find $S_n - S_{n-1}$. Deduce that the terms of the series are in arithmetic progression.

8. How many terms of the A.P.
   $$8, 11, 14, \ldots$$
   must be taken so that the sum of the series is 435?

9. A contractor agrees to sink a well 100 metres deep at a cost of £30 for the first metre, £50 for the second metre and £20 for each additional metre. Find the cost of the last metre and the total cost.

10. A well-off parent saves £50 on his daughter's first birthday, £55 on the second birthday, £60 on the third birthday and so on, increasing the amount by £5 each birthday. How much will be saved up when the girl reaches her eighteenth birthday?

11. Is the series $S = a + (a + d) + (a + 2d) + \ldots$ convergent?

12. The first term of an arithmetic series is -12, and the last term is 40. If the sum of the series is 196, find the number of terms and the common difference.

13. The twenty-first term of an arithmetic series is $5\frac{1}{2}$, and the sum of the first twenty-one terms is $94\frac{1}{2}$. Find the first term, the common difference and the sum of the first 30 terms.

14. The second term of an arithmetic series is 5 and sixth term is -7. Find the first term, the common difference and the sum of the first twenty terms.

15. The sum of the first twenty terms of an arithmetic series is 510, the sum of the first forty terms being 2220. Find the sum of the first fifty terms of the series.

3.6 Geometric progression (G.P.)

We consider the following sequences :

(i) $1, 2, 4, 8, \ldots$

(ii) $1, \dfrac{1}{2}, \dfrac{1}{4}, \dfrac{1}{8}, \ldots$

(iii) $2, -6, 18, -54, \ldots$

(iv) $x, x^2, x^3, x^4, \ldots$

These sequences have a common feature: the ratio between successive terms is a constant. Thus in (i) this ratio is 2; in (ii) the ratio is $\dfrac{1}{2}$; in (iii) the ratio is -3; and in (iv) the ratio is x.

Definition

A geometric progression (G.P.) is a sequence of terms for which the ratio of any term to that which immediately precedes it is constant for the whole sequence. This ratio is called the **common ratio** of the progression. In general, for a geometric progression with first term a and common ratio r, the terms are

$$a, ar, ar^2, ar^3, \ldots,$$

where a and r can be any real numbers.

The nth term is ar^{n-1}.

Example 3.15

The first term of a geometric progression is a and the third term is equal to the sum of the first and second terms. Find the possible values of the common ratio r.

The terms are $a, ar, ar^2, ar^3, \ldots$

Now $\quad ar^2 = a + ar$

so $\quad ar^2 = a(1 + r)$.

$\therefore \quad\quad r^2 = 1 + r$ ⟨ assuming $a \neq 0$ ⟩

so $\quad r^2 - r - 1 = 0$.

Solve by the quadratic formula

$$\therefore \quad\quad r = \frac{-(-1) \pm \sqrt{(-1)^2 - 4(1)(-1)}}{2} \quad\quad \langle a = 1, b = -1, c = -1 \rangle$$

$$= \frac{1 \pm \sqrt{5}}{2}.$$

In surd form, the common ratio has possible values $\dfrac{1 - \sqrt{5}}{2}, \dfrac{1 + \sqrt{5}}{2}$.

Example 3.16

The sixth term of a G.P. is 24 and the 3rd term is 3. Find the common ratio and the first term.

The 6th term $= ar^5 = 24$.

3rd term $= ar^2 = 3$.

Then $\qquad \dfrac{\text{6th term}}{\text{3rd term}} = \dfrac{ar^5}{ar^2} = r^3 = 8.$

$\therefore \qquad\qquad\qquad r = 2.$

Then since the 3rd term is 3,

$$a(2)^2 = 3$$

so $\qquad\qquad\qquad a = \dfrac{3}{4}.$

Exercises 3.7

1. Write down the next two terms of the following sequences:-
   (a) $2, 6, 18, \ldots$ (b) $25, 5, 1, \ldots$
   (c) $12, -18, 27, \ldots$ (d) $0.2, 0.02, 0.002, \ldots$

2. Find the sixth term of the sequence $2, 4, 8, \ldots$

3. Find the sixth term of the sequence $6, -4, \dfrac{8}{3}, \ldots$

4. Find the fifth term of the sequence $1.2, 1.44, 1.728, \ldots$

5. The first term of a geometric progression (G.P.) is 1.1 and the common ratio is 1.2. Find the sixth term.

6. A young person is appointed to a post at a salary of £5000 with the promise that the salary will increase each year by 10 per cent of that for the previous year. What is the salary after six years?

7. The overhead costs of a business are £2.5 (millions) per year. The directors decide that they shall be reduced by 3 per cent of those for the preceding year. What will be the overhead costs during the fifth year, the first reduction taking place in the first year?

8. The fifth term of a geometric progression is 256 and the second term is 4. Find the first term and the common ratio.

9. The third term of a geometric progression is 2, and the fifth is 18. Find two possible values of the common ratio, and the second term in each case.

10. The three numbers $n-2, n, n+3$ are the first three terms of a geometric progression. Find n, and the term after $n+3$.

11. Find, in its simplified form, the common ratio of the geometric progression
$$\left(\sqrt{2}-1\right), \left(3-2\sqrt{2}\right), \ldots.$$
Find the third term of the progression.

Sum of n terms of a G.P.

Given a geometric progression we can sum the terms of the sequence.

Suppose $S_n = a + ar + ar^2 + \ldots + ar^{n-1}.$ (1)

Multiply (1) by r $\therefore$ $rS_n = ar + ar^2 + \ldots + ar^{n-1} + ar^n.$ (2)

Move terms to the right

Subtract (2) from (1): $S_n(1-r) = a - ar^n = a(1-r^n).$

$\therefore \qquad\qquad\qquad S_n = \dfrac{a(1-r^n)}{1-r}.$

Example 3.17

The seventh term of a G.P. having positive common ratio is 36, the third term is 9. Find the common ratio, and the sum of the first eight terms.

If the first term is a and the common ratio is r then the nth term is ar^{n-1}.

Thus we have $\quad ar^6 = 36, \quad (n = 7)$
$$ar^2 = 9. \quad (n = 3)$$

Then division gives $r^4 = 4$

so $\qquad r^2 = \pm 2$

or $\qquad r = \sqrt{2}$, ignoring $r = -\sqrt{2}$.

> There is no real value of r such that $r^2 = -2$.

Substitution for r in $ar^2 = 9$

gives $\qquad 2a = 9$

so $\qquad a = \dfrac{9}{2}$.

Sum of eight terms $= \dfrac{a(1 - r^n)}{1 - r}$

$$= \frac{\frac{9}{2}\left[1 - \left(\sqrt{2}\right)^8\right]}{1 - \sqrt{2}} = \frac{\frac{9}{2}\left[1 - 2^4\right]}{1 - \sqrt{2}}$$

$$= \frac{135}{2\left(\sqrt{2} - 1\right)} = \frac{135}{2}\left(\sqrt{2} + 1\right).$$

> Check rationalizing

Example 3.18

The sum of the first n terms of a series is $5^n - 1$. Show that the terms of this series are in geometric progression and find the first term and the common ratio.

If $\qquad S_n = a_1 + a_2 + \ldots + a_n$

then $\qquad a_n = S_n - S_{n-1}$
$$= 5^n - 1 - (5^{n-1} - 1)$$
$$= 5^n - 5^{n-1} = 5^{n-1}(5 - 1)$$
$$= 4 \cdot 5^{n-1}.$$

Thus the nth term $a_n = 4 \cdot 5^{n-1}$ which describes a G.P.

Then $\qquad a = 4, r = 5$.

3.7 The sum to infinity of a geometric series

If we consider the nth partial sum, i.e. the sum of the first n terms, of the series

$$S = 1 + \frac{1}{2} + \frac{1}{4} + \ldots + \left(\frac{1}{2}\right)^{n-1} + \ldots,$$

we obtain $\qquad S_n = \sum_{r=1}^{n}\left(\frac{1}{2}\right)^{r-1}$

> terms of a G.P. with $a = 1$, $r = 1/2$

$$= \frac{\left[1-\left(\frac{1}{2}\right)^n\right]}{1-\frac{1}{2}}$$

$$= 2\left[1-\left(\frac{1}{2}\right)^n\right] = 2-\left(\frac{1}{2}\right)^{n-1}.$$

Then as $n \to \infty$, $\qquad \left(\frac{1}{2}\right)^{n-1} \to 0$

and $\qquad\qquad\qquad\qquad S_n \to 2.$

Thus the series $\qquad S = 1 + \frac{1}{2} + \frac{1}{4} + \ldots \quad$ is convergent.

> Partial sums tend to a limit.

In contrast, the series

$$S = 1 + 2 + 4 + \ldots$$

has partial sum $\qquad S_n = \frac{1[2^n - 1]}{2 - 1} = 2^n - 1.$

In this case, as $n \to \infty$, $S_n \to \infty$.

This second series diverges.

It appears therefore that series whose terms are in geometric progression may converge or diverge.

From section 3.6 we saw that for $S = a + ar + ar^2 + \ldots$, the partial sum S_n is

given by $\qquad\qquad S_n = \frac{a(1-r^n)}{1-r}.$

(i) When $|r| < 1$, i.e. $-1 < r < 1$, $r^n \to 0$ as $n \to \infty$, so that

$$S_n \to \frac{a}{1-r}.$$

> $|r|$ means the numerical value of r, ignoring the sign.

(ii) When $|r| > 1$, i.e. $r > 1$ or $r < -1$,

$$S_n \to \pm\infty \quad \text{for } r > 0 \text{ or alternates } (r < 0).$$

Thus S_n does not lend to a limit as $n \to \infty$ for $|r| > 1$, in other words the series does not converge for that range of r.

> a may be positive or negative.

(iii) When $r = 1$,

$$S_n = a + a + a + \ldots + a \quad (n \text{ times})$$

so that $\qquad S_n = na$ and $S_n \to \pm\infty$ as $n \to \infty$.

(iv) When $r = -1$,

$$S_n = a - a + a \ldots$$

and $\qquad\qquad S_n = 0 \quad (\text{even } n)$

$$= a \quad (\text{odd } n).$$

Summary

The geometric series $S = a + ar + ar^2 + \ldots$ converges for $|r| < 1$.

It diverges or oscillates for other values of r.

For a convergent geometric series, we say that $\lim\limits_{n \to \infty} S_n$ is the **sum to infinity**.

Thus, sum to infinity $= \dfrac{a}{1-r}$.

Example 3.19

Write down the sum to infinity of the series
$$S = \frac{1}{4} + \frac{1}{16} + \frac{1}{64} + \ldots$$

In this case $a = \dfrac{1}{4}$, $r = \dfrac{1}{4}$.

Then sum to infinity $= \dfrac{\frac{1}{4}}{1 - \frac{1}{4}} = \dfrac{\frac{1}{4}}{\frac{3}{4}} = \dfrac{1}{3}$.

Example 3.20

Find the limit of the sequence
$$0.1, 0.11, 0.111, 0.111, \ldots$$

The nth term of the sequence is
$$0.111 \ldots 1$$

$\left\{ n \text{ 1s after the .} \right\}$

This decimal is in effect the geometric series
$$\frac{1}{10} + \frac{1}{10^2} + \frac{1}{10^3} + \ldots + \frac{1}{10^n}$$

$\left\{ 0.1 + 0.01 + 0.001 + \ldots \right\}$

As $n \to \infty$, the number of terms increases infinitely and the sum to infinity is
$$\frac{\frac{1}{10}}{1 - \frac{1}{10}} = \frac{1}{9}.$$

$\left\{ a = \dfrac{1}{10}, \ r = \dfrac{1}{10} \right\}$

Thus the limit of $0.1, 0.11, 0.111, \ldots$ is $\dfrac{1}{9}$.

Exercises 3.8

1. Find the sum of the first n terms of the series
   (i) $S = 2 + 6 + 18 + \ldots$
   (ii) $25 + 5 + 1 + \ldots$
   (iii) $12 - 18 + 27 + \ldots$
   (iv) $0.2 + 0.02 + 0.002 + \ldots$

2. Write down the sum to infinity for the various series in (i) - (iv), where it exists.

3. Write down the sum to infinity of

(i) $1 + \dfrac{1}{3} + \dfrac{1}{9} + \ldots$

(ii) $1 - \dfrac{1}{2} + \dfrac{1}{4} - \dfrac{1}{8} + \ldots$

(iii) $0.06 + 0.0006 + 0.000006 + \ldots$

4. Find $\displaystyle\sum_{r=1}^{10} (1.1)^r$.

5. Find the sum of n terms of the series

(i) $1 + x + x^2 + \ldots$

(ii) $1 - x + x^2 + \ldots$

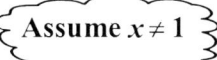

(iii) $a + 1 + \dfrac{1}{a} + \ldots$

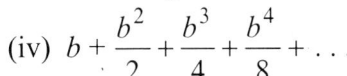

(iv) $b + \dfrac{b^2}{2} + \dfrac{b^3}{4} + \dfrac{b^4}{8} + \ldots$

6. The sum of the first 3 terms of a geometric series is 15 and the first term is 10. Given that the series is convergent, find the sum to infinity.

7. The sum to infinity of a geometric series is 15, the first term being 5. Find the sum to infinity of the series whose terms are the squares of those of the original series.

8. Find the exact value of the following recurring decimals :-

(i) $0.444\ldots$ (ii) $0.424242\ldots$

(iii) $0.4232323\ldots$ (iv) $0.1676676676\ldots$

9. A rubber ball is dropped from a height of 3 metres. At each rebound it rises to a height which is $\dfrac{2}{3}$ of the height from which it has just fallen. Show that the total distance moved by the ball tends to 15 metres.

10. The yearly output of a small coal mine is found to be decreasing by 10 per cent of its previous output. If the production in the first year is valued at £100000 what will be the value of the total output, at current prices.

11. The sum of the first two terms of a geometric series is 12 and the third term is 1. Find (a) the two possible values of the common ratios,
       (b) the sum to infinity of the series with the positive common ratio.

12. The sum of the first two terms of a geometric series is 3; the sum to infinity is 4. Find the possible values of the common ratio.

Chapter 4

Cartesian Coordinate Geometry

Coordinate geometry is concerned with the application of algebraic methods to the solution of certain geometrical problems involving straight lines, curves and surfaces. In this chapter and the next we concentrate on two-dimensional geometry, i.e. that relating to plane figures.

4.1   Coordinates in a plane

It is assumed here that the reader is familiar with plotting points in order to draw simple graphs. In particular, some knowledge of rectangular Cartesian coordinates is assumed.

The position of a point P in a plane is specified by its perpendicular distances from the fixed perpendicular lines $0x$, $0y$. The point P in the diagram has its x-coordinate equal to a, its y-coordinate equal to b.

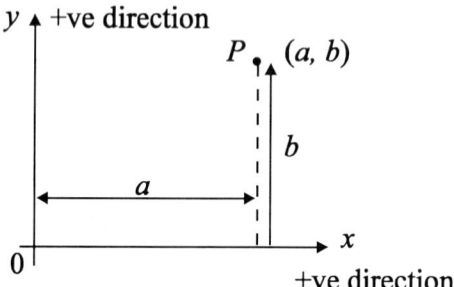

It should be noted in passing that the *x-coordinate* of a point is its perpendicular distance from $0y$ (and similarly for its y-coordinate). Also the distances are directed so that a positive (negative) coordinate is the positive (negative) direction of the axis.

The coordinates are given as an ordered pair with the x-coordinate (often called the *abscissa*) first and the y-coordinate (often called the *ordinate*) second. The point P is referred to as (a, b).

Example 4.1

The points $A(1,2)$, $B(-2, 1)$, $C(2, -3)$, $D(-2, -3)$ are represented as shown.

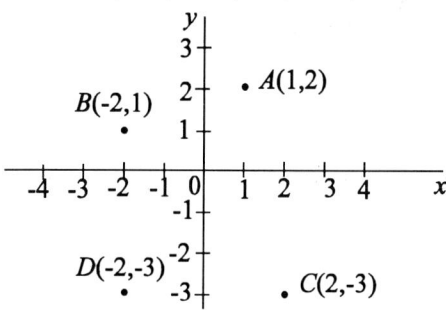

4.2   The distance between two points in a plane

Given the rectangular Cartesian coordinates of two points, we are able to find the distance between them.

Example 4.2

Find the distance between the points $A(2, 3)$ and $B(4,5)$.

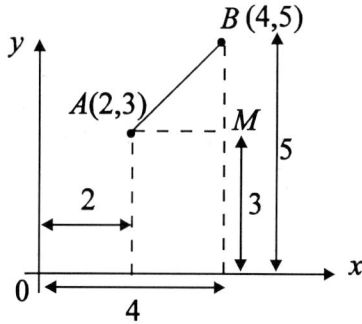

If we represent the points as shown and draw AM parallel to $0x$ as shown, then triangle ABM is right angled.

By Pythagoras' theorem,

$$\begin{aligned}
AB^2 &= AM^2 + MB^2 \\
&= (4-2)^2 + (5-3)^2 \\
&= 2^2 + 2^2 = 8
\end{aligned}$$

so $AB = \sqrt{8}$.

> Sometimes we shall use the symbol Δ to denote triangle.

In general, if $A(x_1, y_1)$ and $B(x_2, y_2)$ are two general points as shown, we then have

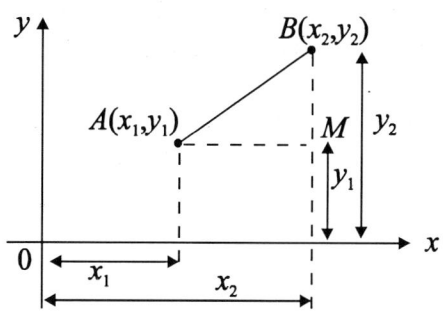

by Pythagoras' theorem,

$$AB^2 = AM^2 + MB^2$$
$$= (x_2 - x_1)^2 + (y_2 - y_1)^2$$

or $\qquad AB = \sqrt{(x_2 - x_1)^2 + (y_2 - y_1)^2}\,.$

In words, we find AB^2 by squaring the difference of the x's, squaring the difference of the y's and adding. This procedure is valid even if some or all of the x's and / or y's are negative.

Example 4.3

Find AB for $A(-2, -1)$ and $B(6, -7)$.

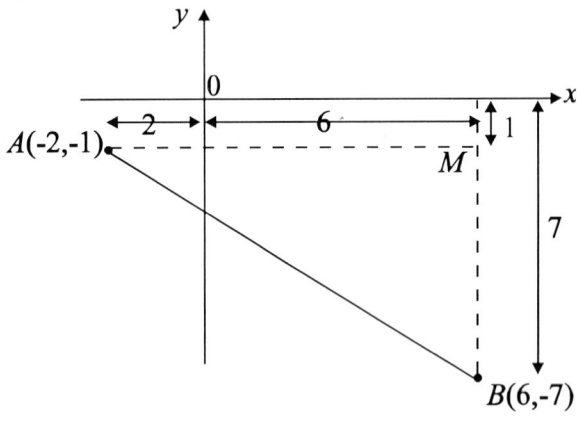

Now $\quad AM = 2 + 6 = 6 - (-2) = x_2 - x_1$,

$\qquad\quad MB = 7 - 1 = -1 - (-7) = y_1 - y_2$,

$\qquad\quad AM^2 = (x_2 - x_1)^2$,

and $\quad MB^2 = (y_1 - y_2)^2 = (y_2 - y_1)^2$

so that $\quad AB^2 = AM^2 + MB^2 = (x_2 - x_1)^2 + (y_2 - y_1)^2$.

When due account is taken of the signs of coordinates, the previous formula always applies.

Rule

The square of the distance between two points is found by squaring the difference of the x's, squaring the difference of the y's and adding those squares.

Exercises 4.1

1. Find the length of the lines joining the following pairs of points :-

   (a) $(1, 2), (2, 4)$ (b) $(1, 2), (-1, 3)$ (c) $(2,1), (0, 2)$

   (d) $(0, 0), (-3, -4)$ (e) $(-2, -3), (-4, -5)$.

2. Given the points $A(1, 3)$, $B(12, 10)$, $C(6, 0)$, show that the triangle ABC is right angled (use Pythagoras' Theorem).

3. Find the length of the lines from the origin 0 to the points (i) $(4, 5)$ (ii) $(-3, 4)$ (iii) $(-3, -5)$.

4. Show that the triangle ABC is isosceles where the points A, B, C are $(-1, -2)$, $(10, 5)$ and $(9, -8)$, respectively.

5. The point A is $(3, 2)$ and the point P is (x, y) where x and y are unknown. Given that $AP = 5$, show that
$$x^2 + y^2 - 6x - 4y - 12 = 0.$$

6. A and B are the points $(1, 2)$ and $(3, 7)$ respectively. P is the point (x, y) where x and y are unknown. Given that $AP = PB$, show that $10y + 4x - 53 = 0$.

7. Prove that the sides AB and BC of the triangle ABC are perpendicular, where A, B, and C are the points $(-2, 1)$, $(7, 4)$ and $(9, -2)$ respectively.

4.3 The midpoint of the straight line joining two given points

Example 4.4
Find the coordinates of the midpoint of the line AB, where A and B are the points $(2, 3)$ and $(4, 7)$.

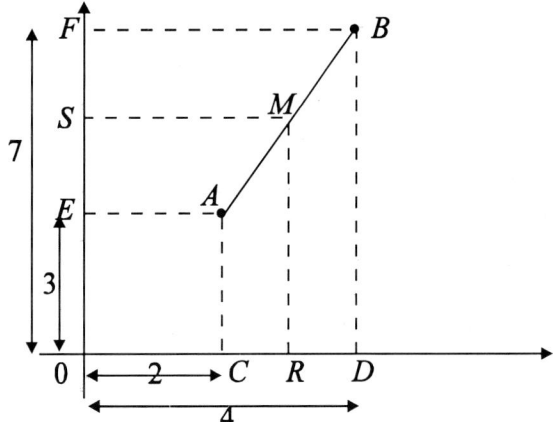

In the diagram, M is the midpoint of AB. It is possible to prove (but we shall not do so here) that R and S are the midpoints of CD and EF, respectively.
Then the x coordinate of $M = OR = OC + CR$
$$= OC + \tfrac{1}{2}CD$$
$$= 2 + \tfrac{1}{2}(4 - 2) = 3.$$
Also the y coordinate of $M = OS = OE + ES$
$$= OE + \tfrac{1}{2}EF$$
$$= 3 + \tfrac{1}{2}(7 - 3) = 5.$$
Thus M is the point $(3, 5)$.

Inspection of the original coordinates shows

$$x \text{ of } M = 3 = \tfrac{1}{2}(x \text{ of } A + x \text{ of } B),$$
$$y \text{ of } M = 5 = \tfrac{1}{2}(y \text{ of } A + y \text{ of } B).$$

This is a general result in fact. If A is the point (x_1, y_1), B is (x_2, y_2) then the above calculations with $OC = x_1$, $OD = x_2$, $OE = y_1$, $OF = y_2$ gives

$$x \text{ coordinate of } M = x_1 + \tfrac{1}{2}CD = x_1 + \tfrac{1}{2}(x_2 - x_1) = \tfrac{1}{2}(x_1 + x_2)$$

and y coordinate of $M = y_1 + \tfrac{1}{2}EF = y_1 + \tfrac{1}{2}(y_2 - y_1) = \tfrac{1}{2}(y_1 + y_2).$

Rule

The midpoint of the line joining the points (x_1, y_1) and (x_2, y_2) has coordinates

$$\left(\frac{x_1 + x_2}{2}, \frac{y_1 + y_2}{2} \right).$$

This result holds when some or all of the coordinates are negative.

Example 4.5

Find the coordinates of the midpoint of the line joining the points $(-1, 4)$ and $(3, -8)$.

Then for the midpoint

$$x = \frac{(-1) + 3}{2} = \frac{-1 + 3}{2} = 1,$$
$$y = \frac{4 + (-8)}{2} = \frac{4 - 8}{2} = -2.$$

Exercises 4.2

1. Find the coordinates of the midpoints of the lines joining the following pairs of points :- (a) $(1, 2), (2, 4)$ (b) $(1, 2), (-1, 3)$ (c) $(2, 1), (0, 2)$
    (d) $(0, 0), (-3, -4)$ (e) $(-2, -3), (-4, -5)$.

2. A, B, and C are the points $(4, 9)$, $(-2, 1)$ and $(6, 7)$, respectively. Show that $\triangle ABC$ is isosceles and find the midpoint of the base AC. Hence find the area of $\triangle ABC$. [Assume that the area of a triangle is $\tfrac{1}{2}$ base $\times$ height.]

3. A, B, M are three points such that M is the midpoint of AB. The coordinates of A and M are $(3, 5)$ and $(-1, 2)$ respectively. Find the coordinates of B.

4. Find the centre and radius of the circle which has the line joining $A(1, 4)$ and $B(3, 8)$ as diameter.

5. The coordinates of the vertices P, Q, R, S of a quadrilateral are respectively $(-1, 2)$, $(5, 4)$, $(7, 0)$ and $(-3, -2)$. A, B, C, D are the midpoints of the sides PQ, QR, RS, SP, respectively. Show that the midpoints of AC and BD coincide.

6.   Show that the triangle with vertices $(-2, 0)$, $(0, 4)$, and $(4, 2)$ is isosceles and right-angled. Find its area.

7.   Show that the figure with vertices $(3, 6)$, $(5, 4)$, $(7, 6)$ and $(5, 8)$ is a square and find its area. [Assume that the area of a square is (length of side)^2.]

We continue our study of coordinate geometry by considering the geometry of straight lines.

4.4. Gradient of a straight line

Let's consider the two straight lines given in the diagram. It is obvious from our usual notions concerning steepness that line II is steeper than line I. The concept of gradient enables us to say how much steeper line II is than line I.

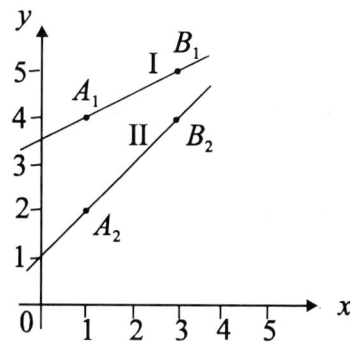

Definition

Gradient of a line is defined as the increase in the y coordinate divided by the increase in the x coordinate between one point on the line and another point on the line.

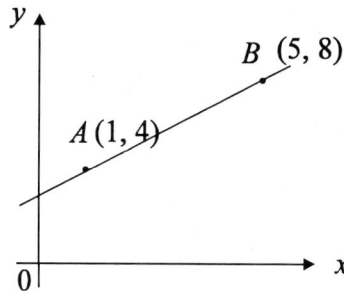

Then for the line shown above:-

$$\text{gradient} = \frac{\text{difference in } y\text{'s for } A \text{ and } B}{\text{difference in } x\text{'s for } A \text{ and } B} = \frac{8-4}{5-1} = \frac{4}{4} = 1.$$

Example 4.6

Find the gradient of the line joining the points (2, 10) and (4, 4).

Then gradient $= \dfrac{\text{difference in } y\text{'s}}{\text{difference in } x\text{'s}} = \dfrac{4-10}{4-2} = \dfrac{-6}{2} = -3.$

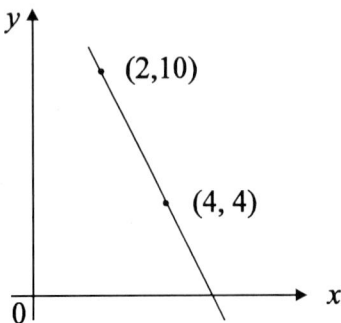

The negative gradient indicates that y decreases as x increases, in other words, the line falls to the right.

It should be noted here and elsewhere that the calculated value of the gradient is independent of the order in which the y's or x's are subtracted.

Example 4.7

Find the slope of the line joining the points (3, −5) and (−4, 9).

$$\text{Gradient} \quad = \frac{-5-9}{3-(-4)} = \frac{-14}{7} = -2$$

$$\text{or} \qquad\quad = \frac{9-(-5)}{-4-3} = \frac{14}{-7} = -2.$$

The gradient of a line is strongly related to the angle that the line makes with the x-axis.

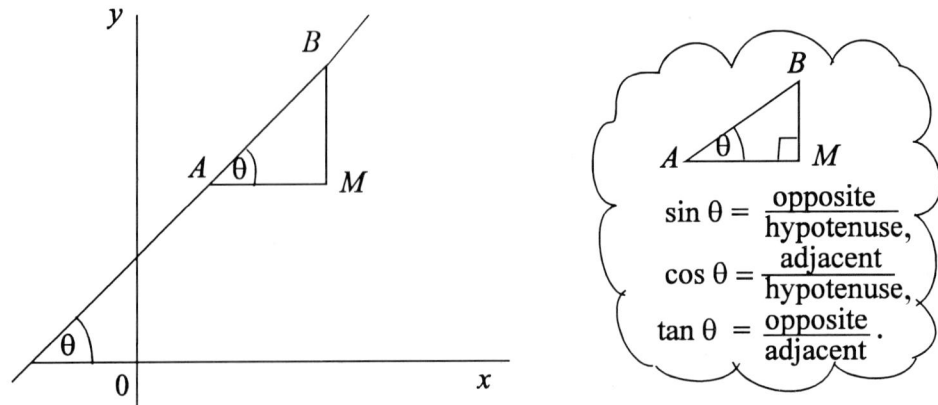

For the line shown above,

$$\text{gradient} = \frac{\text{difference of } y\text{'s}}{\text{difference of } x\text{'s}} = \frac{BM}{MA} = \tan\theta.$$

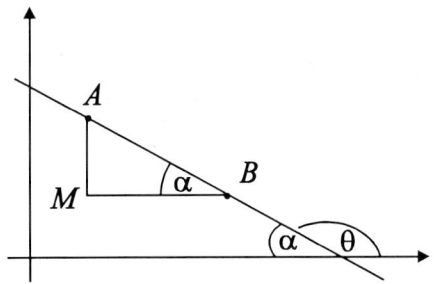

This definition applies whether the gradient is negative or positive. For a negative gradient, as shown above,

$$\text{gradient} = \frac{-AM}{MB} = -\tan\alpha = \tan\theta$$

you are asked to accept here that $\tan(180-\theta) = -\tan\theta$

since $\theta + \alpha = 180^0$.

Definition

The gradient of the line passing through the points $A(x_1, y_1)$, $B(x_2, y_2)$ is

$$\frac{\text{the difference of } y\text{'s}}{\text{the difference of } x\text{'s}} = \frac{y_2 - y_1}{x_2 - x_1} = \tan\theta,$$

or $\frac{y_1 - y_2}{x_1 - x_2}$

where θ is the angle made by the line with the positive x-axis.

Exercises 4.3

1. Find the gradients of the lines joining the following pairs of points :-
   (i) (2, 3), (4, 7)   (ii) (−2, 3), (2, 5)   (iii) (−2, 3), (2, 4)
   (iv) (8, 9), (10, 7)   (v) (−3, 6), (2, −5).

2. $A(1, 5)$, $B(3,11)$, $C(5, 17)$ are three points on a straight line. Three pairs of points can be chosen from these points. Show that the value of the gradient of the line doesn't depend upon which pair of points is chosen.

4.5   Parallel lines

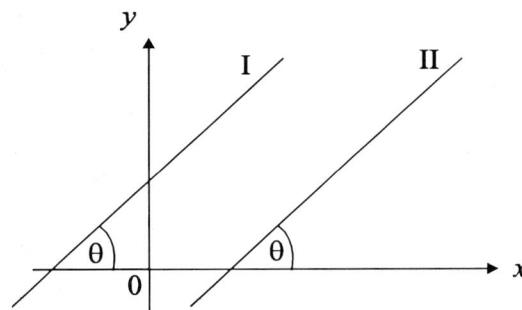

If lines I and II are parallel, they make equal angles with the positive x-axis, θ being the common angle shown in the diagram.

Since gradient $= \tan\theta$, it follows that parallel lines have equal gradients.

Example 4.8

Show that the line joining (3, 7) and (5, 15) is parallel to the line joining (−6, −8) and (2, 24).

The first gradient $= \dfrac{15-7}{5-3} = \dfrac{8}{2} = 4.$

The second gradient $= \dfrac{24-(-8)}{2-(-6)} = \dfrac{32}{8} = 4.$

The gradients are equal so the lines are parallel.

4.6 Perpendicular lines

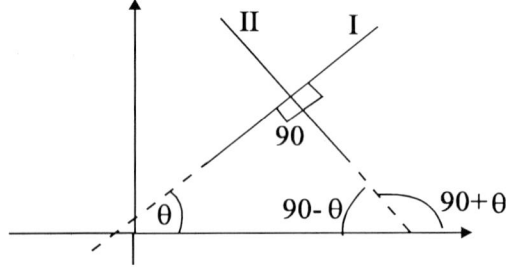

Let's suppose we have two lines I and II intersecting at right angles as shown.

$$\text{gradient of I} = \tan\theta$$
$$\text{gradient of II} = \tan(90+\theta)$$
$$= -\tan(90-\theta)$$
$$= -\frac{1}{\tan\theta}.$$

90 + θ and 90 − θ add up to 180.

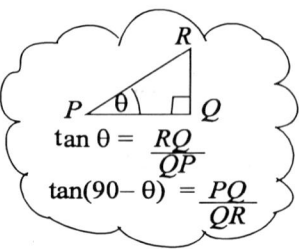

$$\tan\theta = \frac{RQ}{QP}$$
$$\tan(90-\theta) = \frac{PQ}{QR}$$

Thus $\text{gradient of II} = -\dfrac{1}{\text{gradient of I}}$

so gradient of II × gradient of I $= -1.$

Rule

The product of the gradients of two perpendicular lines is −1.

Example 4.9

Show that the line joining (1, 3) and (3, 6) is perpendicular to the line joining (8,6) and (5, 8).

$$\text{First gradient} = \frac{6-3}{3-1} = \frac{3}{2}.$$
$$\text{Second gradient} = \frac{8-6}{5-8} = \frac{2}{-3} = -\frac{2}{3}.$$
$$\text{Product of gradients} = \frac{3}{2} \times -\frac{2}{3} = -1.$$

Hence the lines are perpendicular.

Exercises 4.4

1. Determine whether AB is perpendicular or parallel to CD, or neither :-
    (a) $A(1, 0)$ $B(2, 2)$, $C(2, 6)$ $D(0, 2)$
    (b) $A(-2, 0)$ $B(0, 1)$, $C(-4, 0)$ $D(-3, -2)$
    (c) $A(1, 1)$ $B(-5, -1)$, $C(-3, -3)$ $D(-1, -9)$
    (d) $A(3, 7)$ $B(0, -8)$, $C(3, 12)$ $D(1, 2)$.

2. The points $A(2, 3)$, $B(3, 5)$, $C(2,2)$, $D(a, b)$ form a parallelogram $ABCD$. Find a and b.

3. Show that the points $A(0, 2)$, $B(4, 6)$, $C(3, 7)$, $D(-1, 3)$ form a rectangle $ABCD$. Find the area of this rectangle.

4. The points $A(3, 7)$, $B(6, 1)$ and $C(a, -3)$ form a triangle ABC with $\angle ABC = 90°$. Find a and the area of the triangle.

5. $A(3, -3)$, $B(-5, -3)$ and $C(3, 5)$ form a triangle ABC. D is the midpoint of BC. Show that AD is perpendicular to BC. Find the area of $\triangle ABC$.

6. Show that $P(11, 12)$, $Q(33, 34)$, $R(-22, 23)$ and $S(-44, 1)$ form a parallelogram. Show further that the midpoints of PR and QS coincide.

7. $ABCD$ is a quadrilateral where A, B, C, D are the points $(0, -4)$, $(3, -3)$, $(4, 0)$ and $(a, -1)$, respectively. If the diagonals intersect at right angles, find a.

4.7 The equations of straight lines

We start by considering a formula which involves x and y.

Example 4.10

Given $y = 2x + 1$ draw up a table of values of y for values of x from -2 to 3 in steps of 1. Draw a graph showing the pairs of values of x and y.

x	-2	-1	0	1	2	3
$2x$	-4	-2	0	2	4	6
$y = 2x+1$	-3	-1	1	3	5	7

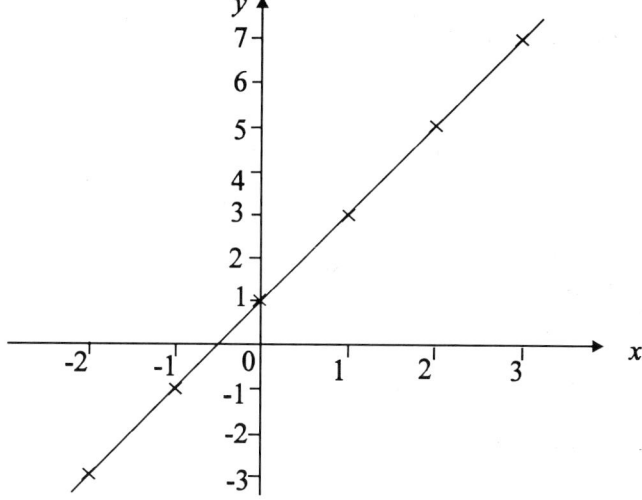

It is seen that a straight line can be drawn through all the points. A little thought indicates the reason for the graph being a straight line. From the table we see that whenever x increases by 1, y always increases by 2, or when x increases by 2, y increases by 4. The important point is that when x increases by a constant amount y increases by a constant (usually not the same as the x increase) amount.

This constant increase of y with x does not occur with $y = x^2 + 1$, as can be seen from the table.

x	-2	-1	0	1	2	3
x^2	4	1	0	1	4	9
$y = x^2+1$	5	2	1	2	5	10

Inspection of the graph in this case reveals that a curve, not a straight line, is obtained.

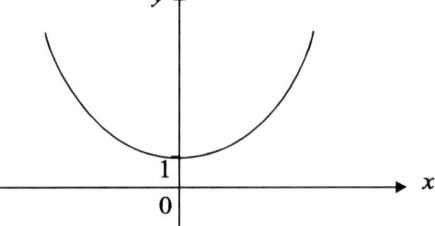

In fact, a straight line graph is only and always obtained when the formula relating x and y is of the form $\alpha x + \beta y + \gamma = 0$, where αx, β, and γ are constants.

> The establishment of this result will be given later.

It should be noted that the relationship is first degree in x and y (i.e. involves only x^1 and y^1). Also, in some cases one or two of the constants may be zero, e.g. $x = 0$, $y = \frac{1}{2}$, $x = -3$ are all equations describing straight lines.

Exercises 4.5

1. Which of the following equations represent straight lines :-
    (a) $y = 2x + 3$,   (b) $y = -3x + 2$ (c) $2y = x^2 + 1$ (d) $2y = -x + 3$
    (e) $y = x^3$ (f) $y = x$ (g) $x = -4$ (h) $y = 5$ (i) $y = 0$

In the above it was asserted that the equation of a straight line is always of the form $\alpha x + \beta y + \gamma = 0$, where αx, β, and γ are constants.

Here we specify straight lines in different ways, and show that this type of equation is always obtained whatever the specification.

(i)   Straight lines of given slope passing through the origin

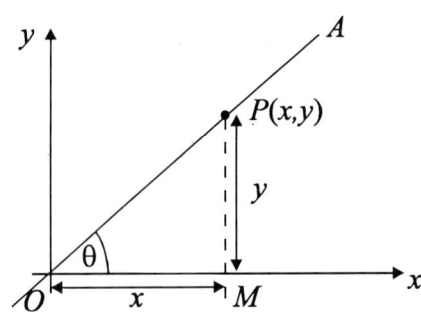

Let's suppose that a straight line OA passes through the origin and makes an angle θ with the positive x-axis direction. $P(x, y)$ is a general point on the line, and PM is perpendicular to the x-axis.

Now $\angle PMO = 90°$ and in $\triangle POM$,

$$\tan \theta = \frac{y}{x}$$

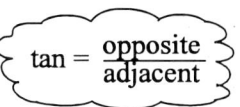

$$\tan = \frac{\text{opposite}}{\text{adjacent}}$$

or $\quad y = x \tan \theta.$

Now if we write the gradient $\tan \theta = m$ then y and x satisfy

$$y = mx \text{ or } y - mx = 0,$$

the equation of the straight line OA.

This is of the form $\alpha x + \beta y + \gamma = 0$, with $\alpha x = -m$, $\beta = 1$, and $\gamma = 0$.

(ii)   Straight line of given slope intersecting the y-axis at a given point.

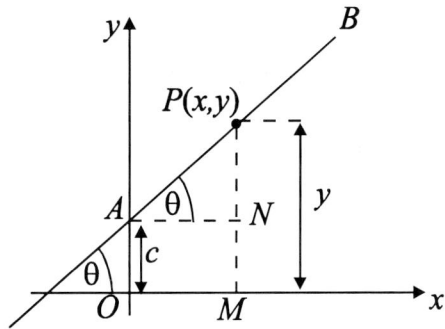

The line AB makes an angle θ with the positive x-axis direction, and crosses the y-axis at A where OA is c. Let $P(x, y)$ be a general point on the line, AN parallel to the x-axis and PM parallel to the y-axis as shown.

Now $\angle PNA = 90°$ and $\angle PAN = \theta.$
In $\triangle PAN$,

$$\tan \theta = \frac{\text{opposite}}{\text{adjacent}} = \frac{PN}{AN} = \frac{y - c}{x}$$

so $\quad y - c = x \tan \theta$

or $\quad y = x \tan \theta + c.$

Writing the gradient $\tan \theta = m$, we obtain

$$y = mx + c$$

or $\quad y - mx - c = 0.$

This is of the form

$$\alpha x + \beta y + \gamma = 0$$

where $\alpha = -m$, $\beta = 1$, $\gamma = -c$.

(iii) Straight line of given slope passing through a fixed point.
The case is a generalisation of (ii) : the given point may not be on the *y*-axis.

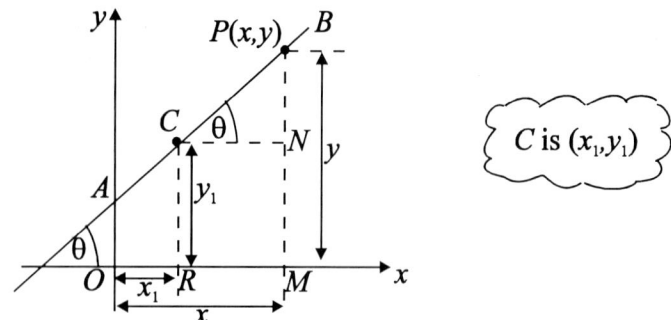

The line *AB* makes an angle θ with the positive *x*-axis direction and passes through the point $C(x_1, y_1)$, where x_1 and y_1 are assumed known. $P(x, y)$ is a general point on the line, *CR* and *PM* are parallel to the *y*-axis and *CN* is parallel to the *x*-axis.

Then $\angle PNC = 90°$ and $\angle PCN = \theta$. In $\triangle PCN$,

$$\tan \theta = \frac{PN}{NC} = \frac{y - y_1}{x - x_1}.$$

$\therefore \qquad (x - x_1) \tan \theta = y - y_1.$

If we write gradient $\tan \theta = m$, then the equation is

$$y - y_1 = m(x - x_1).$$

This form of the equation is often used. However, writing it in the form

$$y - mx - y_1 + mx_1 = 0$$

we identify it as being of the form

$$\alpha x + \beta y + \gamma = 0$$

where $\alpha = -m$, $\beta = 1$, $\gamma = -y_1 + mx_1$.

(iv) The equation of the line passing through two given points.

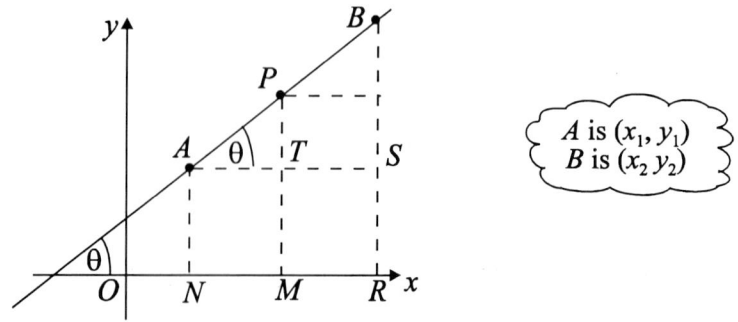

The line *AB* passes through the two points $A(x_1, y_1)$ and $B(x_2, y_2)$, where x_1, x_2, y_1 and y_2 are assumed known. $P(x, y)$ is a general point on *AB*, whilst *AN*, *PM*, and *BR* are parallel to the *y*-axis and *ATS* is parallel to the *x*-axis. The angle made by the line *AB* with the positive *x*-axis is θ which is not known i.e. not given.
Then $\angle PAT = \theta$ and $\angle PTA = \angle BST = 90°$.

From the right angled triangles *PAT, BAS* : -

$$\tan\theta \;=\; \frac{PT}{TA} \;=\; \frac{BS}{SA}. \qquad (1)$$

The details of various lengths are not shown on the diagram but a little thought leads to $ON = x_1$, $OM = x$, $OR = x_2$ and $AN = y_1$, $PM = y$ and $BR = y_2$.

Then
$$
\begin{aligned}
PT &= PM - TM = PM - AN = y - y_1, \\
TA &= NM = OM - ON = x - x_1, \\
BS &= BR - SR = BR - AN = y_2 - y_1, \\
SA &= NR = OR - ON = x_2 - x_1.
\end{aligned}
$$

Then substitute in (1).

$$\therefore \qquad \tan\theta \;=\; \frac{y - y_1}{x - x_1} = \frac{y_2 - y_1}{x_2 - x_1}$$

↑

This can now be ignored.

so
$$y - y_1 \;=\; \frac{y_2 - y_1}{x_2 - x_1}(x - x_1)$$

which is of the form

$$y - y_1 \;=\; m(x - x_1), \qquad (2)$$

where
$$m \;=\; \text{gradient} \;=\; \frac{y_2 - y_1}{x_2 - x_1}.$$

y_1, y_2, x_1, x_2 are known so *m* is known.

Then equation (2) is of the same form as that given in case (iii). In fact (2) is of the form

$$\alpha x + \beta y + \gamma \;=\; 0$$

where $\alpha = -\left(\dfrac{y_2 - y_1}{x_2 - x_1}\right)$, $\beta = 1$, $\gamma = -y_1 + \left(\dfrac{y_2 - y_1}{x_2 - x_1}\right)x_1.$

Summary

The four cases (i) to (iv) indicate that straight lines have equations of the form

$$\alpha x + \beta y + \gamma \;=\; 0$$

where α, β and γ are constants.

In practice, most straight lines can be considered to be of the forms

$$y \;=\; mx + c$$

or
$$y - y_1 \;=\; m(x - x_1).$$

Example 4.11

Find the equation of the straight line having gradient $\frac{1}{3}$ and intercept 4 on the *y*-axis.

From the equation

$$y \;=\; mx + c$$

m is the gradient, *c* is the intercept.

we see that the required equation is

$$y \;=\; \tfrac{1}{3}x + 4$$

or
$$3y \;=\; x + 12$$

or
$$3y - x - 12 \;=\; 0.$$

Example 4.12

Find the equation of the straight line having gradient -2 and which passes through the point $(2,1)$.

From $\qquad y - y_1 = m(x - x_1)$ we obtain immediately

$$y - 1 = -2(x - 2)$$

so $\qquad\qquad y - 1 = -2x + 4$

$\therefore \qquad\qquad\quad y = -2x + 5$

or $\qquad y + 2x - 5 = 0.$

$$m = -2,\ x_1 = 2,\ y_1 = 1.$$

Note

This question and all others involving straight lines can be worked using the other form of the equation of a line :-

$$y = mx + c$$

Here $\qquad m = -2$ (given) but $c = ?$

The equation is therefore

$$y = -2x + c.$$

We are able to find c by noting that the line passes through $(2, 1)$.

Using $x = 2, y = 1$ in the above, we have

$$1 = -2 \times 2 + c.$$

$\therefore \qquad\qquad c = 5$

and thus the required equation is

$$y = -2x + 5, \quad \text{as before.}$$

Example 4.13

Find the equation of the line passing through the points $(2, -1)$ and $(-1, 6)$.

The given points enable us to find the gradient of the line.

Then $\qquad\qquad m = \dfrac{6 - (-1)}{-1 - 2} = \dfrac{7}{-3} = -\dfrac{7}{3}.$

Case (iv) $\quad m = \dfrac{y_2 - y_1}{x_2 - x_1}$

Then $\qquad y - (-1) = -\dfrac{7}{3}(x - 2)$

so $\qquad\qquad y + 1 = -\dfrac{7}{3}x + \dfrac{14}{3}.$

$\therefore \qquad\qquad\quad y = -\dfrac{7}{3}x + \dfrac{11}{3}$

or $\qquad 3y + 7x - 11 = 0.$

or
$$y - 6 = \dfrac{-7(x - (-1))}{3},$$
$$y - 6 = \dfrac{-7x}{3} - \dfrac{7}{3},$$
$$3y + 7x - 11 = 0.$$

<u>Alternatively</u>, we may write

$$y = mx + c$$

where m and c are unknown constants to be determined as follows.

Now when $x = 2, y = -1$ and when $x = -1, y = 6$.

Given points are on the line.

$\underline{x = 2, y = -1} \qquad -1 = 2m + c \qquad (1)$

$\underline{x = -1, y = 6} \qquad 6 = -m + c \qquad (2)$

(1) and (2) are two simultaneous equations for two unknowns m and c.

Subtract (2) from (1).
$$-7 = 3m$$
so
$$m = -\frac{7}{3}.$$
Substitute the value of m into (1).
$$\therefore \quad -1 = 2\left(-\frac{7}{3}\right) + c$$

> Substitute values of m and c into (2) to check

giving
$$c = -1 + \frac{14}{3} = \frac{11}{3}.$$
The equation is therefore
$$y = -\frac{7}{3}x + \frac{11}{3}$$
or $\quad 3y + 7x - 11 = 0,$ as before.

Exercises 4.6

1. Write down the slopes and intercepts on the y-axis for the straight lines :
   (a) $y = 2x$ (b) $y = -x + 1$ (c) $y + 2x - 3 = 0$
   (d) $2y = x - 5$ (e) $4y - 3x + 7 = 0.$

2. Write down the equations of the lines passing through the origin $O\,(0, 0)$ and with the following gradients : - (a) 2 (b) -5 (c) $\frac{7}{2}$ (d) $-\frac{1}{3}$ (e) $0.$

3. Find the equations of the lines passing through the given points and with the given gradient :- (a) $(1, 2), \frac{1}{2}$ (b) $(-1, 2), 3$ (c) $(0, 1), 4$ (d) $(-2, 0), -\frac{1}{2}.$

4. Find the equations of the lines passing through the following pairs of points:-
   (a) $(1, 2), (3, 4)$ (b) $(-1, 3), (2, 3)$ (c) $(0, 1), (2, 0)$ (d) $(-2, -1), (-3, -4).$

5. Write down the equation of the lines which are parallel to the given lines and have the given intercepts on the y-axis :-
   (a) $y = 3x + 2,\ 6$ (b) $y = -\frac{1}{2}x + 1,\ 2$
   (c) $2y = x + 5,\ 4$ (d) $3y - 2x - 7 = 0,\ 6.$

6. Find the equations of the lines which are perpendicular to the given lines and pass through the given points :-
   (a) $y = x + 5, (0, 2)$ (b) $y = -\frac{1}{2}x + 4, (1, 3)$ (c) $3y = -4x + 9, (2, 3)$
   (d) $3y + 5x - 7 = 0, (1, 2)$ (e) $4y + 7x - 3 = 0, (0, 0).$

7. Find the coordinates of the midpoint M of the line joining the points $A(1, 4)$ and $B(3, 2)$. Find also the equation of the line passing through M which is perpendicular to AB. (Such a line is called the <u>perpendicular bisector</u> of AB).

8.   Two parallel lines *AP* and *BQ* pass through the points *A*(3, 0) and *B*(0, 4), respectively. If the point *C*(2, 1) is on the line *AP*, find the equations of *AP* and *BQ*.

9.   Given the points *A*(0, 2), *B*(4, 6), *C*(3, 7) and *D*(1, 5), find the equations of the lines *AC* and *BD*. Check by substitution into these two equations that the point $\left(2, \dfrac{16}{3}\right)$ lies on both lines, i.e. that its coordinates satisfy both equations.

4.8   Cartesian equations of curves

In the previous section we considered straight lines and their equations. What do we mean when we say the equation of a straight line is $2x + 3y - 5 = 0$?

Essentially what we mean is this :- for a point to lie on the line its abscissa (*x*) and ordinate (*y*) must satisfy the equation. In other words, the equation places a restriction upon *x* and *y* in order that the point be on the straight line.

Example 4.14

Do the points (3, 5), (6, 10) lie on the line $y = 2x - 1$?

For (3, 5), $y = 5$ and $2x - 1 = 2 \times 3 - 1 = 5$

so that the equation is satisfied and (3, 5) lies on the line.

For (6, 10), $y = 10$ and $2x - 1 = 2 \times 6 - 1 = 11$

so that the equation is not satisfied and the point does not lie on the line.

To represent a straight line, an equation must be of first degree in *x* and *y*. When the equation is not of first degree in *x* and *y*, the graph will not be a straight line.

Example 4.15

Plot $y = x^2 + x$ for $x = -2, -1, 0, 1, 2$

x	-2	-1	0	1	2
x^2	4	1	0	1	4
$y = x^2 + x$	2	0	0	2	6

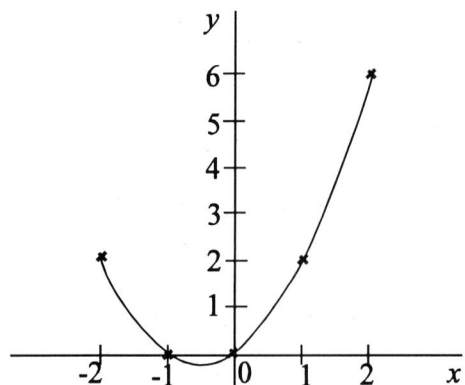

The particular restriction (equation) placed upon *x* and *y* leads to a curved graph.

Rule

When the equation in x and y is *not* of the form

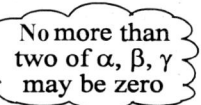

$$\alpha x + \beta y + \gamma \;=\; 0$$

the associated graph will almost always be a curved graph. There are a few exceptions to this rule,

e.g. the equation $\quad x^2 - y^2 = 0$

two straight lines

leads to $\qquad (x - y)(x + y) = 0$

which gives $\qquad x - y = 0$ or $x + y = 0.$

These exceptions may be ignored here because we shall not consider equations involving terms like y^2. Indeed, for the present, we consider equations (restrictions) of the form

y occurs only as y^1

$$y \;=\; f(x),$$

where $f(x)$ is a way of writing some general expression in x. Thus, expressions such as

Previously we used $f(x)$ to denote general polynomials. Here other expressions are allowed.

$$y \;=\; x^2 + 2x + 5$$
$$y \;=\; \sqrt{x + 2}$$
$$y \;=\; \frac{1}{x} + x$$

could be considered, but expressions such as

$$x^2 + y^2 - 2x - 4y + 5 \;=\; 0,$$
$$y^3 \;=\; x^2 + 5$$

would not be.

Exercises 4.7

1. Which of the following equations will lead to curved graphs :-
    (a) $y = (x - 1)(x - 2)$ (b) $y = 3x - 5$
    (c) $y = \dfrac{2}{5x + 17}$ (d) $y = \dfrac{1}{2}(x - 9)$
    (e) $y = x + \dfrac{1}{x}$ (f) $y = x(1 - x).$

2. Draw sketches of graphs between $x = -3$ and $x = 3$ for equations (a), (e) and (f) in question 1.

3. Determine whether the given points lie on the given curves :-
    (a) $y = x^2 + 4,\ (-2, 8)$ (b) $y = \dfrac{1}{x + 1},\ (0, 2)$
    (c) $y = (x - 1)(x - 2),\ (4, 6)$ (d) $y + 3x^2 = 4,\ (1, 1)$
    (e) $\dfrac{2}{x} + y = 3,\ (1, 2).$

4. Find the values of y when $x = 0$ in the following cases :-

(a) $y = (x - 2)(x + 3)$ (b) $y = \dfrac{1}{x + 1}$ (c) $x + 2y = 5$

(d) $y + 2x^2 = 18$ (e) $\dfrac{1}{2x + 5} + 2y = x \quad \left(x \neq -\dfrac{5}{2}\right)$.

5. Find the values of x when $y = 0$ for (a) and (d) in question 4.

4.9   Intersection of curves

Sometimes in coordinate geometry we meet concepts which require no distinction to be made between straight lines and curves. For such a concept, we assume that 'curves' signifies either curves or straight lines.

Intersection is such a concept. The point at which two curves cut is called a point of intersection. At a point of intersection of two curves, the point's coordinates x and y are subject to two restrictions : they must satisfy both equations describing the curves. Thus, to find those coordinates we solve the equations simultaneously.

Example 4.16

Find the point of intersection of the curves

$$y + 6x - 3 = 0$$
and $\qquad 2y + 4x + 7 = 0.$

Straight lines, as it happens.

If the point of intersection is $P(x, y)$ then x and y must satisfy both equations as P lies on both curves. We solve

$$y + 6x - 3 = 0. \quad (1)$$
$$2y + 4x + 7 = 0. \quad (2)$$

$(1) \times 2 - (2).$

Recall chapter 2. Here we make y coefficients equal.

$$12x - 4x - 6 - 7 = 0.$$
$$\therefore \qquad\qquad 8x = 13$$
so $\qquad\qquad x = \dfrac{13}{8}.$

Substitute this value of x in (1).

$$y + 6 \times \dfrac{13}{8} - 3 = 0$$

$$\therefore \quad y = -6 \times \dfrac{13}{8} + 3 = -\dfrac{54}{8} = -\dfrac{27}{4}.$$

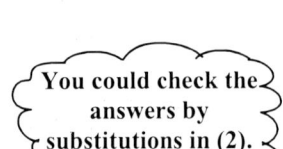
You could check the answers by substitutions in (2).

$\therefore$ Point of intersection is $\left(\dfrac{13}{8}, -\dfrac{27}{4}\right)$.

Example 4.17

Find the point of intersection of $y = x^2 + 8x + 6$ and $y = 3x$.

Solve $\qquad y = x^2 + 8x + 6 \quad (1)$
and $\qquad y = 3x \qquad\qquad\quad (2)$
simultaneously.

Substitute for y from (2) into (1).

$\therefore \qquad 3x = x^2 + 8x + 6$

so $\qquad x^2 + 5x + 6 = 0.$

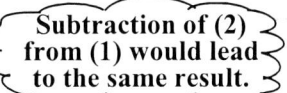

We may find x by factorising or by using the quadratic formula (Chapter 2).

By factorising,

$\qquad (x + 3)(x + 2) = 0.$

$\therefore \qquad x + 3 = 0$ or $x + 2 = 0$

so $\qquad x = -3$ or $x = -2.$

Substitute these values of x into (2).

When $x = -3, \qquad y = 3 \times (-3) = -9.$

When $x = -2, \qquad y = 3 \times (-2) = -6.$

There are two points of intersection, namely

$(-3, -9)$ and $(-2, -6).$

Exercises 4.8

1. Find the points of intersection of the following pairs of curves :-
   (a) $y - 2x + 4 = 0, \; 2y + x - 3 = 0$ \qquad (b) $x + 3y - 5 = 0, \; 3x + y + 4 = 0$
   (c) $y = 2x + 3, \; y = x^2 + 9x + 9$ \qquad (d) $y = x^2 + 4x + 2, \; y = x^2 + 7x + 3$
   (e) $y = x(1 - x), \; y = x(x + 2).$

2. Show that the curves $y = x^2 + 4x - 9$ and $y = 3x^2 + 5x - 6$ do not intersect, i.e. there are no real values of x and y satisfying both equations.

3. Find the coordinates of the point of intersection of $y = 3x^2$ and $y = 3x^{1/2}.$

4. The sides of a triangle are the lines $x = 0, \; 2x + 3y + 5 = 0$ and $3x + 2y - 4 = 0.$ Find the coordinates of the vertices of the triangle.

5. Find the values of a and b if $ax + 2y = 6$ and $3x + by = 6$ intersect at the point $(-1, 2).$ If the lines meet the y-axis at A and B, find the length of $AB.$

6. The equations of the sides AB, BC and CA of $\triangle ABC$ are $x + y = 4, \; x - y = 6$ and $2x + y = 15$ respectively, and D is the midpoint of $BC.$ Find the coordinates of A, B, C, D and verify that $AB^2 + AC^2 = 2AD^2 + 2BD^2.$

7. The vertices of $\triangle PQR$ are $P(0, 2), \; Q(4, 0)$ and $R(6, 8).$ Find the equations of the perpendicular bisectors of the sides PQ and $QR.$ Show that the point of intersection of the perpendicular bisectors is equidistant from P, Q and $R.$

8. Find the equation of the perpendicular from the point $A(2,1)$ to the line $y - 3x + 2 = 0.$ Hence find the perpendicular distance of A from the line.

9. Prove that the diagonals of the parallelogram whose sides are given by $2x + y = 3, \; x + 2y = 3, \; 2x + y = 6, \; x + 2y = 6$ are at right angles to one another.

We return to points of intersection in Chapters 6 and 10.

Chapter 5

Angles and Angular Measure

The use of degrees to measure angles is well known. The use of radians to measure angles is less well known. Both measures are considered in this chapter.

5.1 Degrees and radians

The angle between two intersecting lines OX and OP is defined to be the amount of rotation required to take one of the lines to the other. If the rotation required is anticlockwise, we take the angle to be positive.

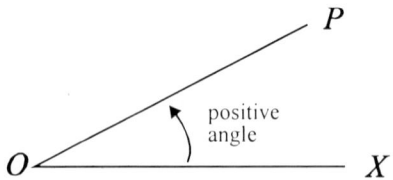

Angles may be measured in degrees or radians.

Degrees

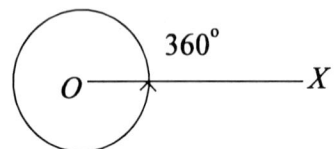

A complete revolution in which the line OX travels a complete circle is defined to be an angle of 360 degrees, written as 360°. Fractions of revolution correspond to angles which are fractions of 360°.

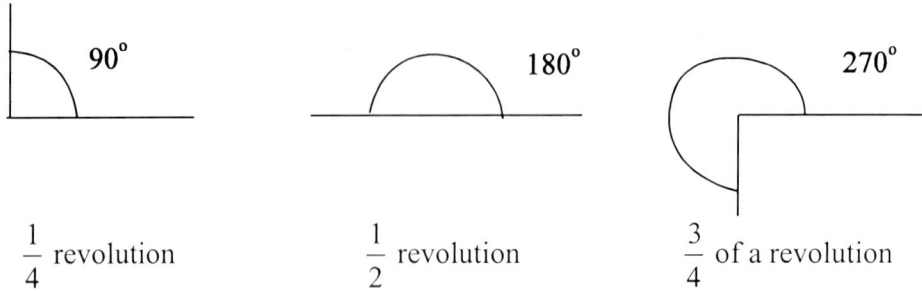

$\dfrac{1}{4}$ revolution $\qquad$ $\dfrac{1}{2}$ revolution $\qquad$ $\dfrac{3}{4}$ of a revolution

Further subdivisions are possible when using degrees. Thus

$$1 \text{ minute } = 1' = \frac{1}{60}\text{th of a degree}$$

$$\text{and} \quad 1 \text{ second } = 1'' = \frac{1}{60}\text{th of a minute}$$

$$= \frac{1}{3600}\text{th of a degree.}$$

Radians

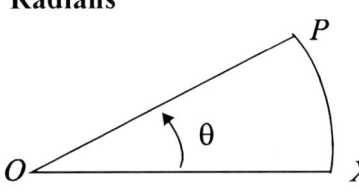

Suppose OX rotates through an angle θ as shown. During this rotation X moves along a circular arc to P.

Definition

The radian measure of the angle is defined by

$$\theta = \frac{\text{arc } PX}{OX} \quad \text{or} \quad \frac{\text{arc } PX}{OP}.$$

Then 1 radian is the angle subtended at the point O when the arc length equals OX or OP.

In a complete revolution, X moves along a circle through a distance $2\pi \times OX$ (i.e. the circumference of the circle). Thus in one complete revolution the angle subtended is

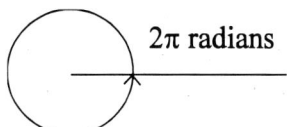

$$\frac{2\pi \times OX}{OX} = 2\pi.$$

Fractions of a complete revolution correspond to angles which are fractions of 2π.

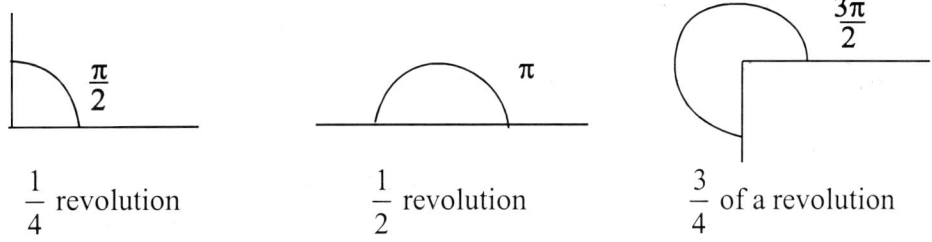

$\dfrac{1}{4}$ revolution $\qquad$ $\dfrac{1}{2}$ revolution $\qquad$ $\dfrac{3}{4}$ of a revolution

To convert from degrees to radians (or vice versa) :-

2π radians is equivalent to $360°$

so 1 radian is equivalent to $\dfrac{360°}{2\pi}$

and x radians is equivalent to $x \times \dfrac{360°}{2\pi}$.

Also $1°$ is equivalent to $\dfrac{2\pi}{360}$ radians

so $y°$ is equivalent to $y \times \dfrac{2\pi}{360}$ radians.

N.B.   To convert angles measured in degrees into radians, the angle must be expressed in decimal form, for example to convert $113° \ 33'$ into radians, first express it as $113.55°$.

Exercises 5.1

1. Draw diagrams to indicate each of the following angles, labelling the angle in both degrees and radians :-

   (i) $\dfrac{1}{8}$ revolution   (ii) $\dfrac{1}{6}$ revolution   (iii) $\dfrac{1}{9}$ revolution

   (iv) $\dfrac{1}{12}$ revolution   (v) $\dfrac{1}{4}$ revolution   (vi) $\dfrac{2}{15}$ revolution.

2. Convert each of the following to radians :-

   (i) 36°   (ii) 54°   (iii) 156°   (iv) 192°   (v) 288°

   (vi) 119.5°

3. Convert each of the following to degrees :-

   (i) $\dfrac{3\pi}{8}$ radians (ii) $\dfrac{\pi}{7}$ radians (iii) 1 radian   (iv) 0.75 radians.

5.2   Length of arc and area of a sector of circle

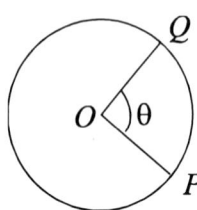

Suppose the arc PQ subtends an angle θ radians at the centre of the circle. Since an angle of 2π radians corresponds to a complete revolution, θ corresponds to a fraction of a revolution, $\dfrac{\theta}{2\pi}$.

The circumference of the circle is $2\pi r$.

> Then the length of the arc PQ is given by $\dfrac{\theta}{2\pi} \times 2\pi r = r\theta.$

The area of the circle is πr^2.

> The area of the sector POQ is given by $\dfrac{\theta}{2\pi} \times \pi r^2 = \dfrac{1}{2}r^2\theta.$

Exercises 5.2

1. Find each of the shaded areas :-

(i)

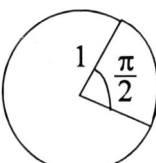

(ii)

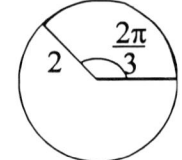

(iii)

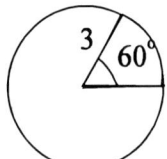

(iv)

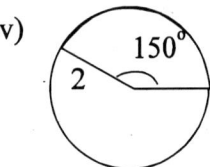

2. Find the length of the arc *PRQ* in each of the following cases :-

    (i)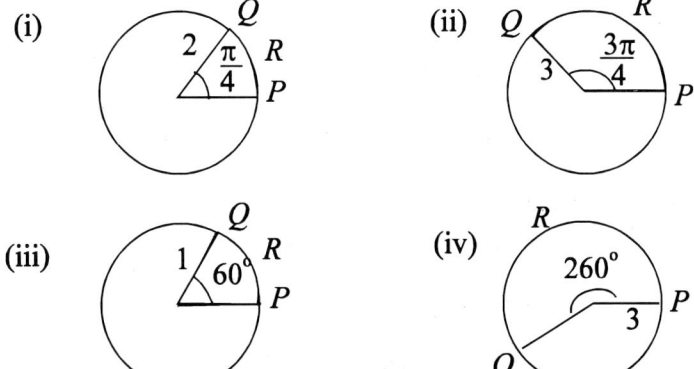

    (ii)

    (iii)

    (iv)

3. Given that the length of the arc is 5cm, find the value of the area of the sector *AOB*.

    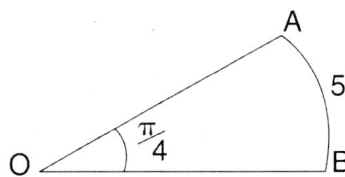

4. Given that the area of the sector *AOB* is 50cm^2, find the value of the perimeter of the sector.

    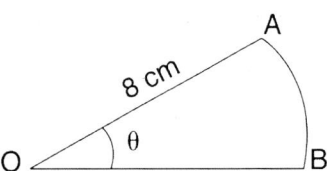

5. Given that the length of the arc *AB* is 12 cm and the area of the sector *AOB* is 48cm^2, find the values of *r* and θ.

    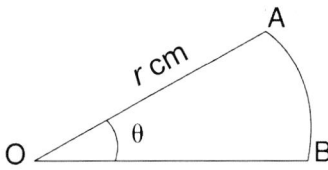

6. Write down expressions for the area *A* cm^2 and the perimeter *P* cm of the sector *AOB* in terms of *r* and θ.

    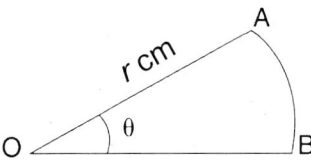

    Given that $P = 20$, show that $A = 10r - r^2$.
    Find, by completing the square, the maximum value of *A*.

5.3 Trigonometric ratios for angles between 0° and 90°

Trigonometric ratios for acute angles are defined in terms of the ratio of sides of right-angled triangles. Suppose triangle *ABC* is such that $\angle CAB = 90°$. We say that $\angle CAB$ is a **right angle**.

Now for the angle $\angle CBA = \theta$, we label *AC* as 'opposite side', *AB* as 'adjacent side'. The side *BC* is usually termed the 'hypotenuse'.

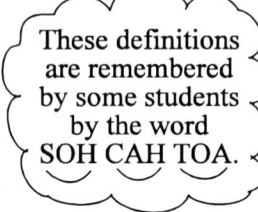

The definitions given below will be familiar.

Then using the words 'opposite' and 'adjacent' to denote 'opposite side' and 'adjacent side' respectively, we define

$$\sin \theta \;=\; \frac{\text{opposite}}{\text{hypotenuse}} \;=\; \frac{AC}{BC}\left(\frac{\text{O}}{\text{H}}\right),$$

$$\cos \theta \;=\; \frac{\text{adjacent}}{\text{hypotenuse}} \;=\; \frac{AB}{BC}\left(\frac{\text{A}}{\text{H}}\right),$$

$$\tan \theta \;=\; \frac{\text{opposite}}{\text{adjacent}} \;=\; \frac{AC}{AB}\left(\frac{\text{O}}{\text{A}}\right).$$

These definitions are remembered by some students by the word SOH CAH TOA.

There are other ratios:-

$$\operatorname{cosec} \theta = \frac{1}{\sin \theta}, \quad \sec \theta = \frac{1}{\cos \theta}, \quad \cot \theta = \frac{1}{\tan \theta}.$$

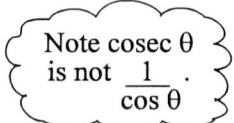

Note cosec θ is not $\dfrac{1}{\cos \theta}$.

Example 5.1

Use the right-angled triangle to find cos θ.

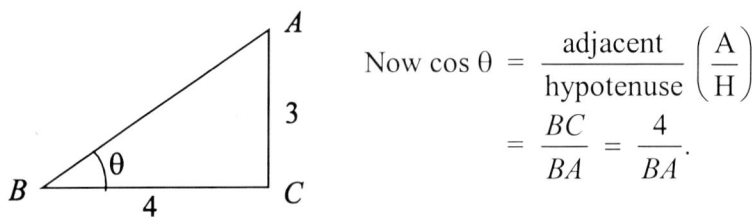

$$\begin{aligned}
\text{Now } \cos \theta &= \frac{\text{adjacent}}{\text{hypotenuse}} \left(\frac{\text{A}}{\text{H}}\right) \\
&= \frac{BC}{BA} = \frac{4}{BA}.
\end{aligned}$$

The hypotenuse *AB* is unknown but may be found by Pythagoras' theorem.

$$AB^2 = 3^2 + 4^2 = 25.$$
$$\therefore \qquad AB = 5.$$

Then $\cos \theta \;=\; \dfrac{4}{5} = 0.8.$

Example 5.2

Use the right angled triangle to find sin φ.

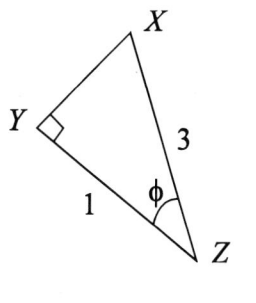

$$\sin \phi = \frac{\text{opposite}}{\text{hypotenuse}} = \frac{XY}{XZ} = \frac{XY}{3}.$$

By Pythagoras,
$$3^2 = 1^2 + XY^2$$
so $$XY^2 = 3^2 - 1^2 = 9 - 1 = 8.$$
∴ $$XY = \sqrt{8}$$

and $$\sin \phi = \frac{\sqrt{8}}{3} = 0.9428, \text{ correct to four decimal places.}$$

Calculators with the appropriate function keys provide the answers to such questions as :-

What is sin 55.6° or cos 0.361 radians or which angle has a tangent equal to 4.1? The inverse or 2nd function or shift key must be pressed to answer questions of the latter type.

Example 5.3

Use your calculator to find (i) sin 0.3 and (ii) cos 63° 46' (iii) cosec 69°3'.

(i) In mathematics when the angle units are not specified, it should be assumed that the angle is measured in radians. Thus, on ensuring your calculator is in radian mode, entering 0.3 and pressing the sin key, you should obtain sin 0.3 = 0.2955, correct to four decimal places.

(ii) Now 63° 46' ≈ 63.7667°.
Then ensuring your calculator is in degree mode, entering 63.7667 and pressing the cos key, you should obtain cos 63.7667° = 0.4420, correct to 4 decimal places.

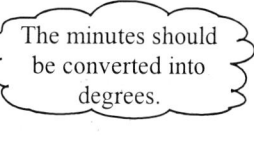

The minutes should be converted into degrees.

(iii) Most calculators do not contain a cosec key. However cosec $= \dfrac{1}{\sin \theta}$. Thus

1. convert 69° 3' to 69.05°,
2. ensure the calculator is in degree mode,
3. enter 69.05 and press sin key to obtain sin 69.05°,
4. enter $\dfrac{1}{x}$ (you may need to press 2nd F or inv or shift key first)

to obtain cosec 69.05° = 1.0708, correct to four decimal places.

Example 5.4
Use your calculator to find the angles in degrees and radians whose
(i) cosine is 0.6357,   (ii) sine is 0.1361,   (iii) tangent is 0.5369.

(i) Your calculator has a cosine key which should enable you to find the angle corresponding to a given cosine. The operation required here may be thought as undoing the cosine and is referred to as finding the **inverse cosine** or $\cos^{-1}$. The inverse cosine is also known as **arccos**.
We require $\cos^{-1}(0.6357)$ or arccos (0.6357). Some calculators have $\cos^{-1}$ or arccos marked on the keyboard. The usual procedure is
(a) enter 0.6357,
(b) press the 2nd F or inv or shift keys and then the cos key.
The result will be displayed as 50.5281° or 0.8819 radians.

(ii) Here we enter 0.1361, press 2nd F or inv or shift keys and then press the sin key. The result is 0.1365 radians or 7.8222°.

(iii) Similarly, $\tan^{-1}(0.5369) = 28.2314°$ or 0.4927 radians.

Exercises 5.3
1.(i)   Find sin θ for each of the following triangles :-

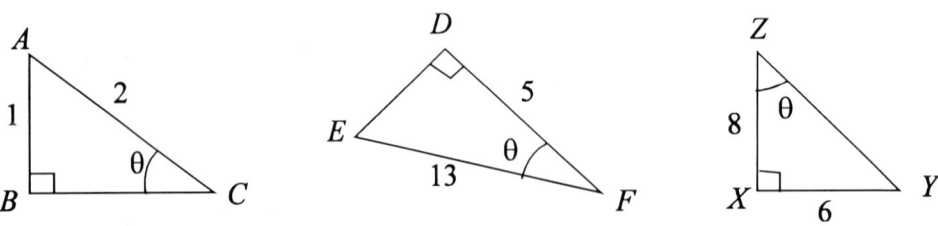

(ii)   Find cos θ for each of the following triangles :-

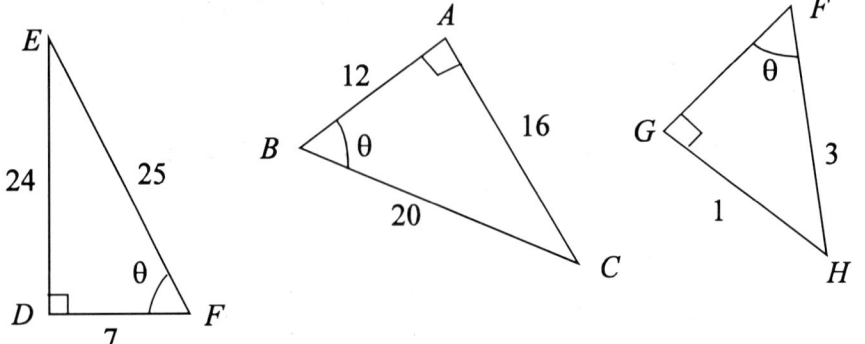

2.   Find the values of tan θ in Question 1.

3.   Find (i) sin 36.31° (ii) cos 26.52° (iii) tan 15°37' (iv) tan 0.6315
(v) sin 0.7128.

4. Find (i) $\sin^{-1}(0.7071)$ (ii) $\tan^{-1}(2)$ (iii) $\cos^{-1}(0.9161)$, giving the answers in degrees and radians.

5. Find the angles θ in degrees in the following :-

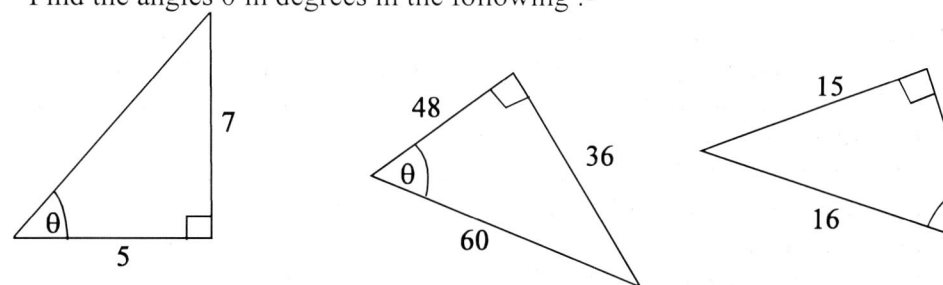

In spite of the access to answers via calculators, knowledge of the trigonometric ratios of some special angles is often useful in calculations.

5.4 Trigonometric ratios for special angles

For the present we consider 30° $\left(\dfrac{\pi}{6}\right)$, 45° $\left(\dfrac{\pi}{4}\right)$, and 60° $\left(\dfrac{\pi}{3}\right)$. Later we consider

the angles θ = 0° (0 radians) and 90° $\left(\dfrac{\pi}{2}\right)$.

(i) 30° $\left(\dfrac{\pi}{6}\right)$

We consider an equilateral triangle *ABC* of side 2 units as shown, where *AD* is the perpendicular bisector of *BC*.

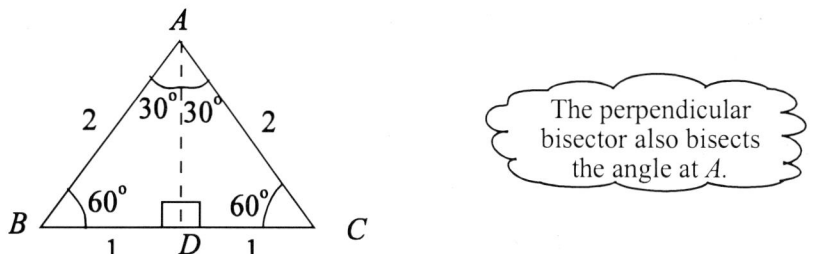

The perpendicular bisector also bisects the angle at *A*.

Now triangle *BAD* is right angled and by Pythagoras' Theorem,
$$2^2 = AD^2 + 1^2$$
so $$AD^2 = 4 - 1 = 3$$
and $$AD = \sqrt{3}.$$
Then $$\sin B\hat{A}D = \frac{BD}{BA}$$

$\dfrac{O}{H}$ for *B$\hat{A}$D*

so
$$\sin 30° = \frac{1}{2}$$

or
$$\sin\left(\frac{\pi}{6}\right) = \frac{1}{2}.$$

Also $\quad \cos B\hat{A}D \quad = \quad \dfrac{AD}{AB}$

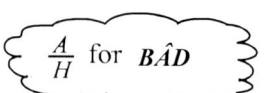
$\dfrac{A}{H}$ for $B\hat{A}D$

so

$$\cos 30° = \dfrac{\sqrt{3}}{2}$$

or

$$\cos \dfrac{\pi}{6} = \dfrac{\sqrt{3}}{2}.$$

Finally, $\quad \tan B\hat{A}D \quad = \quad \dfrac{BD}{AD}$

so

$$\tan 30° = \dfrac{1}{\sqrt{3}}$$

or

$$\tan \dfrac{\pi}{6} = \dfrac{1}{\sqrt{3}}.$$

(ii) $\quad 60° \left(\dfrac{\pi}{3}\right)$

Consider $A\hat{B}D$, which equals 60°, in triangle BAD.

Then $\quad \sin A\hat{B}D \quad = \quad \dfrac{AD}{AB}$

$\dfrac{O}{H}$

so

$$\sin 60° = \dfrac{\sqrt{3}}{2}$$

or

$$\sin \dfrac{\pi}{3} = \dfrac{\sqrt{3}}{2}.$$

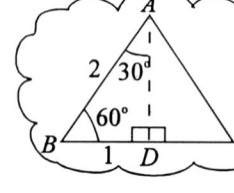

Also $\quad \cos A\hat{B}D \quad = \quad \dfrac{BD}{AB}$

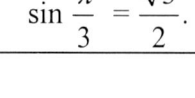
$\dfrac{A}{H}$

so

$$\cos 60° = \dfrac{1}{2}$$

or

$$\cos \dfrac{\pi}{3} = \dfrac{1}{2}.$$

Finally, $\quad \tan A\hat{B}D = \dfrac{AD}{BD}$

$\dfrac{O}{A}$

so

$$\tan 60° = \sqrt{3}$$

or

$$\tan \dfrac{\pi}{3} = \sqrt{3}.$$

(iii) $45°\left(\dfrac{\pi}{4}\right)$

We consider the isosceles right-angled triangle *UVW* as shown.

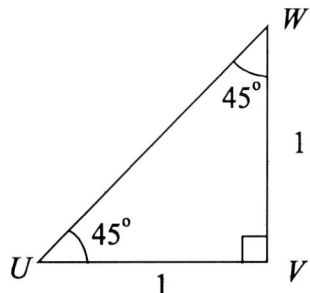

The sides *UV*, *VW* are each of 1 unit and $W\hat{U}V = U\hat{W}V = 45°$.

Then $\qquad\qquad UW^2 = UV^2 + VW^2 = 1^2 + 1^2 = 2.$

$\therefore \qquad\qquad UW = \sqrt{2}.$

Then $\qquad \sin W\hat{U}V = \dfrac{VW}{UW} \qquad \left\{\dfrac{O}{H}\right\}$

so

$$\boxed{\sin 45° = \dfrac{1}{\sqrt{2}}}$$

or

$$\boxed{\sin \dfrac{\pi}{4} = \dfrac{1}{\sqrt{2}}.}$$

Also $\qquad \cos W\hat{U}V = \dfrac{UV}{UW} \qquad \left\{\dfrac{A}{H}\right\}$

so

$$\boxed{\cos 45° = \dfrac{1}{\sqrt{2}}}$$

or

$$\boxed{\cos \dfrac{\pi}{4} = \dfrac{1}{\sqrt{2}}.}$$

Finally, $\qquad \tan 45° = \dfrac{WV}{VU} \qquad \left\{\dfrac{O}{A}\right\}$

so

$$\boxed{\tan 45° = 1}$$

or

$$\boxed{\tan \dfrac{\pi}{4} = 1.}$$

We leave the above trigonometrical ratios in fractional and surd form for ease of manipulation.

The results given in (i), (ii), (iii) are summarised in the following table.

For completeness, the results for 0°, 90°, 180°, 270° and 360° are also given although they have not been established. Angles such as 180° and 270° will be considered by other methods, of course, because it is impossible to draw a right angled triangle (or indeed, any triangle) having one of its angles equal to 180° or 270°.

sin, cos, tan of some special angles			
θ	$\sin \theta$	$\cos \theta$	$\tan \theta$
* 0° (0)	0	1	0
30° $\left(\dfrac{\pi}{6}\right)$	$\dfrac{1}{2}$	$\dfrac{\sqrt{3}}{2}$	$\dfrac{1}{\sqrt{3}}$
45° $\left(\dfrac{\pi}{4}\right)$	$\dfrac{1}{\sqrt{2}}$	$\dfrac{1}{\sqrt{2}}$	1
60° $\left(\dfrac{\pi}{3}\right)$	$\dfrac{\sqrt{3}}{2}$	$\dfrac{1}{2}$	$\sqrt{3}$
* 90° $\left(\dfrac{\pi}{2}\right)$	1	0	undefined
* 180°(π)	0	−1	0
* 270° $\left(\dfrac{3\pi}{4}\right)$	−1	0	undefined
* 360° (2π)	0	1	0

* to be established.

sec θ, cosec θ and cot θ may also be written down.

Exercises 5.4

Find the acute angle θ in the following, without use of a calculator.

1. $\sin 3\theta = \sqrt{\dfrac{3}{2}}$

2. $\cos\left(\theta + 30^\circ\right) = \dfrac{1}{\sqrt{2}}$

3. $\tan\left(\theta - 15^\circ\right) = \dfrac{1}{\sqrt{3}}$

4. $\sin\left(2\theta + \dfrac{\pi}{6}\right) = 1$

5. $\cos\left(4\theta - \dfrac{\pi}{4}\right) = \dfrac{1}{2}$

6. $\sin\left(8\theta + 12^\circ\right) = \dfrac{1}{2}$

7. $\sin\left(5\theta - \dfrac{\pi}{4}\right) = 0$

8. $\tan\left(4\theta + 23^\circ\right) = 1$.

Chapter 6

Further Trigonometry

In Chapter 5, we introduced the definitions of sin, cos, tan for acute angles. Here we

(a)   extend the definitions to angles other than acute,
(b)   use trigonometry to find areas of some plane geometric figures,
(c)   introduce a trigonometric identity,
and
(d)   solve some simple trigonometric equations.

6.1   Trigonometric ratios for general angles

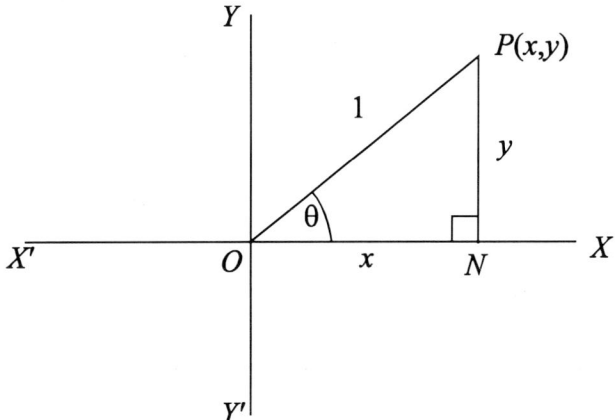

In the diagram, $X'OX$ and $Y'OY$ are two perpendicular axes. OP is a line which is supposed to rotate anticlockwise about O, OP is of length 1 unit.

If P is in the first quadrant as shown then $P\hat{O}X = \theta$ is an acute angle. Drawing PN to complete a right-angled triangle PON, we see that

$$\sin\theta = \frac{PN}{OP} = \frac{y}{1}$$

so $y = \sin\theta$.

Also $\cos\theta = \frac{ON}{OP} = \frac{x}{1}$

so $x = \cos\theta$.

Thus when OP is 1 and P is in the first quadrant with $POX = \theta$, the coordinates of P are $(\cos\theta, \sin\theta)$.

This idea is now extended to angles of any magnitude.

Definition If $P\hat{O}X = \theta$ and $OP = 1$, whatever the value of θ, the coordinates of P are $(\cos\theta, \sin\theta)$ and $\tan\theta = \dfrac{\sin\theta}{\cos\theta}$.

Example 6.1
Find the values of cos 160°, sin 160° and tan 160°.

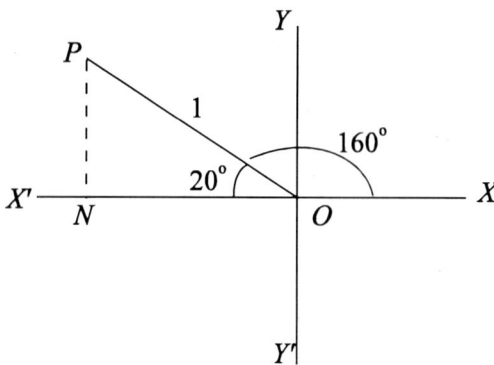

In this case, P lies in the second quadrant.
Now for P, $x < 0$ so cos 160° < 0,
                          $y > 0$ so   sin 160° > 0,
since the coordinates of P are taken to be (cos 160°, sin 160°) by definition.
Further if we drop the perpendicular PN from P to $X'OX$,
$$\cos 160° = -ON,$$
$$\sin 160° = PN.$$
Now $P\hat{O}X' = 20°$ and

$$\frac{ON}{1} = \cos 20°, \quad \frac{PN}{1} = \sin 20°. \qquad \text{Triangle } PON \text{ is right-angled.}$$

∴ $ON = \cos 20°, PN = \sin 20°.$
∴ $\cos 160° = -ON = -\cos 20° = -0.9397,$ (correct to 4 decimal places)
              $\sin 160° = PN = \sin 20° = 0.3420$

and $\tan 160° = \dfrac{\sin 160°}{\cos 160°} = \dfrac{\sin 20°}{-\cos 20°} = -\tan 20° = -0.3640.$

Example 6.2
Find the values of sin 250°, cos 250° and tan 250°.

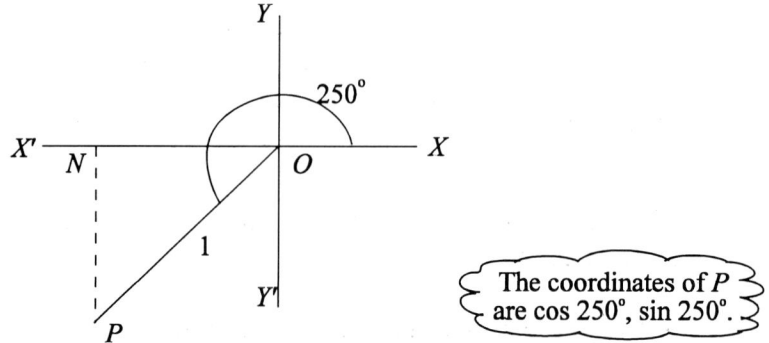

The coordinates of P are cos 250°, sin 250°.

P lies in the third quadrant. Then for the point P,
$$x < 0, \quad y < 0$$
so   cos 250° < 0, sin 250° < 0.
Then if N is the foot of the perpendicular from P to $X'OX$,

$$\cos 250° = -ON,$$
$$\sin 250° = -PN.$$

Now $P\hat{O}N = 70°$ and

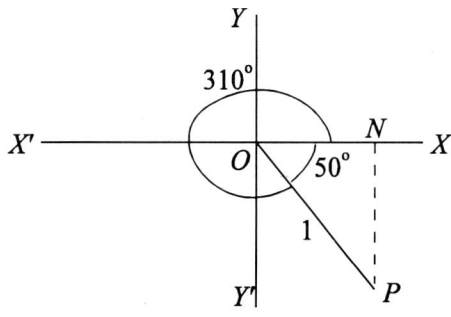

$$\frac{ON}{1} = \cos 70°, \quad \frac{PN}{1} = \sin 70°$$

so $\qquad ON = \cos 70°$ and $PN = \sin 70°$.

Then $\qquad \cos 250° = -ON = -\cos 70° = -0.3420,$

$$\sin 250° = -PN = -\sin 70° = -0.9397,$$

and $\qquad \tan 250° = \dfrac{-\sin 70°}{-\cos 70°} = \tan 70° = 2.7475.$

Example 6.3

Find the values of $\sin 310°$, $\cos 310°$ and $\tan 310°$.

Here P is in the fourth quadrant and $x > 0$, $y < 0$

so $\qquad \cos 310° > 0$, $\sin 310° < 0$.

Then as before, if PN is the perpendicular from P to $X'OX$,

$$\cos 310° = ON,$$
$$\sin 310° = -PN.$$

Now $P\hat{O}N = 50°$ and

$$\frac{ON}{1} = \cos 50°, \quad \frac{PN}{1} = \sin 50°,$$

so $\qquad ON = \cos 50°, \quad PN = \sin 50°.$

Then $\qquad \cos 310° = ON = \cos 50° = 0.6428,$

$$\sin 310° = -PN = -\sin 50° = -0.7660,$$

and $\qquad \tan 310° = \dfrac{\sin 310°}{\cos 310°} = \dfrac{-\sin 50°}{\cos 50°} = -\tan 50° = -1.1918.$

Examples 6.1 – 6.3 illustrate the following rules for assigning values of sin, cos and tan to general angles.

Rules for finding sin, cos and tan of general angles

(i) Determine in which quadrant the angle lies and allocate signs to sin and cos by reference to the signs of x and y.

(ii) Find the acute angle between OP and $X'OX$ and write down the value of sin, cos of the acute angle, and then use (i). Finally, if required $\tan \theta = \sin \theta / \cos \theta$.

After some practise, the quadrant and the acute angle may be found mentally.

Angles greater than 360° are easily accommodated by this rule.

Example 6.4

Find sin 490°, cos 490°, and tan 490°.

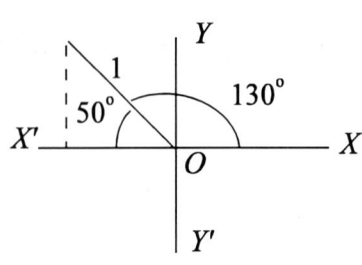

Now 490° is the equivalent to one revolution (360°) plus 130°. The angle 130° is in the second quadrant and the acute angle is 50°.

Then $\cos 490° = \cos 130° = -\cos 50°$,

$\sin 490° = \sin 130° = \sin 50°$,

$\tan 490° = \dfrac{\sin 490°}{\cos 490°} = \dfrac{\sin 50°}{-\cos 50°} = -\tan 50°$.

Finally, the procedure enables us to find the trigonometric ratios for 0°, 180°, 270° and 360°.

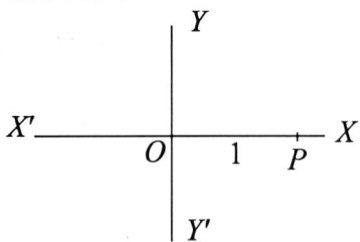

For $\theta = 0°$, the point P lies on the x - axis, with $OP = 1$.

Then $\cos \theta = \cos 0° = 1$,

$\sin \theta = \sin 0° = 0$,

and $\tan 0° = \dfrac{\sin 0°}{\cos 0°} = 0$.

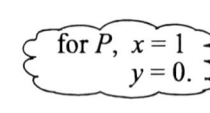

for P, $x = 1$
$y = 0$.

The derivation of the other results are left as exercises.

Exercises 6.1

1   State whether the following values are positive or negative.
(i) sin 162° (ii) sin 325° (iii) cos 279° (iv) tan 220° (v) cos (–33.6°)
(vi) sin 600° (vii) cot 195° (viii) sin (–135°) (ix) sec 140° (x) tan (–158°).

2   Express the following as trigonometric ratios of an acute angle with the proper sign :-
(i) cos 256° (ii) sin 114° (iii) sin (–10°) (iv) tan 183°6' (v) sin 345°
(vi) cos (–248°) (vii) tan 93.1° (viii) cos 585° (ix) tan (–460°).

3   Find, where the quantities are defined :-   sin 90°, cos 90°, tan 90°, sin 180°, cos 180°, tan 180°, sin 270°, cos 270°, tan 270°, sin 360°, cos 360° and tan 360°.

4   In which quadrant does the angle θ lie if
(i) $\sin \theta > 0$, $\cos \theta < 0$,
(ii) $\tan \theta > 0$, $\cos \theta < 0$.

5   For any acute angle, show by means of a sketch that $\sin(180 - \theta) = \sin \theta$ and $\cos(180 - \theta) = -\cos \theta$ and write $\tan(180 - \theta)$ in terms of $\tan \theta$.

6   For any acute angle θ, show that
$$\sin(180 + \theta) = -\sin \theta,$$
$$\cos(180 + \theta) = -\cos \theta$$
and find $\tan(180 + \theta)$ in terms of $\tan \theta$.

7   Show that if θ is acute
$$\sin(-\theta) = -\sin \theta, \quad \cos(-\theta) = \cos \theta$$
and find $\tan(-\theta)$ in terms of $\tan \theta$.

Having defined the trigonometric ratios for general angles, we are able to write down formulae for areas of triangles and parallelograms.

6.2   Areas of triangles and parallelograms

(a)   Triangles

Let's consider first the areas of right-angled triangles such as *ABC* and *XYZ*.

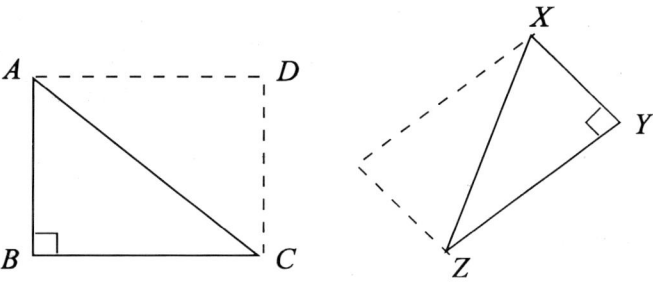

The areas of the triangles may be considered to be exactly half of the areas of the rectangles shown.

The area of rectangle *ABCD* = *AB* × *BC* so that the area of triangle *ABC* is $\frac{1}{2}AB \times BC$.

Similarly, the area of triangle *XYZ* = $\frac{1}{2}ZY \times XY$.

For a right-angled triangle,
area $= \dfrac{1}{2}$ base × height.

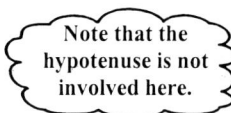

Note that the hypotenuse is not involved here.

Now triangles which are not right-angled can be built up by combining right-angled triangles.

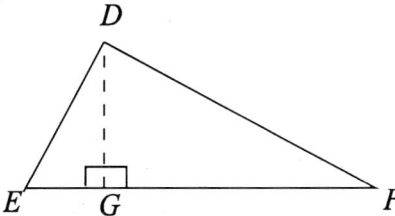   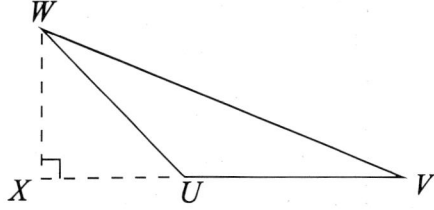

In triangle *DEF*, drop the perpendicular *DG* onto *EF*. Then triangle *DEF*

= triangle *DEG* + triangle *DGF*

so area *DEF*

$= \frac{1}{2}EG \times DG + \frac{1}{2}GF \times DG$

$= \frac{1}{2}(EG + GF) \times DG$

$= \frac{1}{2}EF \times DG$

$= \frac{1}{2}$ base × height.

In triangle *UVW*, drop the perpendicular *WX* onto *VU*. Then triangle *WUX*

= triangle *WXV* – triangle *WXU*

$= \frac{1}{2}XV \times WX - \frac{1}{2}XU \times WX$

$= \frac{1}{2}(XV - XU) \times WX$

$= \frac{1}{2}UV \times WX$

$= \frac{1}{2}$ base × height.

We conclude that

$$\boxed{\text{for any triangle,} \quad \text{area} \ = \ \frac{1}{2} \text{ base} \times \text{height.}}$$

We may express the area of a triangle in terms of one of the triangle's angles.

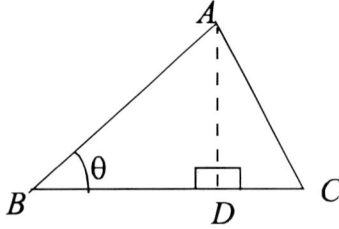

180 − θ

For triangle *ABC*,

$$\text{area} \ = \ \frac{1}{2} BC \times AD$$

$$= \ \frac{1}{2} BC \times BA \sin \theta$$

$$= \ \frac{1}{2} \text{product of two sides}$$

$$\times \sin(\text{angle between those sides}).$$

For triangle *XYZ*,

$$\text{area} \ = \ \frac{1}{2} XY \times WZ$$

$$= \ \frac{1}{2} XY \times ZX \sin (180 - \theta)$$

$$= \ \frac{1}{2} XY \times ZX \sin \theta$$

$$= \ \frac{1}{2} \text{product of two sides}$$

$$\times \sin(\text{angle between those sides}).$$

$$\boxed{\begin{array}{l} \text{Thus for any triangle,} \\ \quad \text{area} \ = \ \frac{1}{2} \times \text{product of two sides} \times \sin \text{ (included angle).} \end{array}}$$

Area of a parallelogram

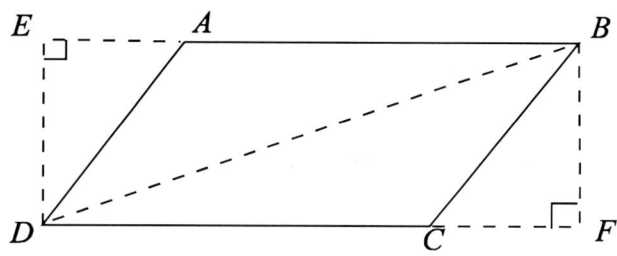

The area of parallelogram $ABCD$

$$= \text{area of triangle } ABD + \text{area of triangle } BCD$$

$$= \frac{1}{2} AB \times DE + \frac{1}{2} DC \times BF$$

$$= \frac{1}{2} DC \times BF + \frac{1}{2} DC \times BF \qquad \left\{ \begin{array}{l} AB = DC \\ DE = BF \end{array} \right.$$

$$= DC \times BF$$

$$= \text{base} \times \text{height}$$

Area of parallelogram $=$ base $\times$ height.

The area may also be expressed in terms of the sine of one of the angles.

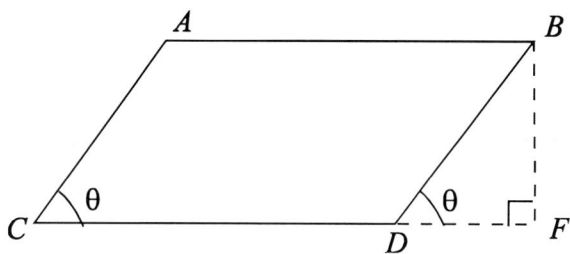

Then if $A\hat{C}D = \theta$ then $B\hat{D}F = \theta$

and $\qquad \dfrac{BF}{BD} = \sin \theta$ $\qquad \left\{ \text{corresponding angles} \right.$

so $\qquad BF = BD \sin \theta$.

Then area of parallelogram $ABCD = DC \times BF$

$$= DC \times BD \sin \theta$$

$$= DC \times AC \sin \theta$$

$$= \text{product of two adjacent sides}$$

$$\times \sin (\text{included angle between sides}).$$

Area of parallelogram $=$ product of two adjacent sides $\times$ sin (included angle).

Exercises 6.2

1   Find the area of each of the following triangles :-

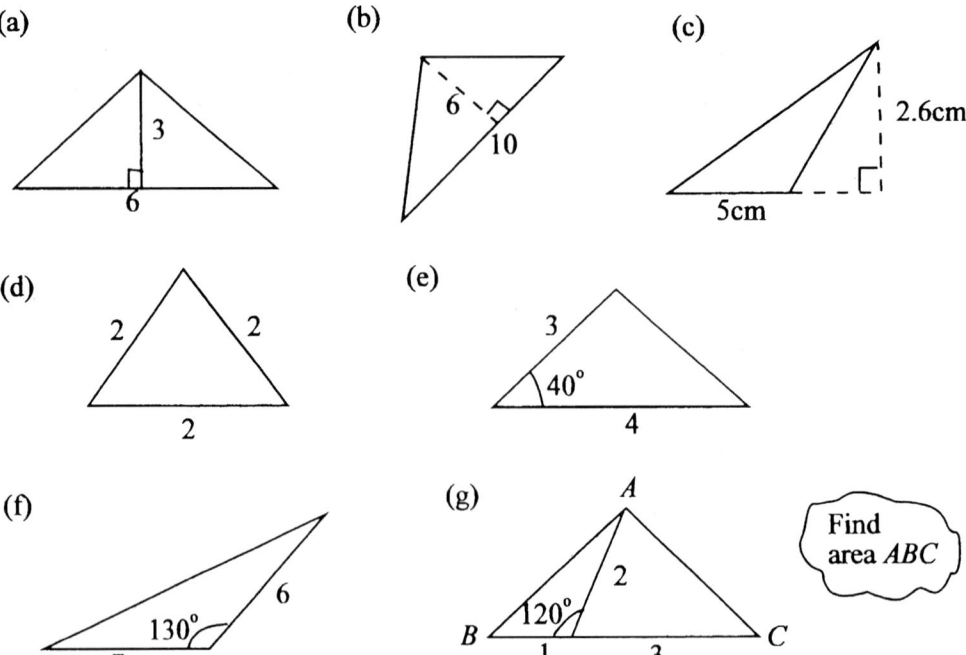

(a)

(b)

(c) 2.6cm / 5cm

(d)

(e)

(f)

(g)   Find area *ABC*

2   Given a circle centre *C*, radius 2 cm and $\angle ACB = 110°$, find the shaded area (Careful!).

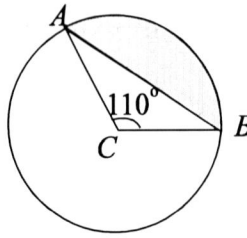

3   Find the areas of the following shapes.

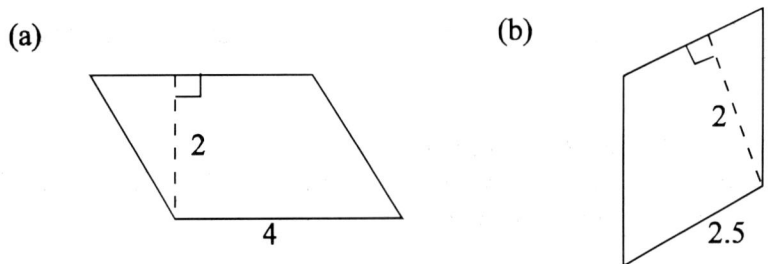

(a)

(b)

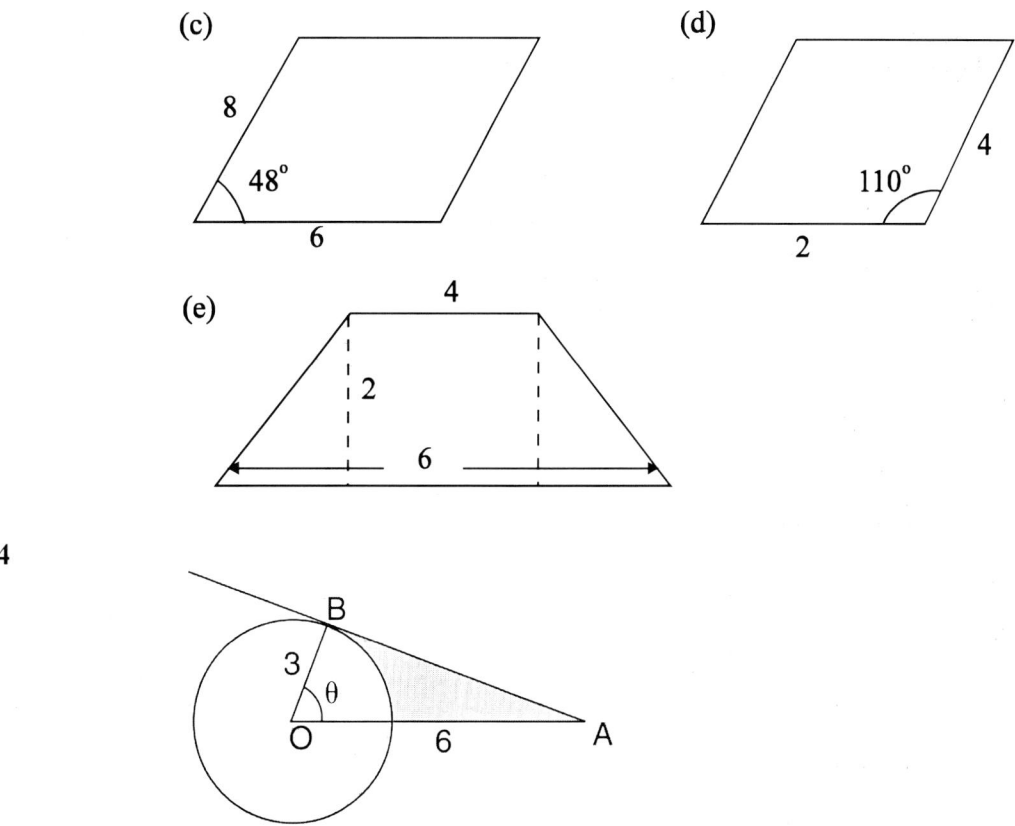

4

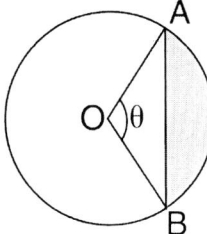

In the diagram, AB is a tangent to a circle of centre O and of radius 3cm; OA is of length 6cm and $A\hat{O}B = \theta$ radians. Find the shaded area in terms of θ.

5   In the diagram, AB is a chord of a circle of centre O and radius r; and

$A\hat{O}B = \theta$ radians. Find the shaded area in terms of r and θ.

N.B. This is an important result which often occurs in questions involving radian measure.

6.3   Graphs of trigonometric functions
In **Section 6.1**, the values of sin, cos and tan were defined for any angle. Using these values, we are able to draw graphs of the functions.

Example 6.5
Complete the following table and plot these points on a graph.

θ (degrees)	0	45°	90°	135°	180°	225°	270°	315°	360°
sin θ	0	0.7071							

The values may be found by means of a calculator or by means of the concepts introduced in section 6.1.

Thus sin 90° = 1, sin 135° = sin 45° ≈ 0.7071, sin 180° = 0,

sin 225° = – sin 45° ≈ – 0.7071, sin 270° = – 1,

sin 315° = – sin 45° ≈ – 0.7071 and sin 360° = 0.

The points are shown below on the graph.

Graph of sin

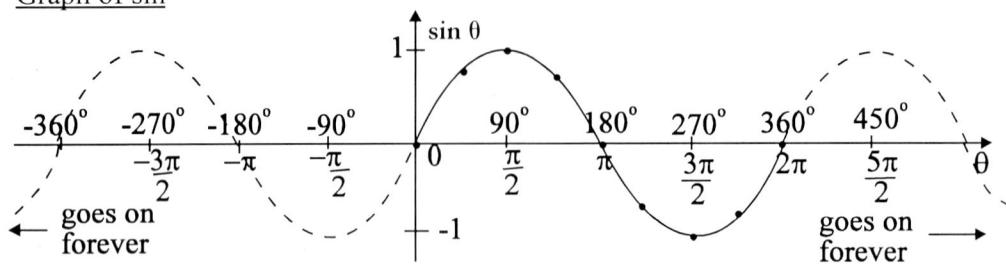

These points may be joined by a smooth curve as shown, illustrating the graph for sin θ in the range 0° – 360° (or 0 to 2π radians).

Generally, the sine of any angle can be related to the sine of an angle in the range 0° – 360° by addition or subtraction of multiples of 360°. The extension of the graph for angles outside the range 0° – 360° is shown by the dotted lines.

The main features of the function sin θ may be noted from the graph.

(i) The maximum value of sin θ is 1 and occurs at . . . – 270°, 90°, 450°, . . . and at intervals of 360°.

$\ldots, -\frac{3\pi}{2}, \frac{\pi}{2}, \frac{5\pi}{2}, \ldots$ at intervals of 2π radians

(ii) The minimum value of sin θ is –1 and occurs at . . . –90°, 270°, 630°, . . . and at intervals of 360°.

$\ldots, -\frac{\pi}{2}, \frac{3\pi}{2}, \frac{7\pi}{2}, \ldots$ at intervals of 2π radians

(iii) sin θ = 0 when θ = . . . –180°, 0, 180°, . . . and at intervals of 180°.

$\ldots, -\pi, 0, \pi, \ldots$ at intervals of π radians

(iv) The shape of the graph of sin θ from θ = 0°(0) to 360°(2π) is repeated over intervals of 360°(2π). The function is said to be periodic or cyclic. We say the period of the graph is 360° or, more usually, 2π (radians). The graph exhibits a wavelike nature and is often referred to as a sine wave.

Graph of cos

The graph of the cosine function cos θ may be plotted in the same way and has the shape shown on the next page.

Check some values
cos 45° = 0.7071
cos 135° = –0.7071
cos 180° = –1

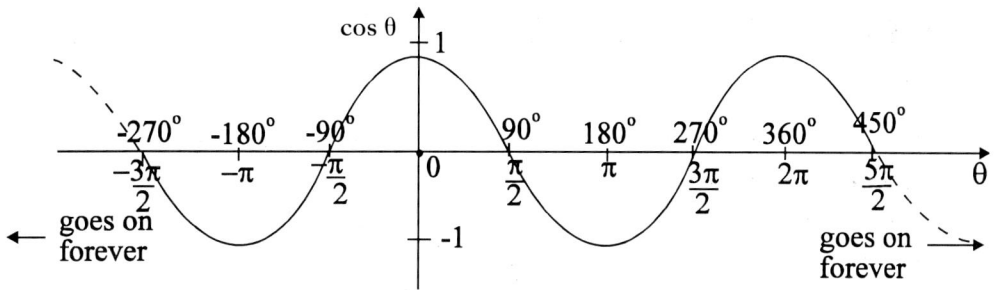

The main features of the function cos θ may be noted from the graph.

(i)   The maximum value of cos θ is 1 and occurs at . . . 0°, 360°, . . ., and at intervals of 360°.

> . . ., 0, 2π, . . . at intervals of 2π radians

(ii) The minimum value of cos θ is − 1 and occurs at . . . −180°, 180°, . . . , and at intervals of 360°.

> . . ., −π, π, . . . at intervals of 2π radians

(iii) cos θ = 0 when θ = . . . − 90°, 90°, . . . , and at intervals of 180°.

> . . ., $\frac{-\pi}{2}, \frac{\pi}{2}$, . . . at intervals of π radians

(iv) The shape of the graph of cos θ from 0 to 360° (0 to 2π) is repeated over intervals of 360° (2π). The function cos θ is also periodic or cyclic with period 360° or 2π radians, and its graph exhibits a wavelike nature similar to that of the sine function. Indeed, inspection of the graphs of sin θ and cos θ indicate that the graph of cos θ can be obtained by moving the graph of sin θ to the left through 90° (or $\frac{\pi}{2}$ radians). For that reason, the graph of cos θ is also often referred to as a sine wave.

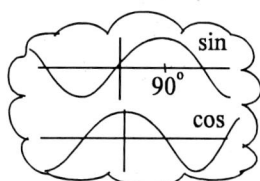

Example 6.6

From the graph of sin θ and given that sin 132° = 0.7431, correct to 4 decimal places, find all angles between −360° and 360° which have their sines equal to 0.7431, correct to 4 decimal places.

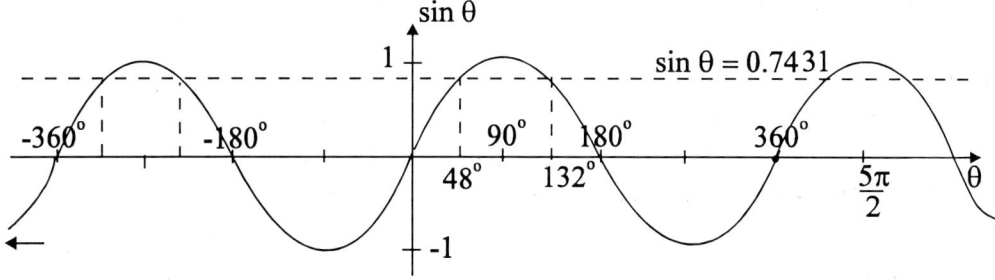

From the graph the angles are − 360° + 48°, −360° + 132°, 48°, 132°, i.e. − 312°, −228°, 48°, 132°.

Graph of tan θ

To draw the graph of tan θ we first construct a table of values for values of θ between 0° and 360° (or 0 to 2π radians).

θ	0	45°	90°	135°	180°	225°	270°	315°	360°
tan θ	0	1	undefined	−1	0	1	undefined	−1	0

The graph is shown below.

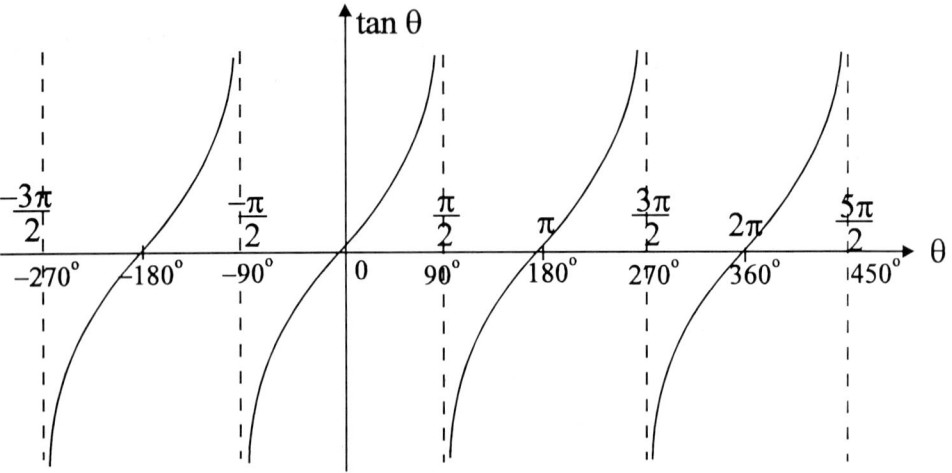

The graph has breaks at θ = . . . , − 270°, − 90°, 90°, . . ., and at intervals of 180° (2π radians). The function is said to be <u>discontinuous</u> at these points. Whilst the graphs of sin θ and cos θ (which are continuous functions) lie entirely between the values −1 and 1, the graph of tan θ stretches indefinitely upwards and downwards.

As θ approaches 90° (or $\frac{\pi}{2}$ radians) from the left, i.e. by gradually increasing values, tan θ increases indefinitely, e.g. tan 88°30' ≈ 38.19, tan 89° ≈ 57.29, tan 89.9° ≈ 572.96; and between 89.9° and 90° tan θ increases without limit. We say that tan θ → ∞ as θ → 90° ($\frac{\pi}{2}$ radians) from below or from the left.

In contrast, as θ approaches 90° from above or the right, tan θ decreases indefinitely: tan 91.5° ≈ − 38.19, tan 90.1° ≈ − 572.96. We say that tan θ → − ∞ as θ → 90° ($\frac{\pi}{2}$ radians) from the right or above.

Thus when θ is just less than 90°, tan θ is a very large positive number; when θ is just greater than 90°, tan θ is a very large negative number. We are unable to assign a definite value to tan 90° or tan $\frac{\pi}{2}$: it is undefined.

$$\tan \theta = \frac{\sin \theta}{\cos \theta}$$
and $\sin 90° = 1$
$\cos 90° = 0$.

The main features of the function tan θ may be noted from its graph, as follows:

(i)   tan θ has neither maximum nor minimum values;

(ii)   tan θ = 0 when θ = . . ., −180°, 0, 180°, . . . at intervals of 180° or π radians;

(iii) the shape of the graph from −90° to 90° is repeated over intervals of 180°: the function is periodic with period 180° (π radians), in contrast to the sine and cosine functions which have period 360° (2π radians).

> tan 210° = tan 30°, for example.

In chapter 4 the link between the points of intersection of graphs and the solution of equations was explored. There the points of intersection were found by solving equations.

Here, the link is considered from the opposite viewpoint: points of intersection are used to make deductions concerning roots of equations.

Example 6.7

Show by sketching the graphs of

$$y = \theta - \frac{\pi}{2} \quad \text{and} \quad y = \sin \theta$$

that the equation

$$2 \sin \theta - \theta + \pi = \theta$$

has a root between $\frac{\pi}{2}$ and π.

We note that where the graphs intersect,

$$\theta - \frac{\pi}{2} = \sin \theta$$

> Equating the *y*s

or $2 \sin \theta - \theta + \pi = \theta$.   (1)

The graphs are shown below.

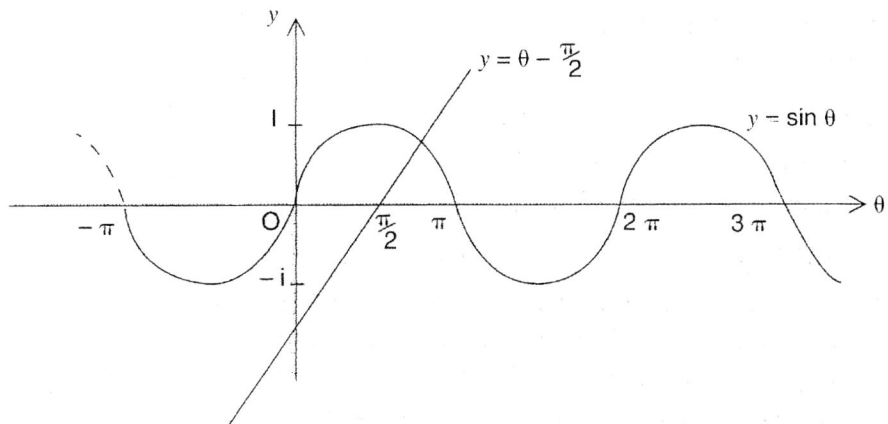

It is seen that the graphs intersect once between $\theta = \frac{\pi}{2}$ and $\theta = \pi$, indicating there is a root of equation (1) in this range of θ.

Exercises 6.3

1   Find all angles between 0 and 360°, inclusive, satisfying the following equations:-

(a) $\sin \theta = \dfrac{1}{\sqrt{2}}$ (b) $\cos \theta = \dfrac{1}{2}$ (c) $\tan \theta = \dfrac{1}{\sqrt{3}}$ (d) $\cos \theta = \dfrac{\sqrt{3}}{2}$

(e) $\cos \theta = 1$ (f) $\tan \theta = 0$ (g) $\sin \theta = -\dfrac{\sqrt{3}}{2}$ (h) $\cos \theta = -1$ (i) $\tan \theta = -1$.

2   Find the values of θ between 0 and $\dfrac{\pi}{2}$ satisfying $\sin 2\theta = \dfrac{1}{\sqrt{2}}$.

3   Without using a calculator, find
(i) $\tan 180°$ (ii) $\tan 360°$ (iii) $\tan 60°$ (iv) $\tan 240°$
(v) $\sin 330°$ (vi) $\cos 420°$ (vii) $\sin 480°$ (viii) $\cos 570°$.

4   Find the values of θ between 0 and π satisfying $\tan 3\theta = \dfrac{1}{\sqrt{3}}$.

5   Find the values of θ between 0° and 180° satisfying

(i) $\sin (\theta + 60°) = \dfrac{1}{2}$ (ii) $\cos (\theta - 45°) = \dfrac{\sqrt{3}}{2}$ (iii) $\tan (\theta - 30°) = 1$.

6   Solve the following equations for values of θ from $0°$ to $360°$, inclusive: -

(a) $\sin^2 \theta = \dfrac{1}{4}$ (b) $\tan^2 \theta = \dfrac{1}{3}$

(c) $\sin 3\theta = -1$ (d) $2\cos 2\theta = 1$

(e) $\tan^2 \theta + \tan \theta = 0$ (f) $2\cos^2 \theta = \cos \theta$

(g) $3\sin^2 \theta + \sin \theta = 0$ (h) $4\cos^3 \theta = \cos \theta$

(i) $\tan \theta = 2\sin \theta$.

7

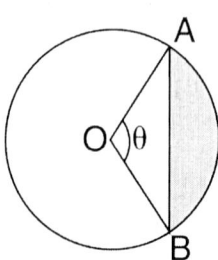

A chord AB subtends an angle θ at the centre of a circle of radius r. Given that the chord bisects the sector OAB, show that
$$\theta = 2\sin \theta.$$

By sketching the graphs of $y = \dfrac{\theta}{2}$ and $y = \sin \theta$, show that there is a root of this

equation between $\dfrac{\pi}{2}$ and θ.

8   By sketching the graphs of $y = \tan\theta$ and $y = 1 + \theta$, show there is a root of the equation

$$\tan\theta = 1 + \theta$$

between $\dfrac{\pi}{4}$ and $\dfrac{\pi}{2}$.

6.4   A trigonometric identity

The trigonometric ratios for general angles were defined in **Section 6.1**. Let's recall the definition.

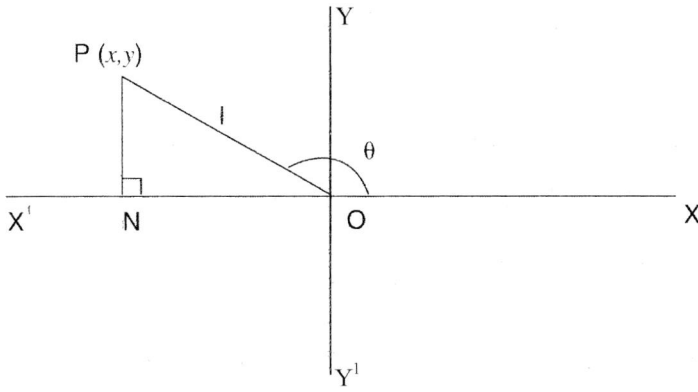

In the diagram, $X'OX$ and $Y'OY$ are the usual perpendicular axes and $\hat{POX} = \theta$.

From the definitions, P has coordinates

$$x = \cos\theta, \qquad y = \sin\theta.$$

> This applies in whichever quadrant P is situated

Then if PN is perpendicular to $X'OX$, the triangle PNO is right-angled.
Let's use Pythagoras' Theorem.
Then $ON^2 + NP^2 = 1$
Since $x = -ON$ and $y = NP$, we have

$$x^2 + y^2 = 1$$

or $\boxed{\cos^2\theta + \sin^2\theta \equiv 1}$

The symbol $\equiv$ is used to stress that the relationship is an identity, i.e. it holds for <u>all</u> values of θ.

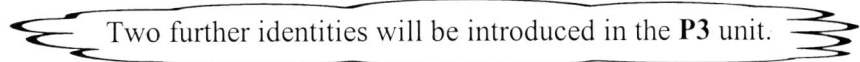
Two further identities will be introduced in the **P3** unit.

Example 6.8

Solve the equation
$$1 + \sin\theta = 2\cos^2\theta,$$
for values of θ between 0° and 360°.

The term in $\cos^2\theta$ on the right hand side indicates that the equations may be written in terms of $\sin\theta$ only.

Then from $\sin^2\theta + \cos^2\theta = 1$, we obtain
$$\cos^2\theta = 1 - \sin^2\theta$$
and the given equation becomes
$$1 + \sin\theta = 2(1 - \sin^2\theta).$$

$\therefore \qquad 2\sin^2\theta + \sin\theta - 1 = 0.$

Then $(2\sin\theta - 1)(\sin\theta + 1) = 0$

$$\sin\theta = \frac{1}{2} \text{ or } -1.$$

Then $\qquad \theta = 30°, 150°$ or 270^0.

> $\sin^2\theta + \cos^2\theta = 1$ so whenever you see $\cos^2\theta$, think of $\sin^2\theta$ and vice versa.

> or use the quadratic formula

> Remember $-90°$ from your calculator is equivalent to $270°$ after adding $360°$.

Example 6.9

Show that
$$(\cos\theta + \sin\theta)^2 + (\cos\theta - \sin\theta)^2 = 2.$$

Now $(\cos\theta + \sin\theta)^2 + (\cos\theta - \sin\theta)^2$

$= \underbrace{\cos^2\theta + \sin^2\theta}_{1} + 2\cos\theta\sin\theta + \underbrace{\cos^2\theta + \sin^2\theta}_{1} - 2\cos\theta\sin\theta$

$= 2.$

> Note there are six terms, not four.

Example 6.10

If $\sin\theta = \dfrac{3}{5}$ find, without using a calculator, the possible values of $\cos\theta$ and $\tan\theta$.

Now $\sin^2\theta + \cos^2\theta = 1$

so $\qquad \cos^2\theta = 1 - \sin^2\theta = 1 - \left(\dfrac{3}{5}\right)^2 = 1 - \dfrac{9}{25} = \dfrac{16}{25}.$

Then $\qquad \cos\theta = \pm\sqrt{\dfrac{16}{25}} = \pm\dfrac{4}{5}.$

Also $\qquad \tan\theta = \dfrac{\sin\theta}{\cos\theta} = \dfrac{\frac{3}{5}}{\pm\frac{4}{5}} = \mp\dfrac{3}{4}.$

Exercises 6.4

1. Find all the values of θ between $0°$ and $360°$ satisfying the following equations,

   (i) $\quad \sin^2\theta + \cos\theta + 1 = 0$ $\qquad$ (ii) $\quad 3 - 3\sin\theta = 2\cos^2\theta$

   (iii) $\quad 1 - \sin\theta = \cos^2\theta$ $\qquad\qquad$ (iv) $\quad \sin^2\theta - \cos^2\theta = 3\cos\theta - 2$.

2. If $\cos\theta = -\dfrac{1}{2}$ and θ is obtuse (i.e. $90° < \theta < 180°$), find, without using a calculator, the values of (i) $\sin\theta$, (ii) $\tan\theta$.

3. If $\cos\theta = -\dfrac{\sqrt{3}}{2}$ and $180° < \theta < 270°$ find, without using a calculator, the values of (i) $\sin\theta$ $\quad$ (ii) $\tan\theta$.

4. If $\sin\theta = -\dfrac{1}{\sqrt{2}}$ and $270° < \theta < 360°$, find, without using a calculator, the value of $\cos\theta$.

5. If $x = a\sin\theta$, write the following in terms of θ,

   (i) $\sqrt{a^2 - x^2}$ $\qquad\qquad$ (ii) $\dfrac{x}{\sqrt{a^2 - x^2}}$.

6. If $y = b\cos\theta$, write the following in terms of θ,

   (i) $\sqrt{b^2 - y^2}$ $\qquad\qquad$ (ii) $\dfrac{\sqrt{b^2 - y^2}}{y}$.

Chapter 7

Differentiation

Differentiation is a process related to the rates of change of functions. Let's start by considering some examples concerned with the steepness of graphs of functions.

7.1   Gradients of straight line graphs

Example 7.1
We compare the graphs of the functions $f(x) = 5x$ and $g(x) = \frac{1}{2}x$.

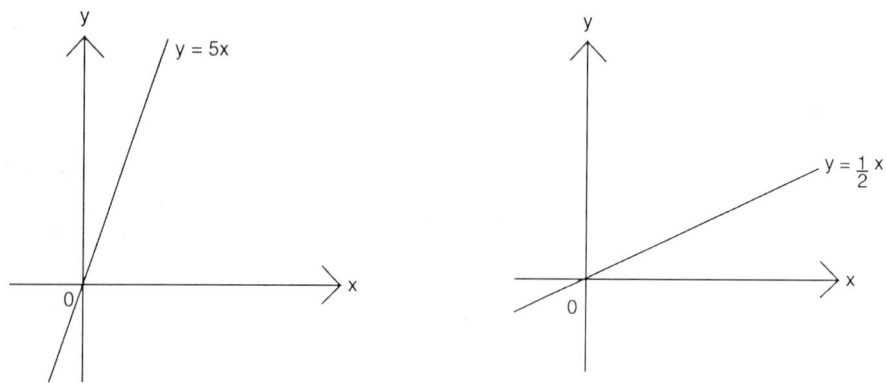

It is observed that both graphs are straight lines and that the first is steeper than the second. To analyse steepness, by analogy with descriptions of hills, we consider the gradients of the lines.

One way of characterising the gradient is to compare the rate at which y changes compared with x for motion along the line.

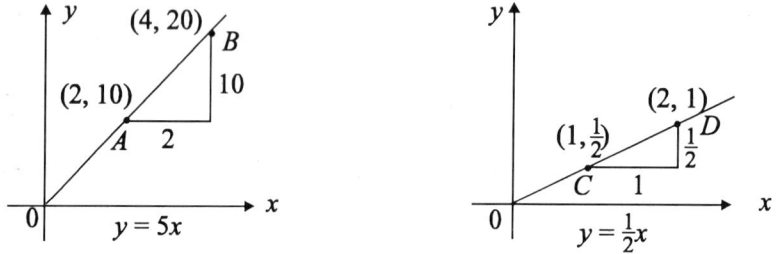

Points $A(2, 10)$, $B(4, 20)$ are taken on the first line, and points $C(1, \frac{1}{2})$, $D(2, 1)$ are taken on the second line. The gradients may be measured as

$$\text{Gradient (or slope)} = \frac{\text{difference of } y\text{'s for } A(C) \text{ and } B(D)}{\text{difference of } x\text{'s for } A(C) \text{ and } B(D)}.$$

These give $\dfrac{20-10}{4-2}$ and $\dfrac{1-\frac{1}{2}}{2-1}$,

i.e.   5   and $\dfrac{1}{2}$.

A few points are worthy of note here.

(i) The calculated gradient (or slope) is greater for the first which ties in with our intuition.

(ii) The numbers 5 and $\frac{1}{2}$ arise in $y = 5x$ and $y = \frac{1}{2}x$.

(iii) The same numbers arise if we take different points on the line. Thus $A'(5, 25)$, $B'(12, 60)$ lie on the first line and give

$$\text{gradient} = \frac{\text{difference of } y\text{'s}}{\text{difference of } x\text{'s}}$$

$$= \frac{60-25}{12-5} = 5.$$

> Check $C'(6,3)$, $D'(20,10)$ lie on the second line and give gradient $= \frac{1}{2}$.

The answers of 5 and $\frac{1}{2}$ for the gradients of $y = 5x$ and $y = \frac{1}{2}x$ respectively indicate that the slope of the line described by $y = mx$ is m.

> 'Slope' will sometimes be used instead of gradient.

Example 7.2

What is the slope of the line given by $y = 7x + 3$?

> The general form of the equation is $y = mx + c$.

The slope of the straight line may be found in the same way as before. Two points are taken on the line, say $(2, 17)$ and $(9, 66)$.

> Check these satisfy $y = 7x+3$.

Then   slope $= \dfrac{66-17}{9-2}$ $\left(\dfrac{\text{difference of } y\text{'s}}{\text{difference of } x\text{'s}}\right)$

$$= \frac{49}{7} = 7.$$

The same result is obtained if any other two points on the line are taken.

> Check $(15, 108)$ and $(28, 199)$.

The slope or gradient of
$$y = 7x + 3 \text{ is } 7.$$

More generally, if
$$y = mx + c, \text{ the slope is } m, \text{ whether}$$
m is positive, zero or negative.

> Beware signs
> For $y = -3x+2$ check with the points $(4,-10)$ and $(10,-28)$ that the slope is -3.

For $y = 8$ (constant), the slope is zero, because $(3, 8)$, $(10, 8)$ are on the line and

$$\text{slope} = \frac{8-8}{10-3} = \frac{0}{7} = 0.$$

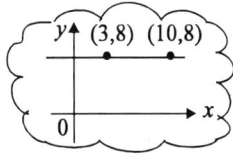

Exercises 7.1

1   Write down the gradients (or slopes) of

  (i) $y = 56x + 3$ (ii) $y = -\dfrac{10}{11}x + 11$ (iii) $y = -7$

  (iv) $y = 13 - 6x$ (v) $y = \dfrac{1}{1000}x + 1000$

  (vi) $3y = x + 6$ (vii) $7y = -3x + 1$.

7.2   Gradients of curves

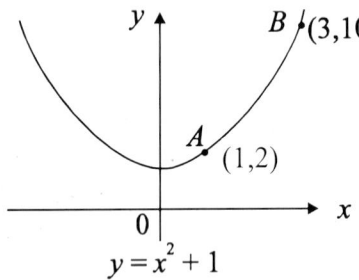

The calculation of the slope of a curve is a more difficult problem. For instance, let's consider the graph of $f(x) = x^2 + 1$ or $y = x^2 + 1$.

Now for the two points A and B on the curve it is clear that the curve is steeper at B than at A.

To make progress in investigating the slope of the curve we exploit our knowledge of slopes of straight lines. Let's adopt the following definition.

Definition

The slope (or gradient) of a curve at a point is the slope of the tangent to the curve at that point. The slope characterises the rate of change of y with x.

The introduction of the tangent to the curve in order to characterise the curve's slope appears reasonable when reference is made to a diagram.

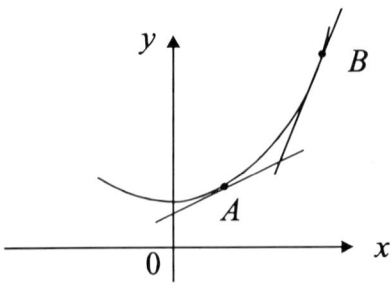

In the diagram, the curve is steeper at B than at A, and the tangent at B is also steeper than the tangent at A.

Thus, one method of measuring the slope of a curve at a point is to draw the tangent to the curve and calculate the slope of this tangent by finding $\dfrac{\text{difference of } y\text{'s}}{\text{difference of } x\text{'s}}$ for two points on the tangent. This method is not recommended because of the difficulty of drawing tangents accurately. A more objective method is preferable.

We study tangents by first considering <u>chords</u> of the curve.

Example 7.3

This refers to the curve $y = x^2 + 1$. Find the slopes of the chords joining the points

(a) $A(1, 2), B_1(2, 5)$ (b) $A(1, 2), B_2(1.7, 3.89)$ (c) $A(1, 2), B_3(1.5, 3.25)$

(d) $A(1, 2), B_4(1.2, 2.44)$ (e) $A(1, 2), B_5(1.01, 2.0201)$.

The sketch (not to scale) shows the relative positions of A and B_1 to B_5.

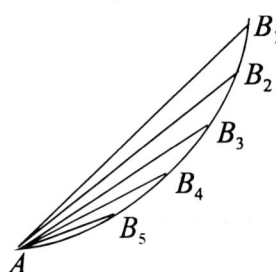

The chords AB_1, AB_2, AB_3, AB_4, AB_5, may be regarded as approximations to the tangent to the curve at A, AB_5 being the most accurate approximation. The slopes of chords AB_1, AB_2, . . . AB_5 are successive approximations of increasing accuracy to the slope of the tangent at A, and therefore by definition, to the slope of the curve at A.

Let's find the slopes of the four (straight line) chords. We recall that if we have two points on a straight line then

$$\text{slope} = \frac{\text{difference of } ys}{\text{difference of } xs}.$$

<u>AB_1</u> $A(1, 2), B_1(2, 5)$

$$\text{slope of } AB_1 = \frac{5-2}{2-1} = 3$$

<u>AB_2</u> $A(1, 2), B_2(1.7, 3.89)$

$$\text{slope of } AB_2 = \frac{3.89-2}{1.7-1} = 2.7$$

<u>AB_3</u> $A(1, 2), B_3(1.5, 3.25)$

$$\text{slope of } AB_3 = \frac{3.25-2}{1.5-1} = 2.5$$

<u>AB_4</u> $A(1, 2), B_4(1.2, 2.44)$

$$\text{slope of } AB_4 = \frac{2.44-2}{1.2-1} = 2.2$$

<u>AB_5</u> $A(1, 2), B_5(1.01, 2.0201)$

$$\text{slope of } AB_5 = \frac{2.0201-2}{1.01-1} = 2.01.$$

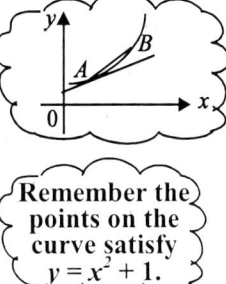

Now the slope of the chord joining A to a point <u>very close</u> to A would be a good approximation to the slope of the tangent at A.

Rather than try more numerical examples along the lines of above, it is useful to generalise and consider a point B near $(1, 2)$ with coordinates $(1 + h, (1 + h)^2 + 1)$.

Remember the points on the curve satisfy $y = x^2 + 1$.

B(1+h,(1+h)²+1)

A(1, 2)

The slope of the chord AB is

$$\frac{\text{difference of } ys}{\text{difference of } xs} = \frac{(1+h)^2 + 1 - 2}{1 + h - 1}$$

$$= \frac{1 + 2h + h^2 + 1 - 2}{h} = \frac{h^2 + 2h}{h} = 2 + h,$$

changing the order of terms for convenience.

This algebraic example conveys more information than numerical examples, namely that the slope of the chord joining $A(1, 2)$ and $B(1 + h, (1 + h)^2 + 1)$ is $2 + h$, and the nearer to zero h is, the closer this slope is to 2. By taking h sufficiently close to zero, the slope of the chord may be made as close to 2 as we please. We conclude that the slope of the tangent to the curve $y = x^2 + 1$ at $(1, 2)$ is 2.

N.B. We cannot take $h = 0$ because one step in obtaining the slope was to divide by h.

The result of example 7.3, whilst instructive, is of limited appeal in that it refers to the particular point $(1, 2)$; a more useful result would be the slope of the curve at any point.

Example 7.4

Following the procedure outlined in example 7.3, find the slope of the tangent (and, therefore, of the curve) at the point $(a, a^2 + 1)$ on the curve $y = x^2 + 1$.

We take the point $(a, a^2 + 1)$ and a neighbouring point $(a + h, (a + h)^2 + 1)$ on the curve.

The slope of the curve joining these points is

$$\frac{\text{difference of } ys}{\text{difference of } xs} = \frac{(a+h)^2 + 1 - (a^2 + 1)}{a + h - a}$$

$$= \frac{a^2 + 2ah + h^2 + 1 - a^2 - 1}{h}$$

$$= \frac{2ah + h^2}{h} = 2a + h.$$

Use brackets around $a^2 + 1$ to avoid errors in signs.

Then as $h \to 0$, the slope of the chord approaches the value $2a$.

Thus the slope of the tangent to the curve $y = x^2 + 1$ at any point is $2 \times x$-coordinate of the point.

The procedure is easily applied to polynomials of higher degree **although you will not be required to do so in the P1 examination.**

To apply the procedure to a polynomial of degree 3 we require knowledge of the following expansion:-

$$(a + b)^3 = a^3 + 3a^2b + 3ab^2 + b^3.$$

This is not required for the examination

We ask you to accept this result; if you do not wish to do so it can be derived from

$$(a+b)^3 = (a+b)(a+b)^2 = (a+b)(a^2 + 2ab + b^2) \text{ etc.}$$

Example 7.5

Find the slope at a point $(a, a^3 + 3a + 2)$ on the curve $y = x^3 + 3x + 2$.
We consider the given point $(a, a^3 + 3a + 2)$ and a neighbouring point
$(a + h, (a + h)^3 + 3(a + h) + 2)$.

Then the slope of the chord joining these points is

$$\frac{\text{difference of } ys}{\text{difference of } xs} = \frac{(a+h)^3 + 3(a+h) + 2 - (a^3 + 3a + 2)}{a + h - a}$$

> Recall expansion for $(a + b)^3$ and let b=h.

$$= \frac{a^3 + 3a^2h + 3ah^2 + h^3 + 3a + 3h + 2 - a^3 - 3a - 2}{h}$$

$$= \frac{3a^2h + 3ah^2 + h^3 + 3h}{h}$$

$$= 3a^2 + 3 + 3ah + h^2, \quad \text{on reordering the terms.}$$

As $h \rightarrow 0$, the slope of chord $\rightarrow 3a^2 + 3$.

$\therefore$ Slope of curve = slope of tangent = $3a^2 + 3$, at the point $(a, a^3 + 3a + 2)$
or the slope of the curve at any point = $3(x\text{-coordinate})^2 + 3$.

The above process of finding the slope of the curve illustrates a process known as
differentiation.

In fact, the actual process is **differentiation from first principles**. Later we
shorten the process of differentiation and give rules which enable it to be done
almost immediately. For the moment, let's look back at the ideas in examples 7.4
and 7.5.

In both cases, we were given equations of curves in
the form $y = f(x)$ and found the slope of the curve at
$(a, f(a))$. In fact, we started by considering the slope
of a chord joining $(a, f(a))$ to a neighbouring point $(a+h, f(a + h))$:-

> Ex 7.4, $f(x) = x^2 + 1$
> Ex 7.5, $f(x) = x^3 + 3x + 2$

$$\frac{\text{difference of } ys}{\text{difference of } xs} = \frac{f(a + h) - f(a)}{h}.$$

> e.g. in Ex 7.5
> $\frac{(a+h)^3 + 3(a+h) + 2 - (a^3 + 3a + 2)}{h}$

After some tidying up, we imagined h to become smaller and smaller, i.e. to tend
to zero, and identified the final result as the slope of the curve at $(a, f(a))$.

We make some further observations on the process.

(i) It is unnecessary to introduce the letter 'a' to denote a general point : the letter x is
equally valid. Thus in example 7.4 the slope at the point $(x, x^2 + 1)$ is $2x$; and in
example 7.5 the slope at the point $(x, x^3 + 3x + 2)$ is $3x^2 + 3$. Thus we may
consider the ratio $\dfrac{f(x+h) - f(x)}{h}$ instead of $\dfrac{f(a+h) - f(a)}{h}$.

(ii) A convenient way of writing the slope of the function $f(x)$ is to use the symbol
$f'(x)$. Thus we have shown
that if $f(x) = x^2 + 1$ then $f'(x) = 2x$,
and if $f(x) = x^3 + 3x + 2$ then $f'(x) = 3x^2 + 3$.
The function $f'(x)$ is called the <u>derivative</u> or <u>derived function</u> of $f(x)$.

(iii) The process of differentiating involves the final stage of letting $h \to 0$ and deciding upon the limit of the final expression.

Drawing on the points considered in (i), (ii), (iii), we say that the derived function $f'(x)$ of $f(x)$ is given by

$$f'(x) = \lim_{h \to 0} \frac{f(x+h) - f(x)}{h}.$$

We use this result in the following example.

Example 7.6 (Non-examinable, but very important)

Given $f(x) = x^3 - 4x + 1$ find $f'(x)$, i.e. find the derived function $f'(x)$ or differentiate $f(x)$.

See expansion for $(a+b)^3$ with $a = x, b = h$

$$\text{Now} \quad f'(x) = \lim_{h \to 0} \frac{f(x+h) - f(x)}{h}$$

$$= \lim_{h \to 0} \frac{(x+h)^3 - 4(x+h) + 1 - (x^3 - 4x + 1)}{h}$$

$$= \lim_{h \to 0} \frac{x^3 + 3x^2h + 3xh^2 + h^3 - 4x - 4h + 1 - x^3 + 4x - 1}{h}$$

$$= \lim_{h \to 0} \frac{3x^2h + 3xh^2 + h^3 - 4h}{h}$$

$$= \lim_{h \to 0} 3x^2 + 3xh + h^2 - 4$$

$$= 3x^2 - 4.$$

Thus if $\quad f(x) = x^3 - 4x + 1$

then $\quad f'(x) = 3x^2 - 4.$

Exercises 7.2

1   Find the slope of the chord joining the points (2, 8) and (2.1, 9.261) on the curve $y = x^3$.

2   Find the slope of the chord joining the points (2,16) and $(2 + h, 3(2 + h)^2 + 4)$ on the curve $y = 3x^2 + 4$. By letting $h \to 0$, find the slope of the curve at (2,16).

3   Find the slope of the curve $y = x^3 - 3x + 1$ at the point (3, 19).

4   If $f(x) = 2x^2 + 3x - 4$, show that $\dfrac{f(x+h) - f(x)}{h} = 4x + 3 + 2h$ and hence find $f'(x)$.

5   Given $f(x) = 7x^2 - 3x + 10$, find $f'(x)$ from first principles.

6   Differentiate $f(x) = x^3 - x^2 + 4$ from first principles.

7   Differentiate the following from first principles

   (i) $3x^3$ (ii) $2x^2$ (iii) $6x$ (iv) $3x^3 + 2x^2 + 6x$.

   What is the relationship between the answers to (i), (ii), (iii) and (iv)?

Note on limits

The process of finding a limit is an essential component of differentiating functions from first principles. To recall, given a function f(x) then

$$f'(x) = \lim_{h \to 0} \frac{f(x+h) - f(x)}{h}.$$

Thus, for example, if f(x) = x^2,

$$f'(x) = \lim_{h \to 0} \frac{(x+h)^2 - x^2}{h}$$

$$= \lim_{h \to 0} (2x + h)$$

check this

$$= 2x.$$

The argument is that as $h \to 0$, $2x + h \to 2x$.

The following question is often raised by students. As <u>in effect</u> we set $h = 0$ in $2x + h$ to obtain $2x$, why don't we put $h = 0$ earlier in the calculation?

To respond to this question, we note that we first consider the slope of the chord joining the points (x, f(x)) and ($x + h$, f($x + h$)) and a chord requires two end points for its definition, so $h \neq 0$. During the limiting process we suppose h becomes smaller and smaller (without allowing it to take the value zero), and observe in the above example that $2x + h$ becomes <u>closer</u> and <u>closer</u> to $2x$ <u>without attaining the value $2x$</u>.

It should also be noted that if we set $h = 0$ in $\dfrac{f(x+h) - f(x)}{h}$ we obtain $\dfrac{0}{0}$ which is undefined.

7.3 The delta notation

An alternative method of presenting differentiation uses the delta prefix.
In mathematics, the letter is often used to mean 'small increase' so that

δx means small increase in x,

δy means small increase in y, and so on.

To find the slope of the curve $y = x^2 + 1$ at the point (2, 5) using this notation, we proceed as follows.

Let A be the point (2, 5) and let δx, δy be corresponding increments in x and y so that B is the point (2 + δx, 5 + δy) on the curve.

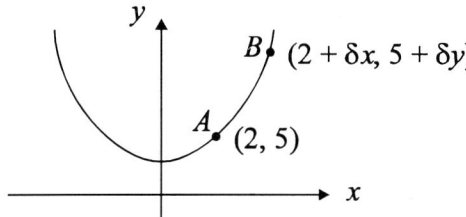

To relate to our previous work in section 7.2 we note that $\delta x = h$ and $\delta y = f(2 + h) - f(2)$ with $f(x) = x^2$.

Since B lies on the curve $y = x^2 + 1$,

$$5 + \delta y = (2 + \delta x)^2 + 1$$

or

$$\delta y = (2 + \delta x)^2 - 4$$

$$= 4\delta x + (\delta x)^2.$$

Then $$\frac{\delta y}{\delta x} = 4 + \delta x.$$

The slope (or gradient) at $(2, 5)$ is found by letting δx become smaller and smaller i.e. letting $\delta x \to 0$.

Then

slope $= \lim_{\delta x \to 0}(4 + \delta x)$

$= 4.$

We write $\lim_{\delta x \to 0}\frac{\delta y}{\delta x} = \frac{dy}{dx},$

thus if $y = x^2 + 1$ then

$\frac{dy}{dx} = 4$ at $(2, 5)$.

> $\frac{f(2+h)-f(2)}{h}$
> $= 4 + h$ if $f(x) = x^2$

> Compare with $\lim(4 + h).$ $h \to 0$

> If $f(x) = x^2 + 1$ then $f'(2) = 4.$

As in section 7.2, we are able to find the gradient at any point on the curve.

Example 7.7

If $y = x^3 - x + 2$, find $\frac{dy}{dx}$ at the point $(x, x^3 - x + 2)$.

Now $y = x^3 - x + 2.$ (1)

Let $\delta x, \delta y$ be corresponding increments in x and y respectively so that

$y + \delta y = (x + \delta x)^3 - (x + \delta x) + 2.$ (2)

Subtracting (1) from (2), we obtain

$\delta y = (x + \delta x)^3 - (x + \delta x) + 2 - (x^3 - x + 2)$

$= x^3 + 3x^2\delta x + 3x(\delta x)^2 + (\delta x)^3 - x - \delta x + 2 - x^3 + x - 2$

$\therefore \quad \delta y = (3x^2 - 1)\,\delta x + 3x(\delta x)^2 + (\delta x)^3$

and $\frac{\delta y}{\delta x} = 3x^2 - 1 + 3x\delta x + (\delta x)^2.$

> Note the use of brackets when subtracting.

Then $\frac{dy}{dx} = \lim_{\delta x \to 0}\frac{\delta y}{\delta x} = \lim_{\delta x \to 0}(3x^2 - 1 + 3x\delta x + (\delta x)^2)$

$= 3x^2 - 1.$

> Note expansion for $(a+b)^3$ with $a = x, b = \delta x.$

Thus if $y = x^3 - x + 2$, then

$\frac{dy}{dx} = 3x^2 - 1.$

Example 7.8

If $y = \frac{1}{x}$, find $\frac{dy}{dx}$.

> It is assumed that $\frac{dy}{dx}$ at the general point is required.

Now $y = \frac{1}{x}.$ (1)

Let $\delta x, \delta y$ be corresponding increments in x and y respectively so that

$y + \delta y = \frac{1}{x + \delta x}.$ (2)

Subtract (1) from (2).

$$\delta y = \frac{1}{x + \delta x} - \frac{1}{x}$$

$$= \frac{x - (x + \delta x)}{(x + \delta x)x}$$

$$= \frac{-\delta x}{(x + \delta x)x}.$$

using the common denominator to subtract fractions

Then
$$\frac{\delta y}{\delta x} = \frac{-1}{(x + \delta x)x}$$

and
$$\frac{dy}{dx} = \lim_{\delta x \to 0} \frac{\delta y}{\delta x} = \lim_{\delta x \to 0} \frac{-1}{(x + \delta x)x} = -\frac{1}{x.x} = -\frac{1}{x^2}.$$

Thus if
$$y = \frac{1}{x}, \quad \frac{dy}{dx} = -\frac{1}{x^2}.$$

Exercises 7.3

1. Given $y = x^2$ and $\delta x, \delta y$ are corresponding increments in x and y respectively, show that
$$\delta y = 2x\delta x + (\delta x)^2$$
and hence show that
$$\frac{dy}{dx} = 2x.$$

2. Given $y = x^3$, apply the procedure adopted in question 1 to show that
$$\delta y = 3x^2\delta x + 3x(\delta x)^2 + (\delta x)^3.$$

Find $\dfrac{dy}{dx}$.

3. Given $y = x$, apply the procedure adopted in question 1 to show that
$$\delta y = \delta x.$$

Hence find $\dfrac{dy}{dx}$.

4. Given $y = 1$, show that
$$\delta y = 0.$$

Deduce the value of $\dfrac{dy}{dx}.$

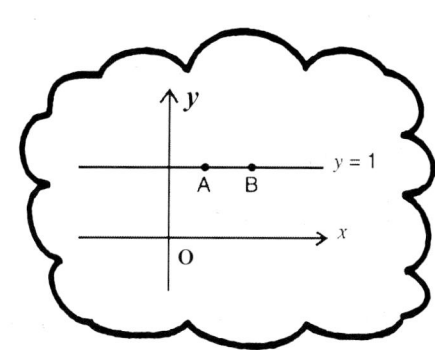

5. If $y = 3x^2 - 5x + 7$, show that
$$\delta y = (6x - 5)\delta x + 3(\delta x)^2.$$

6. If $y = 5x^3 + 3x^2 + 2x + 1$, show that
$$\delta y = (15x^2 + 6x + 2)\delta x + (15x + 3)(\delta x)^2 + 5(\delta x)^3.$$

Deduce the value of $\dfrac{dy}{dx}$.

7. Find $\dfrac{dy}{dx}$ in the following cases:-

   (i) $\quad y = 6x$ (ii) $\quad y = 2x^2$ (iii) $\quad y = 3x^3$

   (iv) $\quad y = 3x^3 + 2x^2 + 6x.$

8. What is the relationship between the answers to (i), (ii), (iii) and (iv)?

   Given $y = \dfrac{1}{x^2}$, show that

   $$\delta y = \dfrac{-2x\delta x - (\delta x)^2}{(x + \delta x)^2 x^2}.$$

   Hence show that

   $$\dfrac{dy}{dx} = \dfrac{-2}{x^3}.$$

9. Given that

   $$y = \dfrac{1}{2x + 3}.$$

   show that

   $$\delta y = \dfrac{-2\delta x}{(2x + 2\delta x + 3)(2x + 3)}.$$

   Hence show that

   $$\dfrac{dy}{dx} = \dfrac{-2}{(2x + 3)^2}.$$

   { Harder }

10. Given that

    $$y = \dfrac{1}{6x + 1},$$

    show that $\dfrac{dy}{dx} = \dfrac{-6}{(6x + 1)^2}.$

    { Harder }

The differentiation of functions, whether using the f or δ notation, from first principles is often tedious. The tedium is avoided by drawing up a catalogue of results for some basic functions and developing rules for use with this catalogue.

7.4 Differentiation of some basic functions

Summarising the results of example 7.8 and questions 1, 2, 3, 4, 8 of exercises 7.3, we have

$$D(1) = 0,$$
$$D(x) = 1,$$
$$D(x^2) = 2x,$$
$$D(x^3) = 3x^2,$$
$$D(x^{-1}) = -1x^{-2},$$
$$D(x^{-2}) = -2x^{-3}.$$

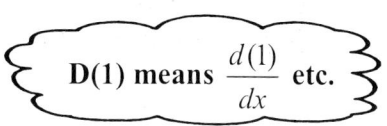

D(1) means $\dfrac{d(1)}{dx}$ **etc.**

All these results obey the general rule

$$D(x^n) = nx^{n-1}$$

or $\qquad f(x) = x^n, f'(x) = nx^{n-1}.$

> We assume now without proof that
> if $\quad f(x) = x^n \quad$ then
> $\qquad f'(x) = nx^{n-1}$
> is valid for all values of n, whether integer, fractional, positive or negative, or zero.

(I)

Example 7.9

If $\qquad f(x) = \dfrac{1}{x^3} = x^{-3},$

$$f'(x) = -3x^{-3-1}$$

$$= -3x^{-4} = -\dfrac{3}{x^4}.$$

$n = -3$

From Rule I

Example 7.10

If $\qquad y = x^{\frac{3}{2}}, \qquad \left(n = \tfrac{3}{2}\right)$

$$\dfrac{dy}{dx} = \dfrac{3}{2}x^{\frac{3}{2}-1} \qquad \text{(from Rule I)}$$

$$= \dfrac{3}{2}x^{\frac{1}{2}} = \dfrac{3}{2}\sqrt{x}.$$

Example 7.11

If $\qquad f(x) = \dfrac{1}{x^{\frac{7}{2}}} = x^{-\frac{7}{2}} \qquad \left(n = -\tfrac{7}{2}\right)$

then $\qquad f'(x) = -\dfrac{7}{2}x^{-\frac{7}{2}-1}$

$$= -\dfrac{7}{2}x^{-\frac{9}{2}} = \dfrac{-7}{2x^{\frac{9}{2}}}.$$

Rule I can also be applied to the differentiation of constants; because

$$f(x) = c \qquad \text{or} \qquad y = c,$$

See question 4, exercise 7.3

where c is a constant, may be written

$$f(x) = x^0 \qquad \text{or} \qquad y = x^0.$$

Then $\quad f'(x) = 0x^{0-1} \quad$ or $\quad \dfrac{dy}{dx} = 0x^{0-1}$

(anything)^0 = 1

so $\quad f'(x) = 0 \quad$ or $\quad \dfrac{dy}{dx} = 0.$

This says slope of $y = c$ is 0.

This result is worthy of display as a second rule.

> If $\quad f(x) = \text{constant},$
> $\qquad f'(x) = 0$
> or $\qquad y = \text{constant},$ $\qquad$ (II)
> $\qquad \dfrac{dy}{dx} = 0.$

Example 7.12

Find $\dfrac{dy}{dx}$ if $y = 8.$

$$\dfrac{dy}{dx} = 0 \quad \text{by Rule II.}$$

The third rule relates to the differentiation of functions such as $f(x) = 3x^9$.
Consider $f(x) = 3x^9$,

$$f(x) = -6x^{\frac{3}{2}},$$

or more generally, $f(x) = Cx^n$,
where C and n are constants.

> The rule is if $f(x) = Cx^n$
> then $\qquad\qquad f'(x) = Cnx^{n-1}$ $\qquad$ (III)

The rule is derived from

$$f'(x) = \lim_{h \to 0} \frac{C(x+h)^n - Cx^n}{h}.$$

We don't pursue this here.

Then for $f(x) = 3x^9$,
$$f'(x) = 3 \times 9x^8 = 27x^8;$$

and if $\quad y = -6x^{\frac{3}{2}}$

then $\quad \dfrac{dy}{dx} = -6 \times \dfrac{3}{2}x^{\frac{3}{2}-1} = -9x^{\frac{1}{2}}.$

Here $C = -6.$

Before concluding this section, we give, without proof at this stage, a rule for differentiating the sum of functions. In question 7 of exercises 7.2, you were asked to differentiate $3x^3 + 2x^2 + 6x$. It is straightforward to show from first principles that if

$$f(x) = 3x^3 + 2x^2 + 6x$$

then $\quad f'(x) = 9x^2 + 4x + 6.$

If we apply Rule II to the separate functions $3x^3, 2x^2, 6x$ we obtain $9x^2, 4x, 6$.

$$\begin{cases} C = 3, n = 3 \\ C = 2, n = 2 \\ C = 6, n = 1 \end{cases}$$

Then if $\quad f(x) = 3x^3 + 2x^2 + 6x,$

$$\qquad\qquad\downarrow\qquad\downarrow\qquad\downarrow$$

$$f'(x) = 9x^2 + 4x + 6.$$

Thus the first principles differentiation of $f(x)$ shows that for this polynomial function the final result could have been found by differentiating term by term. This rule applies to all types of functions, in fact. Thus if

$$y = 3x^2 + \frac{1}{x} + 9,$$

$$\qquad\quad\downarrow\qquad\downarrow\qquad\qquad\downarrow$$

$$\frac{dy}{dx} = 6x + (-1)x^{-1-1} + 0 = 6x - \frac{1}{x^2}.$$

Addition Rule

> Differentiation of expressions involving sums or subtractions of terms involving powers of x can be achieved by differentiating each term separately and adding or subtracting each term as appropriate.

(IV)

Example 7.13

Differentiate (i) $3x^7 - 6x^5 + \dfrac{9}{x^2} + 3$ (ii) $(x - 1)(x + 2)$ (iii) $\dfrac{3x^4 - 2x^{\frac{3}{2}} + 3}{\sqrt{x}}$

(i) Term by term differentiation gives

$$3 \times 7x^6 - 6 \times 5x^4 + 9 \times -2 \times x^{-3} + 0$$

$$\quad\downarrow\qquad\qquad\downarrow\qquad\qquad\downarrow\qquad\qquad\downarrow$$

$$\text{rule III}\qquad\text{rule III}\qquad\text{rule III}\qquad\text{rule II}$$

with $C=3, n=7 \quad C=-6, n=5 \quad C=9, n = -2$

$$= 21x^6 - 30x^4 - \frac{18}{x^3}.$$

(ii) We expand $(x - 1)(x + 2)$ to obtain

$$x^2 + 2x - x - 2 = x^2 + x - 2.$$

Then term by term differentiation gives

$$2x + 1 - 0 = 2x + 1.$$

(iii) We first divide out to obtain

$$3x^{\frac{7}{2}} - 2x + \frac{3}{\sqrt{x}}, \text{ recalling that } \sqrt{x} = x^{\frac{1}{2}}.$$

Then differentiating term by term gives

$$3 \times \frac{7}{2} \times x^{\frac{5}{2}} \quad - 2 \quad + \quad 3 \times -\frac{1}{2} \times x^{-\frac{1}{2}-1}$$

Rule III   Rule III   Rule III

$(C = 3, n = \frac{7}{2})$ $(C = -2, n = 1)$ $(C = 3, n = -\frac{1}{2})$

$$= \frac{21}{2} x^{\frac{5}{2}} - 2 - \frac{3}{2x^{\frac{3}{2}}}.$$

Before leaving this chapter, we recall that we started by asking how we could characterise the steepness of a curve. The concept of differentiation was introduced to find the gradient of a tangent to the curve. Then if the curve is given by $y = f(x)$ we defined the gradient of the curve (and of the tangent) to be $\frac{dy}{dx}$ or $f'(x)$. We conclude this chapter by returning to the concept of tangent to a curve.

Example 7.14

A curve is described by the equation $y = x^3 - 2x^2 + 4$. Find the slope of the tangent to the curve at the point $(2, 4)$.

Now for $y = x^3 - 2x^2 + 4$, the slope of the tangent at a point is given by

$$\frac{dy}{dx} = 3x^2 - 4x.$$

When $x = 2$, $\qquad \frac{dy}{dx} = 3(2)^2 - 4 \times 2 = 4.$

Example 7.15

Find the values of x at which the slopes of the tangents to the curve $y = 2x^3 + 3x^2 - 6x + 2$ are equal to 6.

Slope of the tangent is $\qquad \frac{dy}{dx} = 6x^2 + 6x - 6.$

Required values of x satisfy $6x^2 + 6x - 6 = 6$ (given)

so $\qquad\qquad 6x^2 + 6x - 12 = 0$

or $\qquad\qquad 6(x^2 + x - 2) = 0.$

Then $\qquad\qquad x^2 + x - 2 = 0$

or $\qquad\qquad (x + 2)(x - 1) = 0.$

$\therefore \qquad\qquad\qquad\qquad x = -2 \text{ or } 1.$

Example 7.16

Find the values of x at which the tangents to the graph of
$$f(x) = x^3 - 2x^2 - 4x + 8 \text{ are parallel to the } x\text{-axis.}$$
Slope of the tangent is
$$f'(x) = 3x^2 - 4x - 4.$$
When the tangent is parallel to the x-axis,
$$f'(x) = 0$$

> The x-axis has zero gradient or slope.

so
$$3x^2 - 4x - 4 = 0.$$
This factorises to give
$$(3x + 2)(x - 2) = 0$$

> or use the quadratic formula

so
$$x = -\frac{2}{3} \text{ or } 2.$$

Exercises 7.4

1 Differentiate with respect to x:-

(i) $9x^{10}$ (ii) $\dfrac{3}{x^4}$ (iii) 7 (iv) $2x^{\frac{3}{2}}$ (v) $\dfrac{9}{x^{\frac{2}{3}}}$ (vi) $2x^2 - 9x$

(vii) $3x^3 + 9x^2 - 4$ (viii) $(x + 2)(x - 3)$ (ix) $\dfrac{x^2 + 2x + 4}{x}$ (x) $(x + 1)^2$

(xi) $(x - 1)(\sqrt{x} + x)$ (xii) $1 + \dfrac{2}{x} + \dfrac{2}{x^2} + \dfrac{4}{x^3}$.

2 Find the gradients of the given curves at the given points :-

(i) $y = x^2 + 9$ where $x = 3$ (ii) $y = 3x^3 - 5$ where $x = 1$

(iii) $y = \dfrac{1}{x}$ where $x = 2$ (iv) $y = (3x + 1)(x - 5)$ where $x = 0$

(v) $y = 1 + \dfrac{2}{x}$ where $x = 2$ (vi) $y = x^3 + 2x^2 + 3x + 6 + \dfrac{4}{x}$ where $x = 1$.

3 Find $\dfrac{dy}{dx}$ in the following cases and hence find the points on the curves where the

tangents have the given slopes.

(i) $y = x^2 + 4$ $(m = -8)$ (ii) $y = x^3 + x + 2$ $(m = 1)$

(iii) $y = 3x^2 - 2x + 4$ $(m = 10)$ (iv) $y = (x + 1)(x + 3)$ $(m = -18)$

(v) $y = 2x + \dfrac{1}{x}$ $(m = -2)$ (vi) $y = -\dfrac{1}{x^3}$ $(m = 27)$

(vii) $y = x^3 + x^2 + x + 4$ $(m = 9)$.

4 Find the slope of the tangent to the curve $y = 2x - x^3$ at the point $(1, 1)$.

5 Find the slope of the tangent to the graph of the function $f(x) = (x + 2)(x - 3)$ at the point where $x = 2$.

6 Find the gradients of the graph of $f(x) = x^2 - 2x - 3$ at the points where the graph crosses the x-axis.

7 Find the gradients of the tangents to the curve $y = x^2 - x$ at $x = \dfrac{1}{2}$ and $x = \dfrac{3}{2}$. For what value of x is the gradient of the curve equal to zero?

8 Find the coordinates of the points on the graph of $y = x^3 - 3x^2 + 6$ at which the tangents are parallel to the x-axis.

Chapter 8

Applications of Differentiation

In section 2.4 we considered maximum and minimum values of quadratic functions by completing the square. Here we use differentiation to investigate maximum and minimum values of functions. Before doing so, we consider the relationship between the derivative of a function and the slope of the tangent to the associated curve.

8.1   Increasing and decreasing functions

Example 8.1

Given $f(x) = 2x^3 - 3x^2 - 12x + 6$
we see immediately that
$$f'(x) = 6x^2 - 6x - 12$$
$$= 6(x^2 - x - 2)$$
$$= 6(x + 1)(x - 2).$$

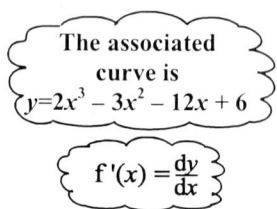

The associated curve is $y = 2x^3 - 3x^2 - 12x + 6$

$f'(x) = \dfrac{dy}{dx}$

Now $f'(x)$ is the slope of the tangent at a point on the curve.
Now when $x < -1$ or $x > 2$,
$$f'(x) > 0$$
and when $-1 < x < 2$,
$$f'(x) < 0.$$

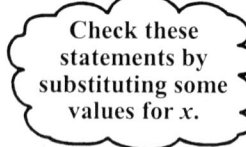

Check these statements by substituting some values for x.

Also $f'(x) = 0$ when $x = -1, 2$.

Now $f'(x) = \dfrac{dy}{dx}$ was derived by considering limiting slopes of chords.

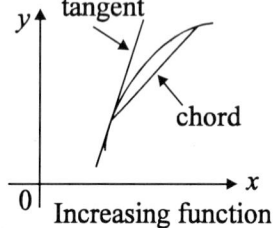

Increasing function

For an <u>increasing function</u> y increases with x and thus $\dfrac{\text{change in } y}{\text{change in } x}$ is positive.

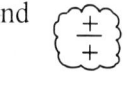

This fraction remains positive during the limiting process and therefore $f'(x) > 0$.

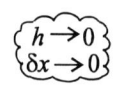

$h \to 0$
$\delta x \to 0$

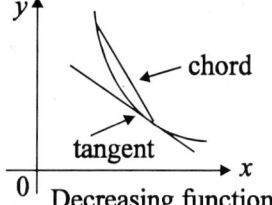

Decreasing function

For a <u>decreasing function</u>, y decreases as x increases and thus $\dfrac{\text{change in } y}{\text{change in } x} < 0$.

This fraction remains negative during the limiting process and $f'(x) < 0$.

When the tangent is parallel to the *x*-axis as in the diagrams given below, the slope is zero, i.e. f'(*x*) = 0.

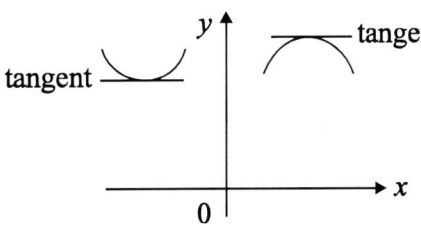 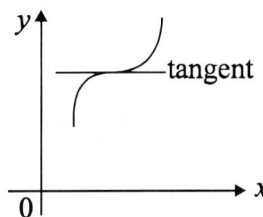

In summary,

f'(*x*) > 0   increasing function,
f'(*x*) < 0   decreasing function,
f'(*x*) = 0   the tangent is parallel to the *x*-axis.

Example 8.2

The function is both increasing and decreasing, over different values of *x*.

From Example 8.1, for
$$f(x) = 2x^3 - 3x^2 - 12x + 6,$$
$$f'(x) = 6(x+1)(x-2).$$

The function increases when $x < -1$ or $x > 2$ and decreases when $-1 < x < 2$.

Also the tangent to $y = f(x)$ is parallel to the *x*-axis when $x = -1, 2$. $\dfrac{dy}{dx} = 0$

Exercises 8.1

1   Find the ranges of *x* for which f(*x*) is (a) increasing   (b) decreasing in the following cases.

(i) $f(x) = x^2 - 3x + 6$ (ii) $f(x) = 2x^3 + 3x^2 - 12x + 1$

(iii) $f(x) = x + \dfrac{1}{x}$ (for $x > 0$)   (iv) $f(x) = 6 - 3x - x^2$

(v) $f(x) = x^4 - 8x + 10$ (vi) $f(x) = x^5 - 15x^3 - 3$.

2   For which values of *x* are the tangents to the associated curves in question 1 parallel to the *x*-axis?

8.2   Stationary points and their classification

Quadratic functions have graphs which have one or other of the general shapes shown below.

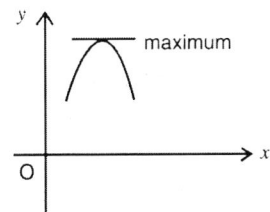 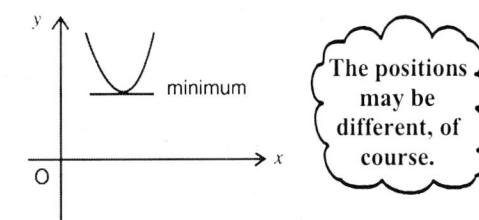

The positions may be different, of course.

The left hand graph has one maximum point (a crest) and the right hand graph has a minimum point (a trough).

A common feature of maximum and minimum points is that the tangents at such points are parallel to the *x*-axis, i.e.

$$\frac{dy}{dx} = 0.$$

$$f'(x) = 0$$

Here we consider functions which may have more complicated graphs, such as the one shown below.

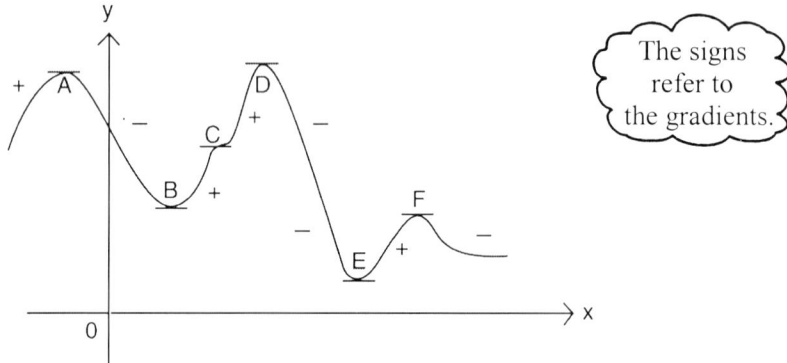

The signs refer to the gradients.

Points on a graph where $\dfrac{dy}{dx} = 0$ are known as **stationary points**, the associated value being a **stationary value**.

In the diagram, there are stationary points at A, B, C, D, E and F. Let's categorise these points.

<u>Points A, D, F</u>

At each of these points, the gradient changes from positive to negative and the graph has crests or **maximum points**.
The values of *y* at such points are **maximum values**.

The graph changes from climbing to falling.

<u>Points B, E</u>

At each of these points, the gradient changes from negative to positive and the graph has troughs or **minimum points**.
The values of y at such points are **minimum values**.

The graph changes from falling to climbing.

N.B.
The maximum and minimum are strictly **local** maximum and **local** minimum points. The qualifying 'local' is useful because it underlines that a maximum (minimum) point must not be understood as the overall maximum (minimum) point. Indeed, in the diagram the (local) maximum value at F is smaller than the (local) minimum value at B.

The point C

At the point C, $\dfrac{dy}{dx} = 0$ since the tangent is parallel to the *x*-axis. However, it is clear that C is neither a maximum nor a minimum point: the graph does not stop climbing although it is (locally) flat at C. Indeed,

$$\frac{dy}{dx} > 0$$

both to the left and right of C. A point such as C where $\dfrac{dy}{dx} = 0$ but does not change sign is called a **stationary point of inflexion (S.P.I.).**

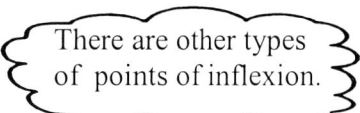

There are other types of points of inflexion.

Summary

$$\frac{dy}{dx}$$

Change of sign of $\dfrac{dy}{dx}$ *(or f'(x))* test for stationary points

At a stationary point

$$\frac{dy}{dx} = 0.$$

(i) $\dfrac{dy}{dx}$ changes from + to –, maximum point

(ii) $\dfrac{dy}{dx}$ changes from – to +, minimum point   (I)

(iii)   no change of sign in $\dfrac{dy}{dx}$, stationary point of inflexion.

Similar statements apply to $f'(x)$.

Exercises 8.2

1   On each of the following diagrams:-

a)   mark in the stationary points and the sign of $\dfrac{dy}{dx}$,

b)   classify the stationary points as maximum, minimum or points of inflexion.

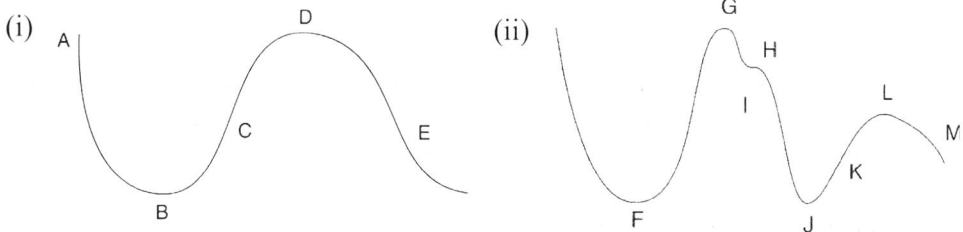

(i)   (ii)

(iii)

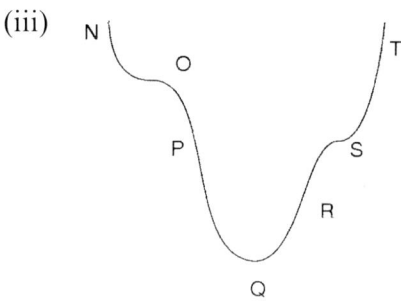

8.3 Use of the sign of $\dfrac{dy}{dx}$ to classify stationary points

Graphs of functions are not always available to assist us in investigating stationary points. However, Rule I may be used in such cases.

Example 8.3

Find and classify the stationary points of

$$y = x^4 + 4x^3 + 25$$

Now $\dfrac{dy}{dx} = 4x^3 + 12x^2 = 4x^2(x+3)$

and for a stationary point

$$\frac{dy}{dx} = 0.$$

$$\therefore 4x^2(x+3) = 0.$$

Don't cancel x^2 without considering the possibility that $x^2 = 0$.

Then $x^2 = 0$ or $x+3 = 0$
i.e. $x = 0, -3$.

There are two stationary points. Now let's investigate the nature of those stationary points, by considering the sign of $\dfrac{dy}{dx}$ on either side of each point.

$\underline{x = 0}$

When x is just below 0, say –0.1,

$$\frac{dy}{dx} = 4(-0.1)^2(-0.1+3) = 0.116 > 0.$$

When x is just above 0, say 0.1,

$$\frac{dy}{dx} = 4(0.1)^2(0.1+3) = 0.124 > 0.$$

Thus $\dfrac{dy}{dx} > 0$ either side of $x = 0$.

<u>$x = -3$</u>

When x is just below -3, say -3.1,
$$\frac{dy}{dx} = 4(-3.1)^2(-3.1+3) = -3.844 < 0.$$
When x is just above -3, say -2.9,
$$\frac{dy}{dx} = 4(-2.9)^2(-2.9+3) = 3.364.$$

$$\therefore \frac{dy}{dx} < 0 \text{ to the left of } x = -3,$$
$$> 0 \text{ to the right of } x = -3.$$

The signs of $\frac{dy}{dx}$ are entered in the table as shown below:

Value of x	L	-3	R		L	0	R
Sign of $\frac{dy}{dx}$	$-$	0	$+$		$+$	0	$+$

      Min   Inflexion

Thus, there is a minimum when
$$x = -3, y = (-3)^4 + 4(-3)^3 + 25$$
$$= -2$$
and a point of inflexion when
$$x = 0, y = (0)^4 + 4(0)^3 + 25 = 25.$$

It is advisable to write $\frac{dy}{dx}$ in a factorised form and care should be taken when $\frac{dy}{dx}$ involves a negative numerical factor.

Example 8.4

Find and classify the stationary values of the function given by
$$f(x) = 3 + 12x - 3x^2 - 2x^3.$$
Then $f'(x) = 12 - 6x - 6x^2$

$$= -6(x^2 + x - 2)$$
$$= -6(x+2)(x-1).$$

> **Don't cancel the -6: its presence is crucial.**

For a stationary point,
$$f'(x) = 0$$
so that $-6(x+2)(x-1) = 0$
$$\therefore x = -2, 1.$$
There are two stationary values.

Now let's use the sign test on $f'(x)$.

<u>$x = -2$</u>
When x is just less than -2, say -2.1,
$$\frac{dy}{dx} = -6(-2.1+2)(-2.1-1)$$
$$= -1.86 < 0.$$
When x is just greater than -2, say -1.9,
$$\frac{dy}{dx} = -6(-1.9+2)(-1.9-1)$$
$$= 1.74 > 0.$$
$$\therefore \frac{dy}{dx} < 0 \text{ to the left of } x = -2,$$
$$> 0 \text{ to the right of } x = -2.$$

<u>$x = 1$</u>
When x is just less than 1, say 0.9,
$$\frac{dy}{dx} = -6(0.9+2)(0.9-1)$$
$$= 1.74 > 0.$$
When x is just greater than 1, say 1.1,
$$\frac{dy}{dx} = -6(1.1+2)(1.1-1)$$
$$= -1.86 < 0.$$
$$\therefore \frac{dy}{dx} > 0 \text{ to the left of } x = 1,$$
$$< 0 \text{ to the right of } x = 1.$$

The signs of $\frac{dy}{dx}$ are entered in the table shown below.

Value of x	L	-3	R		L	0	R
Sign of $\frac{dy}{dx}$	$-$	0	$+$		$+$	0	$+$

Minimum   Maximum

There is a minimum when $x = -2$

and $f(x) = 3 + 12(-2) - 3(-2)^2 - 2(-2)^3$

$\qquad = -17$

and a maximum when $x = 1$

with $f(x) = 3 + 12(1) - 3(1)^2 - 2(1)^3$

$\qquad = 10.$

Exercises 8.3

Use the change of sign test for $\dfrac{dy}{dx}$ or $f'(x)$ to classify the stationary points of the following.

1. $y = x^2 - 2x + 3$

2. $f(x) = 9 + 6x - x^2$

3. $y = 5 + 24x - 9x^2 - 2x^3$

4. $f(x) = x^4 - 4x^3$

5. $y = -5x^6 + 6x^5 + 2$

6. $f(x) = x^3(x - 2)$

7. $y = x^2$

8. $y = -x^3$

9. $y = -x^4.$

8.4 Second derivative tests for maximum and minimum points

The derivative of a function of x is also a function of x. This function may also be differentiable, in which case the derivative of the first derivative is called the second derivative of the original function. Similarly, the derivative of the second derivative is called the third derivative, and so on. Thus if

$$f(x) = 7x^8,$$
$$f'(x) = 7 \times 8x^7 = 56x^7,$$
$$f''(x) = 56 \times 7x^6 = 392x^6,$$
$$f'''(x) = 392 \times 6x^5 = 2352x^5.$$

or $y = 7x^8,$ $\qquad \dfrac{dy}{dx} = 56x^7,$ $\qquad \dfrac{d}{dx}\left(\dfrac{dy}{dx}\right) = \dfrac{d^2y}{dx^2} = 392x^6,$

$$\dfrac{d}{dx}\left(\dfrac{d^2y}{dx^2}\right) = \dfrac{d^3y}{dx^3} = 2352x^5.$$

Exercises 8.4

Prove each of the following differentiations.

1   (i) $y = 3x^4 - 2x^3 + 6x$, $\dfrac{d^2y}{dx^2} = 36x^2 - 12x$.

   (ii) $f(x) = \dfrac{3+x}{x^2}$, $f''(x) = \dfrac{18}{x^4} + \dfrac{2}{x^3}$.

   (iii) $y = \sqrt{x} + \dfrac{1}{\sqrt{x}}$, $\dfrac{d^2y}{dx^2} = -\dfrac{1}{4x^{3/2}} + \dfrac{3}{4x^{5/2}}$.

   (iv) $f(x) = x^4 + x^3 + x^2 + x + 1$, $f'''(x) = 24x + 6$.

   (v) $y = x^3 - \dfrac{3}{x}$, $\dfrac{d^4y}{dx^4} = -\dfrac{72}{x^5}$.

The second derivative may be used to classify stationary points. Let's consider the various possibilities graphically.

<u>Maximum point</u>

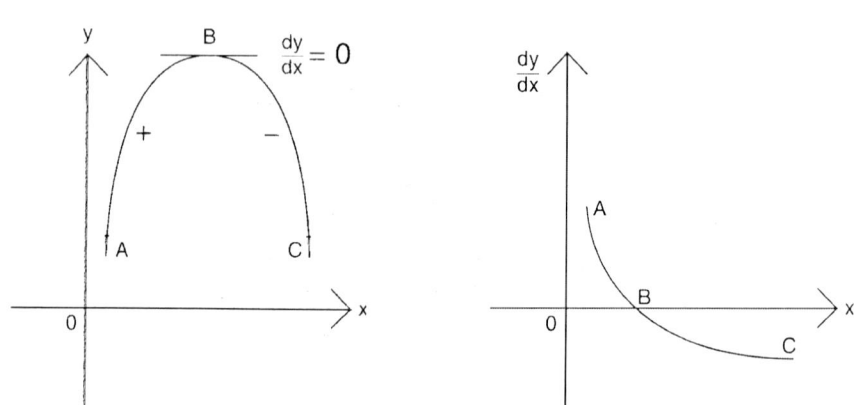

The left hand diagram shows a typical maximum point with neighbouring points A and C. At the point A $\dfrac{dy}{dx} > 0$; at the point C, $\dfrac{dy}{dx} < 0$.

The right hand diagram shows the graph of $\dfrac{dy}{dx}$ against x. The particular shape of this $\dfrac{dy}{dx}$ graph is unimportant: the essential point is that the graph falls from A to C, and $\dfrac{dy}{dx} = 0$ at B. Thus, the $\dfrac{dy}{dx}$ graph has a negative gradient at A, B and C, in particular at B.

Now the gradient of $\dfrac{dy}{dx}$ is $\dfrac{d}{dx}(\dfrac{dy}{dx}) = \dfrac{d^2y}{dx^2}$.

To summarise, at the maximum point B,

$$\frac{dy}{dx} = 0$$

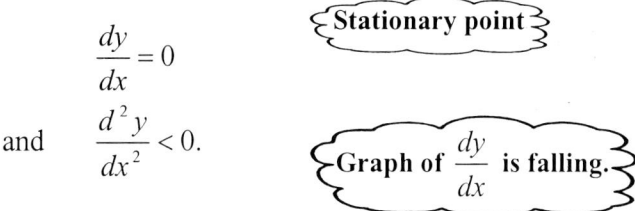

Stationary point

and $\quad \dfrac{d^2y}{dx^2} < 0.$

Graph of $\dfrac{dy}{dx}$ is falling.

Minimum point

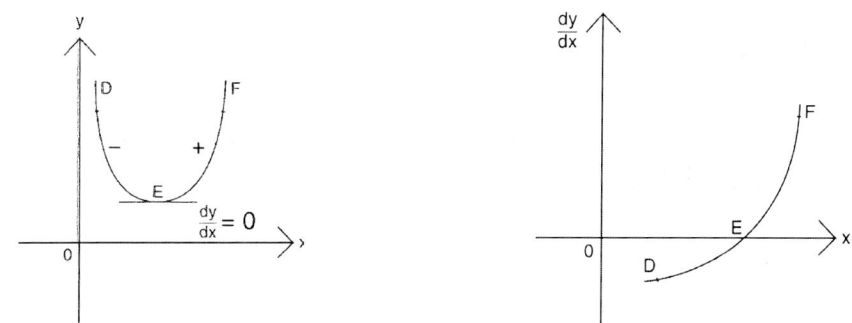

A similar argument for the minimum point E leads to

$$\frac{dy}{dx} = 0$$

Stationary point

and $\quad \dfrac{d^2y}{dx^2} > 0.$

Graph of $\dfrac{dy}{dx}$ is climbing

Stationary point of Inflexion

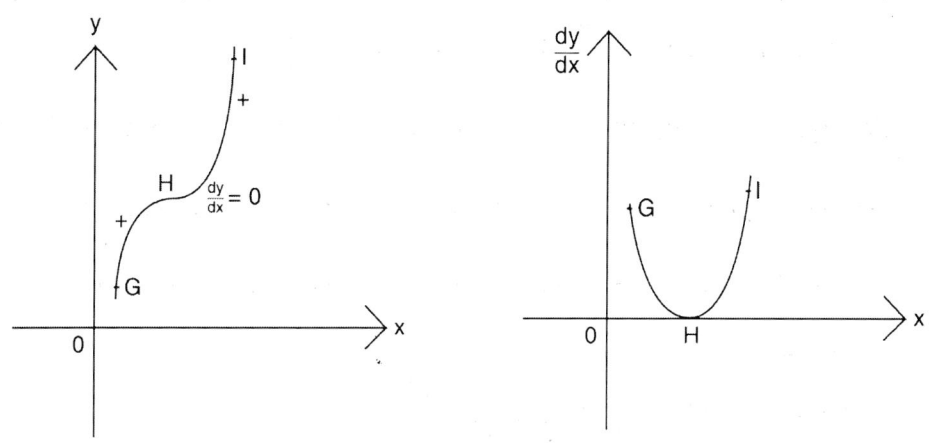

The left hand diagram shows a stationary point of inflexion (S.P.I.).

The right hand diagram shows the general shape

of $\dfrac{dy}{dx}$ against x.

The essential features of the $\dfrac{dy}{dx}$ graph are

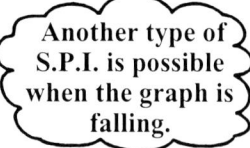

Another type of S.P.I. is possible when the graph is falling.

(i)   the graph is falling at G, so that

$$\frac{d}{dx}\left(\frac{dy}{dx}\right)<0$$

A falling graph has a negative gradient

       i.e. $\dfrac{d^2y}{dx^2}<0.$

(ii)   at H, $\dfrac{dy}{dx}$ has a minimum value,

       i.e.   H is a stationary point for $\dfrac{dy}{dx}$.

$$\therefore \frac{d}{dx}\left(\frac{dy}{dx}\right)=0$$

       or $\dfrac{d^2y}{dx^2}=0.$

(iii)   The graph is rising at I, so that

$$\frac{d}{dx}\left(\frac{dy}{dx}\right)>0$$

       or $\dfrac{d^2y}{dx^2}>0$ at I.

A similar argument applies for the other type of S.P.I. shown below.

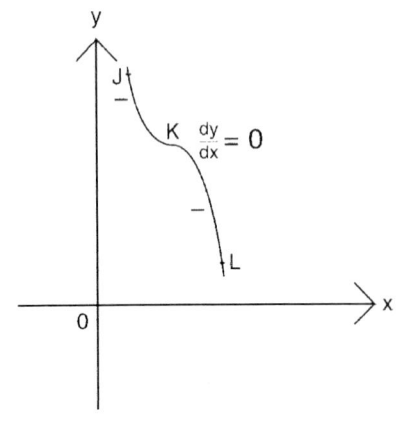

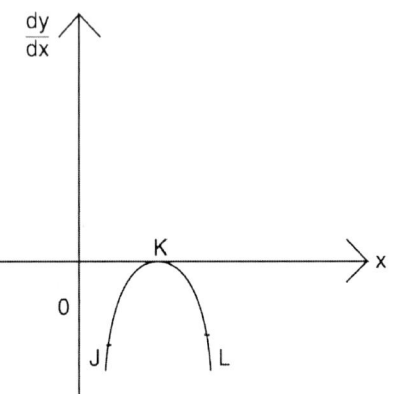

Then $\dfrac{d^2y}{dx^2}>0$ at J,

$\dfrac{dy}{dx}$ **graph is rising**

$\dfrac{d^2y}{dx^2} = 0$ at K,

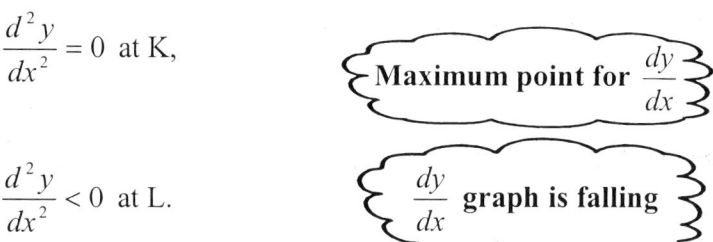

Maximum point for $\dfrac{dy}{dx}$

$\dfrac{d^2y}{dx^2} < 0$ at L.

$\dfrac{dy}{dx}$ **graph is falling**

The results for the two types of S.P.I. can be combined as follows:-

$\dfrac{dy}{dx} = 0,$

Stationary point

$\dfrac{d^2y}{dx^2} = 0$

and $\dfrac{d^2y}{dx^2}$ changes sign in moving through the point.

The full summary of the procedure for using second derivatives to classify stationary points is given below.

Summary

$\dfrac{dy}{dx} = 0$ (Stationary point)

$f'(x) = 0$

<u>Maximum point</u>

$\dfrac{d^2y}{dx^2} < 0$

at the point.

$f''(x) < 0$

<u>Minimum point</u>

$\dfrac{d^2y}{dx^2} > 0$

at the point.

$f''(x) > 0$

<u>Stationary point of Inflexion</u>

$\dfrac{d^2y}{dx^2} = 0$ at the point,

$f'(x) = 0$

$\dfrac{d^2y}{dx^2}$ changes sign as we pass through the point.

Example 8.5

Investigate the function

$$f(x) = x^2 + \frac{432}{x} \qquad (x > 0)$$

for maximum and minimum points.

For a stationary point,

$$f'(x) = 0.$$

Now

$$f'(x) = 2x - \frac{432}{x^2}.$$

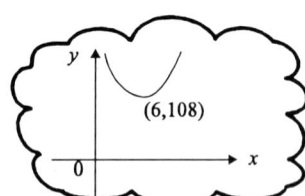
$$\frac{432}{x} = 432x^{-1}$$

Then $f'(x) = 0$ gives

$$2x - \frac{432}{x^2} = 0$$

or

$$x^3 = \frac{432}{2} = 216.$$

$$\therefore \qquad x = 6.$$

The second derivative test requires $f''(x)$.

Then

$$f''(x) = 2 + \frac{432 \times 2}{x^3}.$$

When $x = 6$, $\quad f''(6) = 2 + \frac{864}{6^3} = 2 + \frac{864}{216} = 6.$

> The precise value of f''(6) is unimportant, the sign is the central issue.

Thus

$$f''(6) > 0$$

and so the point at $x = 6$ is a minimum point.

When $x = 6$, the value of the function is

$$f(6) = 6^2 + \frac{432}{6} = 108.$$

> y
>
> (6,108)
>
> 0 x

Thus $y = x^2 + \dfrac{432}{x}$ has a minimum point at (6, 108).

Example 8.6

Find the maximum and minimum points for the curve given by

$$y = x^3 - 3x^2 - 9x + 5.$$

For a stationary point,

$$\frac{dy}{dx} = 0.$$

We also require $\dfrac{d^2 y}{dx^2}$ to distinguish between

> These are the plurals of maximum and minimum.

maxima and minima.

Then

$$\frac{dy}{dx} = 3x^2 - 6x - 9,$$

$$\frac{d^2 y}{dx^2} = 6x - 6.$$

$\dfrac{dy}{dx} = 0$ gives $3x^2 - 6x - 9 = 0.$

> remember to divide throughout by 3

$$\therefore \qquad 3(x^2 - 2x - 3) = 0$$

or $\quad 3(x-3)(x+1) = 0.$

$\therefore \qquad\qquad x = 3 \text{ or } -1.$

When $x = -1$, $\quad \dfrac{d^2y}{dx^2} = 6(-1) - 6 = -12 < 0$

which corresponds to a maximum point.

When $x = 3$, $\quad \dfrac{d^2y}{dx^2} = 6(3) - 6 = 12 > 0$

which corresponds to a minimum point.

Also, when $x = -1$,

$\qquad\qquad y = (-1)^3 - 3(-1)^2 - 9(-1) + 5 = 10.$

When $x = 3$, $\quad y = (3)^3 - 3(3)^2 - 9(3) + 5 = -22.$

Thus $(-1, 10)$, $(3, -22)$ are maximum and minimum points, respectively on the curve.

The curve is broadly of the shape shown, when we note that $y = 5$ when $x = 0$.

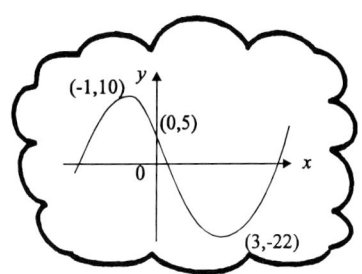

Example 8.7

Find and classify the stationary points for

$$y = x^4 - 2x^3 + 3.$$

We require $\dfrac{dy}{dx}$ and $\dfrac{d^2y}{dx^2}$.

$$\frac{dy}{dx} = 4x^3 - 6x^2 = 2x^2(2x - 3),$$

$$\frac{d^2y}{dx^2} = 12x^2 - 12x = 12x(x - 1).$$

For stationary points,

$$\frac{dy}{dx} = 0$$

so that $2x^2(2x - 3) = 0.$

Then $x = 0$ or $x = \dfrac{3}{2}.$

We use $\dfrac{d^2y}{dx^2}$ to classify the stationary points.

$\underline{x = 0}$

$$\frac{d^2y}{dx^2} = 12(0)(0 - 1) = 0.$$

Thus $x = 0$ may correspond to a point of inflexion but we must

check that there is a change of sign of $\dfrac{d^2y}{dx^2}$.

Many students forget to do this.

Let's consider two values close to $x = 0$, one on each side, say ± 0.1.

$\underline{x = -0.1}$

$$\frac{d^2 y}{dx^2} = 12(-0.1)(-0.1-1)$$

$$= 1.32 > 0.$$

$\underline{x = 0.1}$

$$\frac{d^2 y}{dx^2} = 12(0.1)(0.1-1)$$

$$= -1.08 < 0.$$

Thus $\dfrac{d^2 y}{dx^2}$ changes sign around $x = 0$

and $\dfrac{d^2 y}{dx^2} = 0$ at $x = 0$.

Thus $x = 0$ corresponds to a S.P.I.

When $x = 0$, $y = (0)^4 - 2(0)^3 + 3 = 3$.

$\therefore$ There is a S.P.I. at $(0, 3)$.

Let's consider the other stationary point.

$\underline{x = \dfrac{3}{2}}$

$$\frac{d^2 y}{dx^2} = 12\left(\frac{3}{2}\right)\left(\frac{3}{2}-1\right) = 9 > 0.$$

There is a minimum point.

When $x = \dfrac{3}{2}$, $y = \left(\dfrac{3}{2}\right)^4 - 2\left(\dfrac{3}{2}\right)^3 + 3 = \dfrac{21}{16}$.

$\therefore$ There is a minimum point

at $x = \dfrac{3}{2}$, $y = \dfrac{21}{16}$.

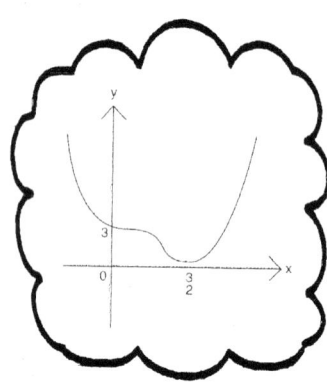

In the last three examples, we gave sketches of the curves in question. Sketching will be the subject of our next section. In the meantime, the following questions do not require sketches.

Exercises 8.5

Investigate the following for stationary points, using the second derivative to classify the points.

1     $y = \dfrac{x^3}{3} - x^2 - 3x + \dfrac{11}{3}$

2     $y = 2 - 4x - \dfrac{5}{2}x^2 - \dfrac{1}{3}x^3$

3     $f(x) = x^4 - 8x^2$

4     $f(x) = 5x - x^5$

5     $y = x^3 + 6x^2$

6     $y = 4 + 3x - x^3$

7     $f(x) = x^2 + \dfrac{9}{x^2}$ $(x \neq 0)$

8     $y = \dfrac{x^4 + 48}{4x}$ $(x \neq 0)$.

8.5   Curve sketching

In the last section, stationary points were investigated without drawing graphs. In fact, stationary points are often valuable aids in sketching graphs, particularly when the general shape and position are required. In such cases, it is not necessary to find a full table of values.

We use the following procedure to sketch graphs.

Procedure

> (a)   Find the value of y when $x = 0$.
>
> (b)   If possible, find the value of x when $y = 0$.
>
> (c)   Find and classify the stationary points.
>
> (d)   Sketch the graph.

Example 8.8

Sketch the graph of $y = x^4 + 4x^3$.

Let's work through the procedure indicated.

     (a)   When $x = 0$, $y = (0)^4 + 4(0)^3 = 0$.

     (b) $y = 0$ when $x^4 + 4x^3 = 0$,

           i.e. $x^3(x + 4) = 0$.

           $\therefore \ x = 0, -4$.

From (a), (b), (0, 0) and (−4, 0) lie on the curve.

(c)   Stationary points

$$\text{Now } \frac{dy}{dx} = 4x^3 + 12x^2 = 4x^2(x+3),$$

$$\frac{d^2y}{dx^2} = 12x^2 + 24x = 12x(x+2).$$

For stationary points,

$$\frac{dy}{dx} = 0$$

so that $4x^2(x+3) = 0$.

$$\therefore x = 0, -3.$$

There are two stationary points at

$$x = 0, \quad y = 0^4 + 4(0)^3 = 0$$

and $\quad x = -3, y = (-3)^4 + 4(-3)^3 = -27.$

Let's use $\dfrac{d^2y}{dx^2}$ to classify the stationary points.

(i) $x = -3$

$$\frac{d^2y}{dx^2} = 12(-3)(-3+2)$$

$$= 36 > 0.$$

There is a minimum point at $(-3, -27)$.

(ii) $x = 0$

$$\frac{d^2y}{dx^2} = 12(0)(0+2) = 0.$$

It appears that $(0, 0)$ is a possible S.P.I. but we must check for

sign of $\dfrac{d^2y}{dx^2}$ about $x = 0$.

We check signs at $x = \pm\ 0.1$.
When $x = -0.1$,

$$\frac{d^2y}{dx^2} = 12(-0.1)(-0.1+2)$$

$$= -2.28 < 0.$$

When $x = 0.1$,

$$\frac{d^2y}{dx^2} = 12(0.1)(0.1+2)$$

$$= 2.52 > 0.$$

Thus $\dfrac{d^2y}{dx^2}$ changes sign and there is a S.P.I. at $(0, 0)$.

(d)   Now we sketch the curve.
        Let's put in the information derived in (a), (b), (c).

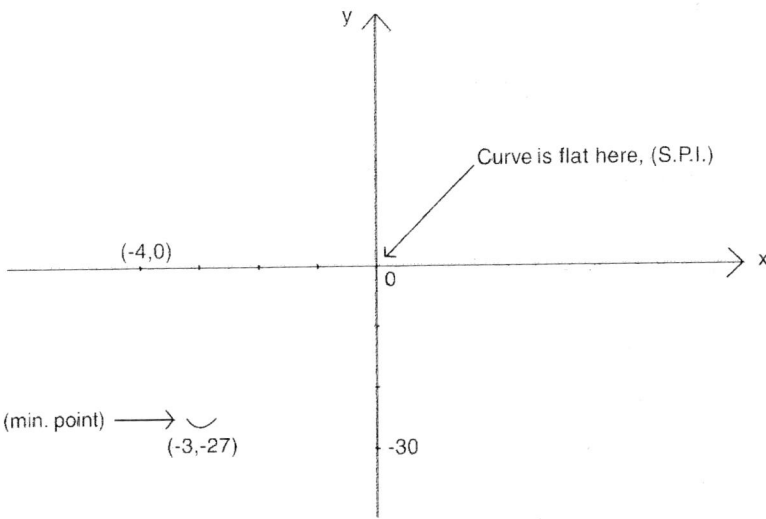

A little thought leads to the shape of the graph shown below.

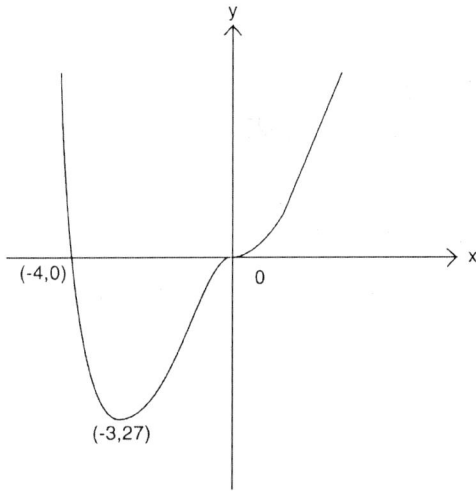

Example 8.9

We return to example 8.4 which was concerned with $y = 3 + 12x - 3x^2 - 2x^3$.

Let's work through the procedure for sketching graphs.

(a)   When $x = 0$, $y = 3$.

(b)   When $y = 0$, we have
        $3 + 12x - 3x^2 - 2x^3 = 0$.

It is not easy to find x from this equation so we do not proceed further along this route.

(c)   <u>Stationary points</u>

It was established earlier that there is a minimum point at $(-2, -17)$ and a maximum point at $(1, 10)$.

(d) Now we sketch the curve by using the information derived in (a), (b) and (c). The curve may be completed as shown.

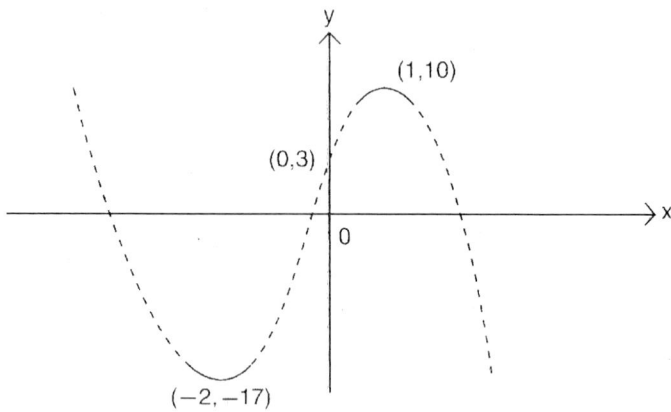

We note in passing that the graph intersects the x-axis at three points. We conclude that the equation

$$3 + 12x - 3x^2 - 2x^3 = 0 \qquad \{ \text{Set } y = 0 \}$$

has three real roots, two of which are negative.

Exercises 8.6
Sketch the graphs of the following curves.

1. $y = 3x^2 - x^3$ 2. $y = x^3 - 6x^2$ 3. $y = x^3 - 2x^2 + x + 4$

4. $y = 3x^4 - 8x^3 + 1$ 5. $y = x^4 + 32x + 32$ 6. $y = 4x^5 - 5x^4$.

8.6   Practical problems involving maxima and minima
The technique of finding (local) maxima and minima may often be used to solve practical problems. We work an example before stating some rules that could usefully be applied to such problems.

Example 8.10
A wooden box is to be built to contain 4 cubic metres. It is to have an open top and a square base. Find the dimensions of the box in order that the surface area is a minimum.

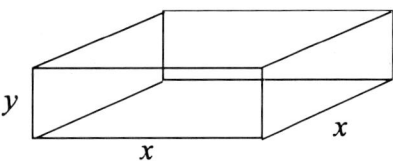

Let x = length of the square side in metres,
   y = height of the box in metres.

Since the volume of the box is given, y may be found in terms of x.

$\therefore$ $x^2 y = 4$

so $y = \dfrac{4}{x^2}.$

The surface area A = area of base + area of 4 side faces

$$= x^2 + 4xy = x^2 + 4x.\dfrac{4}{x^2}.$$

$\therefore$ $A = x^2 + \dfrac{16}{x}$ $(x > 0).$

The minimum value of A is required as x varies from 0 to ∞.

Now a (local) minimum point occurs when $\dfrac{dA}{dx} = 0$ and $\dfrac{d^2 A}{dx^2} > 0.$

Now $\dfrac{dA}{dx} = 2x - \dfrac{16}{x^2}$

and $\dfrac{d^2 A}{dx^2} = 2 + \dfrac{32}{x^3}.$

$\therefore$ $\dfrac{dA}{dx} = 0$ gives $2x - \dfrac{16}{x^2} = 0.$

$\therefore$ $x^3 = 8$

and $x = 2.$

Also $\dfrac{d^2 A}{dx^2} = 2 + \dfrac{32}{x^3} = 2 + \dfrac{32}{2^3} = 6 > 0.$

Thus $x = 2$ corresponds to a local minimum point. We note also that

     $A \to \infty$ as $x \to 0$

and $A \to \infty$ as $x \to \infty.$

Thus the local minimum is the overall minimum.

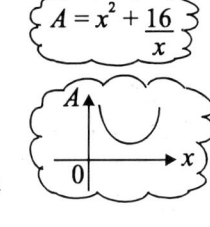

When $x = 2$, $A = 2^2 + \dfrac{16}{2} = 12..$

The minimum surface area is 12 m^2, when the base is a

square of 2 m and the height is $\dfrac{4}{2^2} = 1$ metre.

The single stationary value is the overall minimum value.

Before working another example, we summarise the procedure for working practical problems in maxima and minima.

Procedure for applications of maxima and minima

1   Set up the function whose maximum or minimum value is required in the problem.

2   If the resulting expression contains more than one variable, attempt to eliminate variables so that the expression may be written in terms of one variable only.

3   Apply the rules for finding maximum and minimum values.

4   Decide whether the local maximum (or minimum) is the overall maxima and minima by considering the values of the function at the end values of the domain of the function. If there is only one maximum or minimum value it is the overall maximum or minimum value.

5   If possible, sketch a graph to check the work.

Example 8.11

A sports field is to have the shape of a rectangular area *PQRS* with semicircular areas at opposite ends on *QR* and *PS* as diameters. Its perimeter is to be 400 m and the rectangular area *PQRS* is to be a maximum. Find the dimensions of the rectangle.

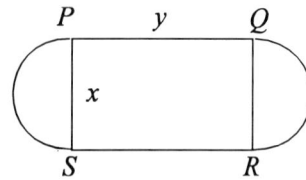

If the dimensions of the rectangle are x m and y m, the area $A = xy$.   (1)

Two variables are involved. It is given that

     perimeter = 400 m.

$\therefore \qquad 2y + \pi\dfrac{x}{2} + \pi\dfrac{x}{2} = 400$ ⟨ Eliminate y ⟩

or $\qquad 2y + \pi x = 400.$

$\therefore \qquad y = 200 - \dfrac{\pi x}{2}.$

Then substitute for y in formula (1) for A.

$\therefore \qquad A = x\left(200 - \dfrac{\pi x}{2}\right).$

For maximum, $\qquad \dfrac{dA}{dx} = 0, \quad \dfrac{d^2A}{dx^2} < 0.$

Now $\qquad \dfrac{dA}{dx} = 200 - \pi x, \quad \dfrac{d^2A}{dx^2} = -\pi.$

Then $\qquad 200 - \pi x = 0.$

$\therefore \qquad x = \dfrac{200}{\pi}.$

Also $\dfrac{d^2 A}{dx^2} < 0$

∴ $\qquad x = \dfrac{200}{\pi}$ corresponds to a maximum.

We note $A = 0$ when $x = 0$, $x = \dfrac{400}{\pi}$.

Thus the local maximum corresponds to the overall maximum.

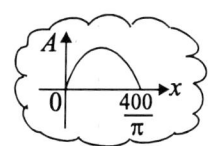

$$\text{Maximum area} = \dfrac{200}{\pi}\left(200 - \dfrac{\pi}{2} \times \dfrac{200}{\pi}\right)$$

$$= \dfrac{200 \times 100}{\pi}$$

$$= 6366 \text{ m}^2 \text{ approx.}$$

The single stationary value is the overall maximum value.

When there is more than one stationary value it is possible that the local maximum (minimum) value is not the overall maximum (minimum). This possibility is illustrated in the diagram given below.

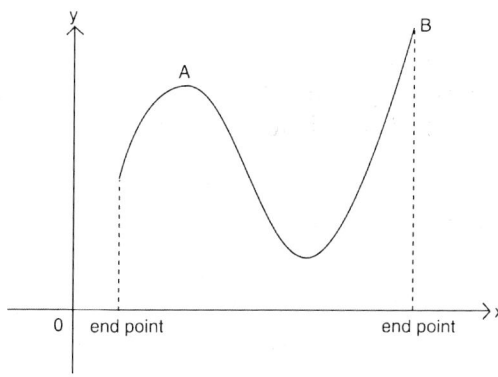

Over the set of values of x considered there are two stationary values. Whilst the curve has a local maximum at A, the value of y at B is greater. The overall maximum is the value of y at B.

Thus, where there is more than one stationary point the local maximum or minimum value should be compared with the end values.

Example 8. 12

A right circular cylinder is to be made so that the sum of its diameter and height is 2m. Given that the cylinder has maximum volume, find its height and radius.

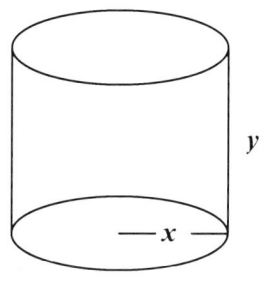

If the radius is x m and the height is y m the volume is given by

$$V = x^2 y \ m^3 \quad (1)$$

Two variables x and y are involved.
It is given that

$$2x + y = 2. \quad (2)$$

Substitute for y from (2) into (1)

$$\therefore V = x^2(2-2x) = 2x^2(1-x)$$

and we note that

$$0 \le x \le 1.$$

For a maximum value,

$$\frac{dV}{dx} = 0, \qquad \frac{d^2V}{dx^2} < 0.$$

Now $\dfrac{dV}{dx} = 4x - 6x^2 = x(4-6x),$

$$\frac{d^2V}{dx^2} = 4 - 12x.$$

Then $\dfrac{dV}{dx} = 0$ gives

$$x(4-6x) = 0$$

so that $x = 0, x = \dfrac{2}{3}.$

When $x = 0, \dfrac{d^2V}{dx^2} = 4 > 0$

which corresponds to a local minimum.

When $x = \dfrac{2}{3}, \dfrac{d^2V}{dx^2} = 4 - 12\left(\dfrac{2}{3}\right) = -4 < 0$

which corresponds to a local maximum.
The local maximum value is

$$V = 2\left(\frac{2}{3}\right)^2\left(1 - \frac{2}{3}\right)$$

$$= \frac{8}{27}\ m^3.$$

At the end points, $x = 0$ and $x = 1$

and $V = 2(0)^2(1-0) = 0$

and $V = 2(1)^2(1-1) = 0.$

The local maximum value is greater than the end values and is therefore the overall maximum.

Thus maximum value $= \dfrac{8}{27}m^3$

when the radius $= \dfrac{2}{3}m$, height $= 2 - 2\left(\dfrac{2}{3}\right) = \dfrac{2}{3}m.$

Exercises 8.7

1   A sector of a circle encloses an area of 36 m². Find the least possible perimeter of the sector.

2   An open cylindrical vessel is to be constructed from a piece of tin of area 64π cm². Find the radius and height of the tin for maximum volume.

3   An open box is to be made from a square piece of cardboard of side 24 cm. The box is formed by cutting out squares of side x cm out of the corners and then folding up the cardboard to form the sides. Show that the volume V of the box is given by $V = 4(12 - x)^2 x$. Find the maximum volume.

4   Assuming the strength of a beam with rectangular cross section is constant $\times$ breadth $\times$ (depth)², what are the dimensions of the strongest beam that can be sawed out of a round log whose diameter is 75 cm?

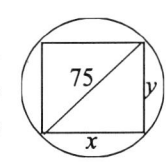

5   A one-man manufacturer of radios finds that he can sell x radios per week at £S each where $S = (75 - x)$. The cost of production is $£(500 + 15x + \frac{1}{5}x^2)$. Show that the maximum profit is obtained when production is 25 radios per week.

6   A rectangular field $ABCD$ is to be enclosed by a rectangular fence and then divided into two lots by a fence parallel to the side AB. If the area of the field is A_1 m² show that the minimum length of fencing required is $2\sqrt{6A_1}$ m.

7   A solid rectangular block of wood has a square base. The sum of the height and any one side of the base is 30cm. Find the maximum volume of the block.

8   A window is in the shape of a rectangle surmounted by a semi circle whose diameter is the width of the window. If the perimeter is 4m, find the maximum area of the window.

Chapter 9

Integration - The Indefinite Integral

The preceding two chapters have been concerned with the differentiation of functions. Thus, the polynomial function $x^3 - 3x^2 + 2x + 1$ becomes $3x^2 - 6x + 2$ when differentiated, for example.

Indefinite integration is concerned with the inverse problem : for example, finding the function which must be differentiated to give $x^4 + 3$, we say that we seek the integral of $x^4 + 3$.

9.1 The indefinite integral

Example 9.1

If we differentiate $f(x) = \dfrac{x^5}{5} + 3x + 7$

and $\qquad\qquad g(x) = \dfrac{x^5}{5} + 3x - 2$

we obtain $\qquad f'(x) = \dfrac{5x^4}{5} + 3 = x^4 + 3$

and $\qquad\qquad g'(x) = \dfrac{5x^4}{5} + 3 = x^4 + 3.$

Now $x^4 + 3$ can be obtained by differentiating $\dfrac{x^5}{5} + 3x +$ any constant, in other words, the integral of $x^4 + 3$ is $\dfrac{x^5}{5} + 3x +$ any constant.

This is written $\qquad \displaystyle\int x^4 + 3 \ dx = \dfrac{x^5}{5} + 3x + k.$ $\qquad\qquad$ (1)

(i) In (1) '$\int$' is an elongated 'S'.

(ii) dx refers to the variable and essentially is short hand for 'the differentiation (and integration) is with respect to x'.

We advise you to cultivate the habit of always writing dx (or dy, or whichever letter is involved) when writing integrals.

(iii) k is any constant. This is often omitted in writing down indefinite integrals. We shall always write down this so-called <u>arbitrary</u> constant.

(iv) Expressions such as $x^4 + 3$ which are to be integrated are called integrands.

Indefinite integration is thus the process of finding which function has to be differentiated to produce the integrand.

Example 9.2

(i)
$$\int 7x^6 \, dx = x^7 + k,$$

because $\dfrac{d}{dx}(x^7 + k) = 7x^6.$

(ii)
$$\int x^{10} + 4x^3 \, dx = \frac{x^{11}}{11} + x^4 + k$$

because $\dfrac{d}{dx}\left(\dfrac{x^{11}}{11} + x^4 + k\right) = \dfrac{11x^{10}}{11} + 4x^3 = x^{10} + 4x^3.$

We sum up the process of indefinite integration, therefore, as finding the expression which when differentiated gives the integrand :-

$$\int \text{integrand} \, dx = \text{expression} + k$$

or $\qquad \dfrac{d}{dx}(\text{expression} + k) = \text{integrand}.$

> Letters other than x may be used, of course.

Exercise 9.1

Complete the following, differentiating your answers to check that they produce the given integrands :-

(i) $\qquad \int 3x^2 \, dx = \boxed{} + \boxed{k}$

(ii) $\qquad \int 4x^3 \, dx = \boxed{} + \boxed{k}$

(iii) $\quad \int 5x^4 + 6x^5 \, dx = \boxed{} + \boxed{k}$

The expression $\int f(x) \, dx + k$ is called the indefinite integral of $f(x)$.

As with differentiation, a catalogue of functions and techniques is an essential requirement for making progress in indefinite integration.

9.2 Techniques and rules

Example 9.3

To find $\int cx^n \, dx$, where c and n are constants, we seek the function to be differentiated to give cx^n.

Now differentiation reduces powers of x by one so to find the definite integral of cx^n we explore the differentiation of cx^{n+1}.

> $\dfrac{d}{dx}(x^3) = 3x^2$
> $\dfrac{d}{dx}\left(\dfrac{6}{7}x^5\right) = \dfrac{30x^4}{7}$

Now since $\qquad \dfrac{d}{dx}(cx^{n+1}) = (n+1)cx^n$

> too big by factor of $n+1$

we note that $\dfrac{d}{dx}\left(\dfrac{c}{n+1}x^{n+1}\right) = \dfrac{(n+1)}{n+1}cx^n = cx^n.$

> divide out the factor $n+1$

and thus

Rule I $\qquad \boxed{\displaystyle\int cx^n \, dx = \frac{c}{n+1}x^{n+1} + k \quad (n \neq -1)}$

> for powers of x add one to the power and divide by the new power

N.B. The proviso $n \neq -1$ is to avoid division by zero. This case will be considered in **P2**.

Example 9.4

(i) $\qquad \int 3x^7 dx = \dfrac{3x^8}{8} + k.$

(ii) $\qquad \int \dfrac{4}{x^3} dx = \int 4x^{-3} = \dfrac{4x^{-3+1}}{-3+1} + k$

$\qquad\qquad\qquad\qquad = \dfrac{4x^{-2}}{-2} + k = -2x^{-2} + k$

$\qquad\qquad\qquad\qquad = -\dfrac{2}{x^2} + k.$

> Add one to the power and divide by the new power, noting $-3+1 = -2$.

(iii) $\qquad \int 5x^{\frac{7}{2}} dx = \dfrac{5x^{\frac{7}{2}+1}}{\frac{7}{2}+1} + k = \dfrac{5x^{\frac{9}{2}}}{\frac{9}{2}} + k$

$\qquad\qquad\qquad\qquad = \dfrac{10x^{\frac{9}{2}}}{9} + k.$

> $\dfrac{1}{9/2} = \dfrac{2}{9}$

When integrating a constant, we can use the previous result with $n = 0$ since $cx^0 = c$.

> (anything)^0 = 1

Then $\qquad\qquad \int c dx = \dfrac{cx^{0+1}}{1} + k$

$\qquad\qquad\qquad\quad = cx + k$

so

$\qquad$ Rule II $\qquad \boxed{\int c dx = cx + k}$

Example 9.5

$$\int 6 dx = 6x + k,$$

$$\int dx = x + k, \text{ since } \int dx \text{ is the same as } \int 1 dx.$$

We recall that when differentiating a sum of a finite number of functions, we were able to differentiate term by term. Since integration reverses differentiation we may integrate term by term.

Example 9.6

(i) $\int x^2 + 3x + 2 + \dfrac{1}{x^2}\, dx$ $= \dfrac{x^3}{3} + \dfrac{3x^2}{2} + 2x + \dfrac{x^{-2+1}}{-2+1} + k$

$= \dfrac{x^3}{3} + \dfrac{3x^2}{2} + 2x + \dfrac{x^{-1}}{-1} + k$

$= \dfrac{x^3}{3} + \dfrac{3x^2}{2} + 2x - \dfrac{1}{x} + k.$

> For each term add one to the power and divide by the new power, Rule I.

Generally,

Rule III $\quad \boxed{\int f(x) + g(x) + h(x) + ... \, dx = \int f(x)dx + \int g(x)dx = \int h(x)dx + ... k}$

where we note that we need only write one arbitrary constant.
Finally we note that the request 'integrate y^2 with respect to y' is equivalent to find ? in

$$\int y^2 dx = \boxed{?} + \boxed{k} \ .$$

The answer is $\dfrac{y^3}{3}$, of course, by rule I.

Exercises 9.2

The following make use of rules, I, II and III. In some of the later questions you will find it necessary to rewrite some of the expressions before integrating.
Integrate the following with respect to the appropriate letter, omitting the constant of integration .

(i) x^8

(ii) $x^{\frac{2}{3}}$

(iii) -6

(iv) $\dfrac{3}{x^3}$

(v) $\sqrt{x}$

(vi) $\dfrac{1}{x^{10}}$

(vii) $-\dfrac{9}{x^5}$

(viii) $\dfrac{1}{\sqrt{x}}$

(ix) $\dfrac{1}{y^{\frac{7}{2}}}$

(x) $4 - 6x - x^3$

(xi) $x + \dfrac{1}{x^2}$

(xii) $\dfrac{1}{2}\sqrt{x} + \dfrac{1}{2\sqrt{x}}$

(xiii) $x(x + 1)$

(xiv) $\left(y^2 + \dfrac{1}{y^2}\right)^2$

(xv) $\dfrac{x + \sqrt{x}}{x}$

(xvi) $\sqrt{x}\left(3\sqrt{x} + 1\right)$

(xvii) $\dfrac{1}{x^4} + 2x^{\frac{1}{4}} + 3x^{-\frac{1}{4}}$

(xviii) $\left(\sqrt{y} + 2\right)\left(\sqrt{y} - 3\right)$

(xix) $\dfrac{x^3 + 2x^2 - 3x}{\sqrt{x}}$

(xx) $\dfrac{y^2 + 1}{y^2}$

(xxi) $y^n \ (n \neq -1).$

Chapter 10

More Integration – The Definite Integral

In this chapter, we give further consideration to integration and introduce an important application of the process, namely the evaluation of areas under curves. The evaluation of such areas involves the concept of the **definite integral**.

To set the scene, let's return briefly to the concept of indefinite integration. When finding an indefinite integral, we included an arbitrary constant of integration. Under certain circumstances we are able to assign particular values to the constant of integration.

10.1   Finding the constant of integration

Example 10.1

Given that $\dfrac{dy}{dx} = x$, and $y = 2$ when $x = 1$, find y.

Now y, when differentiated, gives x so by the definition of indefinite integral,

$$y = \int x\,dx = \frac{x^2}{2} + k. \quad (1)$$

The constant k is arbitrary at this stage. However since $y = 2$ when $x = 1$, we may substitute these values in (1) to obtain

$$2 = \frac{1}{2} + k.$$

$$\therefore \qquad k = 2 - \frac{1}{2} = \frac{3}{2}.$$

Substitution for k in (1) then gives

$$y = \frac{x^2}{2} + \frac{3}{2} = \frac{1}{2}(x^2 + 3).$$

Example 10.2

Given $f'(x) = \dfrac{1}{\sqrt{x}}$ and $f(9) = 4$, find $f(x)$.

Now $f'(x)$ is the derived function of $f(x)$. To find $f(x)$ we seek the expression which when differentiated gives $\dfrac{1}{\sqrt{x}}$.

Then $\quad f(x) = \displaystyle\int \dfrac{1}{\sqrt{x}}\, dx + k = 2\sqrt{x} + k.$ (1)

Now $f(9) = 4$. Substitution of $x = 9$ in (1)
gives $4 = 2\sqrt{9} + k.$
$$\therefore k = 4 - 2\sqrt{9} = 4 - 2\times(3) = -2.$$
Substitution for k in (1) gives
$$f(x) = 2\sqrt{x} - 2.$$

Rule I,
Section, 9.2.

Exercises 10.1

Find y or $f(x)$ in the following cases.

1. $\dfrac{dy}{dx} = x^3$, given $y = 3$ when $x = 2$.

2. $\dfrac{dy}{dx} = 3x^2 + 2x + 1$, given $y = 0$ when $x = 2$.

3. $f'(x) = 2x + \dfrac{1}{x^2}$, given $f(1) = 0$.

4. $f'(x) = 3\sqrt{x} + \dfrac{1}{x^2} + 2$, given $f(1) = 6$.

10.2 The area under a curve

We consider the curve FG given by the equation $y = f(x)$ as shown.

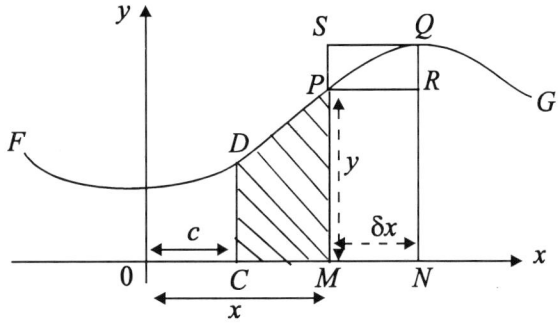

The curve is a general one and has been given the particular shape for convenience of drawing.

In the figure, CD is a fixed y coordinate corresponding to the value $x = c$ and MP is a variable coordinate y.

Now if we suppose M to change position then the shaded area $CDPM$ will change, i.e. the value of the shaded area depends upon $OM = x$. Thus if A is the shaded area we show the dependence of this shaded area by writing A as $A(x)$. For the special case y when the graph is that of $y = x$ (i.e. f(x) = x), $A(x) = \frac{1}{2}(x^2 - c^2)$, for example.

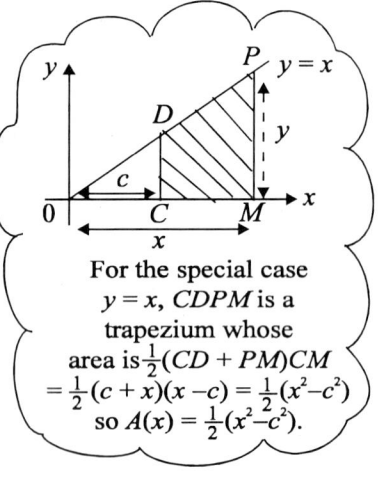

For the special case
$y = x$, $CDPM$ is a
trapezium whose
area is $\frac{1}{2}(CD + PM)CM$
$= \frac{1}{2}(c + x)(x - c) = \frac{1}{2}(x^2 - c^2)$
so $A(x) = \frac{1}{2}(x^2 - c^2)$.

If N is a point close to M so that $MN = \delta x$ (i.e. $ON = x + \delta x$) the area $CDQN$ may be written as $A(x) + \delta A(x)$ so that area $MPQN = \delta A(x)$.

[In passing, note that for the trapezium

$$A(x) = \frac{1}{2}(x^2 - c^2), \quad A(x) + \delta A(x) = \frac{1}{2}((x + \delta x)^2 - c^2)$$

and

$$\delta A(x) = \frac{1}{2}((x + \delta x)^2 - c^2) - \frac{1}{2}(x^2 - c^2)$$

$$= x\delta x + \frac{(\delta x)^2}{2} \ ].$$

Completing the rectangles $MNRP$ and $MNQS$, we see that area $MNRP < \delta A(x) <$ area $MNQS$,

noting that $\delta A(x)$ is the area under the arc PQ.

Thus $MP.\delta x < \delta A(x) < NQ. \delta x$.

Division by δx gives

$$MP < \frac{\delta A(x)}{\delta x} < NQ.$$

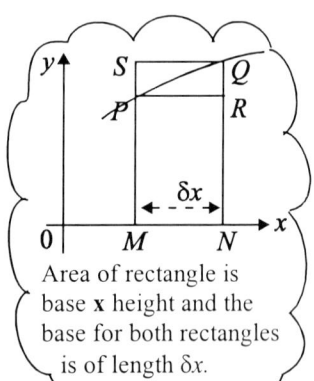

Area of rectangle is
base x height and the
base for both rectangles
is of length δx.

Now as $\delta x \to 0$, MP remains fixed and NQ approaches MP as a limit (since $y = $ f(x) is continuous), and we obtain

$$\lim_{\delta x \to 0} \frac{\delta A(x)}{\delta x} = MP$$

or

$$\frac{dA(x)}{dx} = MP$$

or

$$\frac{dA(x)}{dx} = \text{f}(x).$$

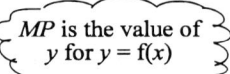

MP is the value of
y for $y = $ f(x)

[For the trapezium under the line $y = x$,

$$\delta A(x) = x dx + \frac{(\delta x)^2}{2}$$

so

$$\frac{\delta A(x)}{\delta x} = x + \frac{\delta x}{2}$$

$\therefore \quad \lim_{\delta x \to 0} \frac{\delta A(x)}{\delta x} = \frac{dA}{dx} = x = MP$ in this case.]

Generally, $\dfrac{dA(x)}{dx} = f(x)$

and $A(x) = \int f(x)d(x)$ by the definition of integration.

Let $F(x)$ be a function which is obtained when $f(x)$ is integrated.

Then $A(x) = F(x) + k.$ (1)

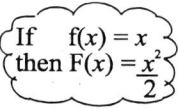

The arbitrary constant may be found by noting that when M and C coincide the shaded area has value zero, i.e. $A = 0$ when $x = c$.

$\therefore$ $A(c) = 0.$

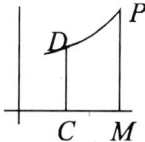

Substitution of $x = c$ in (1) gives

$$A(c) = 0 = F(c) + k.$$

$\therefore$ $k = -F(c).$

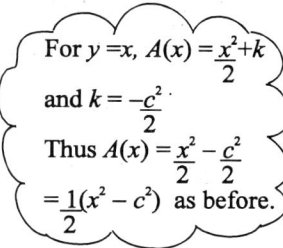

For $y = x$, $A(x) = \dfrac{x^2 + k}{2}$

and $k = -\dfrac{c^2}{2}$.

Thus $A(x) = \dfrac{x^2}{2} - \dfrac{c^2}{2}$

$= \dfrac{1}{2}(x^2 - c^2)$ as before.

Substitution for k in (1) then gives

$$A(x) = F(x) - F(c).$$

If we require the area between the points C and D where $OD = d$, this is $A(d)$ given by

$$A(d) = F(d) - F(c),$$

where $F(x) = \int f(x)d(x)$.

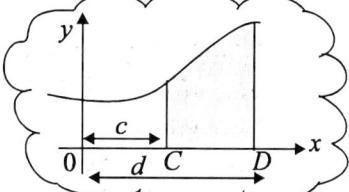

For the case of $y = x$, the area between $x = c$, $x = d$ is as shown in the bubble.

Here $f(x) = x$, $F(x) = \dfrac{x^2}{2}$ and

$$A(d) = F(d) - F(c) = \frac{1}{2}(d^2 - c^2).$$

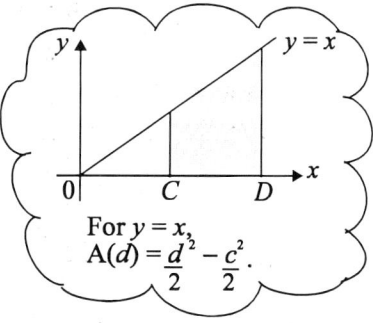

For $y = x$,

$A(d) = \dfrac{d^2}{2} - \dfrac{c^2}{2}$.

Example 10.3

Find the area under the curve $y = x^2$ between the lines $x = 2$, $x = 3$ and the x-axis.

Here $f(x) = x^2$ and

$$F(x) = \int x^2 dx = \frac{x^3}{3}.$$

Required area $= F(3) - F(2)$

$$= \frac{3^3}{3} - \frac{2^3}{3} = \frac{19}{3} = 6\frac{1}{3}.$$

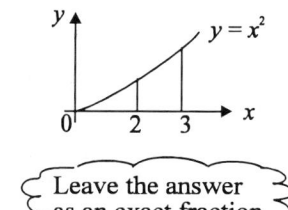

Leave the answer as an exact fraction.

Example 10.4

Find the area between the curve $y = x^3 + x$, the lines $x = 1$, $x = 2$ and the x-axis.

Here $\qquad f(x) = x^3 + x$

and $\qquad F(x) = \int f(x)dx = \dfrac{x^4}{4} + \dfrac{x^2}{2}$.

Required area $= F(2) - F(1)$

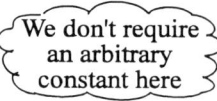

We don't require an arbitrary constant here

$$= \dfrac{2^4}{4} + \dfrac{2^2}{2} - \left(\dfrac{1^4}{4} + \dfrac{1^2}{2} \right)$$

$$= \dfrac{21}{4} = 5\dfrac{1}{4}.$$

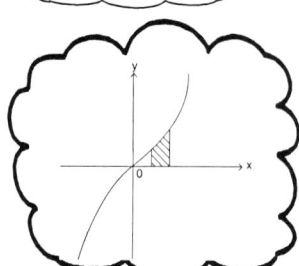

The area between $y = f(x)$, $x = c$, $x = d$ and the x-axis can be represented as

$$\int_{c}^{d} f(x)dx = \left(F(x) \right)_{x=d} - \left(F(x) \right)_{x=c}$$

which can be written as

$$\int_{c}^{d} f(x)dx = \left[F(x) \right]_{c}^{d}.$$

$F'(x) = f(x)$

Example 10.5

Evaluate (i) $\int_{1}^{3} 2x + x^2 dx$

(ii) $\int_{4}^{9} \sqrt{x} + \dfrac{1}{\sqrt{x}} dx$

(i) $\qquad \int_{1}^{3} 2x + x^2 dx = \left[x^2 + \dfrac{x^3}{3} \right]_{1}^{3}$

$f(x) = 2x + x^2$

$F(x) = x^2 + \dfrac{x^3}{3}$

$c = 1, d = 3.$

$$= 3^2 + \dfrac{3^3}{3} - \left(1^2 + \dfrac{1^3}{3} \right)$$

$$= 18 - 1\dfrac{1}{3} = \dfrac{50}{3} \text{ or } 16\dfrac{2}{3}.$$

(ii) $\qquad \int_{4}^{9} \sqrt{x} + \dfrac{1}{\sqrt{x}} dx = \left[2x^{\frac{3}{2}} + 2\sqrt{x} \right]_{4}^{9}$

$$= 2(9)^{\frac{3}{2}} + 2\sqrt{9} - \left[2(4)^{\frac{3}{2}} + 2\sqrt{4} \right]$$

$$= 54 + 6 - 16 - 2(2) = 40.$$

$$= (18 + 6) - (5\tfrac{1}{3} + 4)$$

$$= 24 - 9\tfrac{1}{3}$$

$$= 14\tfrac{2}{3}$$

Integrals such as $\int\limits_c^d f(x)dx$ are known as <u>definite integrals</u> because the answer doesn't involve any arbitrary or unknown constants.

Example 10.6

Represent the area between the curve $y = x^3$ and the lines $x = 2$, $x = 3$ and the x-axis as a defininte integral. Evaluate this definite integral.

The part of the curve lies above the x-axis so that the area will be given by $\int\limits_2^3 x^3 dx$.

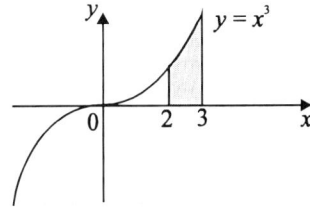

Evaluation of this definite integral gives

$$\int\limits_2^3 x^3 dx = \left[\frac{x^4}{4}\right]_2^3 = \frac{3^4}{4} - \frac{2^4}{4}$$

$$= \frac{81}{4} - \frac{16}{4} = \frac{65}{4}.$$

A word of caution is appropriate concerning the use of definite integrals to evaluate areas. The use of a sketch is recommended, the following example showing the difficulty that may arise.

Example 10.7

Use definite integration to evaluate the area between the curve $y = x^3$ between the lines $x = -2$, $x = 2$ and the x-axis.

Without a sketch, we write the area as $\int\limits_{-2}^2 x^3 dx$

which becomes $\left[\frac{x^4}{4}\right]_{-2}^2 = \frac{2^4}{4} - \frac{(-2)^4}{4} = 4 - 4 = 0.$

The surprising result is understood when we consider a sketch of $y = x^3$, between $x = -2$, $x = 2$.

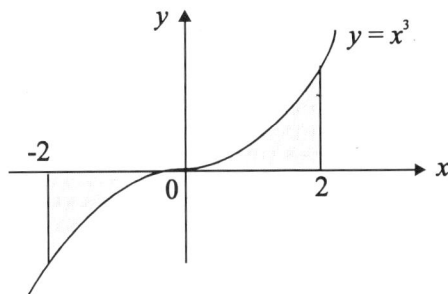

The definite integral $\int\limits_{-2}^2 x^3 dx$ gives the algebraic sum of the shaded areas. The shaded area on the left is evaluated as a negative number because the curve is below the x-axis; the area on the right is evaluated as a positive number because the curve is above the x-axis. The 'positive' and 'negative' areas cancel each other over the range.

The 'negative' area is given by

$$\int_{-2}^{0} x^3 \, dx \quad = \quad \left[\frac{x^4}{4} \right]_{-2}^{0} = \frac{0^4}{4} - \frac{(-2)^4}{4} = -4 \, .$$

The 'positive' area is evaluated as

$$\int_{0}^{2} x^3 \, dx \quad = \quad \left[\frac{x^4}{4} \right]_{0}^{2} = \frac{2^4}{4} - \frac{0^4}{4} = 4 \, .$$

To obtain the total shaded area we require

$$\int_{0}^{2} x^3 \, dx \; - \; \int_{-2}^{0} x^3 \, dx \quad = \; 4 - (-4)$$

$$= \; 8$$

or alternatively by symmetry in this case :-

the required area $= \; 2 \times \int_{0}^{2} x^3 \, dx$

$$= \; 2 \times 4 \; = \; 8.$$

> When areas lie below the x-axis we can arrange for them to give positive answers by introducing a minus sign.

The lesson to be learnt from example 10.7 is an obvious one : when finding areas by definite integrals draw a sketch of the situation.

Sketches are also useful when we are asked to evaluate more complicated areas.

Example 10.8

Sketch the curve $y = x^2$ and the straight line $y = 2x + 3$. Find the points of intersection A and B of the line and the curve, where the x-coordinate of A is less than the x-coordinate of B. Evaluate the area between the chord AB and the curve.

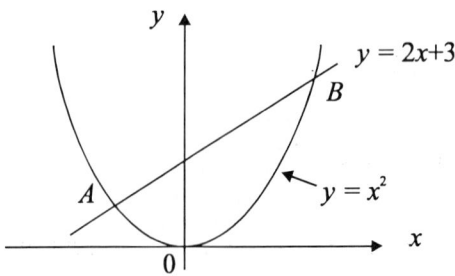

The coordinates of the points of intersection A and B satisfy both
$$y = x^2 \text{ and } y = 2x + 3.$$
Equating the y-coordinates, we obtain
$$x^2 \; = \; 2x + 3$$
i.e. $\qquad x^2 - 2x - 3 \; = \; 0.$
This factorises to give
$$(x + 1)(x - 3) \; = \; 0$$
so $\qquad x = -1 \text{ or } x = 3.$

> or use the quadratic formula

When $x = -1$, $\quad y \; = (-1)^2 = 1,$
$\qquad x = 3, \qquad y \; = 3^2 = 9.$

As it happens, the value of y is not required in this example.

The area between the chord and curve is shown shaded.

> The equation $y = x^2$ as here or $y = 2x+3$ can be used to find the y values.

Shaded area $=$ Area under chord $-$ area under curve

$$= \int_{-1}^{3} 2x + 3\,dx - \int_{-1}^{3} x^2\,dx$$

$$= \left[x^2 + 3x\right]_{-1}^{3} - \left[\frac{x^3}{3}\right]_{-1}^{3}$$

> all areas are above the x-axis so are regarded as positive

$$= 3^2 + 3 \times 3 - ((-1)^2 + 3(-1)) - \left\{\frac{3^3}{3} - \left(\frac{(-1)^3}{3}\right)\right\}$$

$$= 9 + 9 - 1 + 3 - 9 - \frac{1}{3}$$

> use brackets to avoid errors in signs

$$= 10\frac{2}{3}.$$

Example 10.9

Sketch the curve $y = -x^2 + 4x$. The line $y = 3$ intersects the curve in points A and B, where the x-coordinate of A is less than the x-coordinate of B. The curve intersects the x-axis at the origin O and the point C.

Find the area between the arc OA, chord AB, the arc BC and the x-axis.

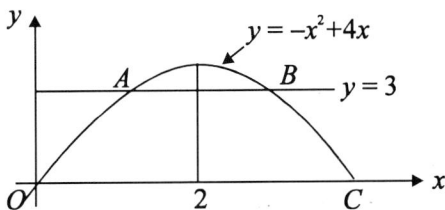

The curve has a maximum point at $x = 2$ and intersects the x-axis at points where $y = 0$, i.e. when

$$-x^2 + 4x \; = 0.$$

$\therefore \qquad x(-x + 4) \; = 0.$

Thus, $\qquad\qquad x \; = 0 \text{ or } 4.$

$x = 4$ corresponds to the point C.

The line $y = 3$ intersects the curve when

$$3 \; = -x^2 + 4x.$$

$\therefore \qquad x^2 - 4x + 3 \; = 0$

so $\qquad (x - 3)(x - 1) \; = 0.$

Thus $\qquad\qquad x \; = 1 \qquad \text{(point } A\text{)}$

or $\qquad\qquad x \; = 3 \qquad \text{(point } B\text{)}.$

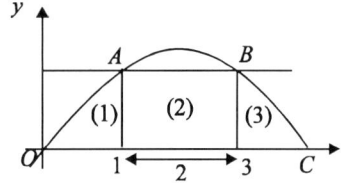

The required area
= area (1) + area (2) + area (3).

$$\text{Area (1)} = \int_0^1 -x^2 + 4x\,dx = \left[-\frac{x^3}{3} + 2x^2\right]_0^1$$

$$= -\frac{(1)^3}{3} + 2(1)^2 - \left(-\frac{0^3}{3} + 2.0^2\right)$$

$$= -\frac{1}{3} + 2 = 1\frac{2}{3}.$$

Area (2) = Area of rectangle of base 2, height 3
= 2 × 3 = 6.

$$\text{Area (3)} = \int_3^4 -x^2 + 4x\,dx = \left[-\frac{x^3}{3} + 2x^2\right]_3^4$$

in fact, area (3)
= area (1)
by symmetry

$$= -\frac{(4)^3}{3} + 2.(4)^2 - \left(-\frac{(3)^3}{3} + 2.(3)^2\right) = 1\frac{2}{3}.$$

The required area $= 1\frac{2}{3} + 6 + 1\frac{2}{3} = 9\frac{1}{3}.$

Exercises 10.2

N.B. You are advised to draw sketches when finding areas.

1. Find the area enclosed between the curve $y = x^2 - 5x + 4$ and the x-axis.

2. Find the area enclosed by the line $y = 7$ and the curve $y = x^2 + 3$.

3. Find the area enclosed by the curve $y = -2x + x^2$, the lines $x = 0$, $x = 3$ and the x-axis.

4. Show that $\int_0^a a^2x - x^3\,dx = \frac{a^4}{4}$.

5. Show that $\int_0^a \left(\sqrt{a} - \sqrt{x}\right)^2 dx = \frac{a^2}{6}$.

6. Evaluate $\int_0^1 x^2\left(1 + x^2\right)dx$.

7. Find the area enclosed by the x-axis and that part of the curve $y = 8x - 12 - x^2$ for which y is positive.

8. Calculate the area of the segment of the curve $y = 2\sqrt{x}$ $(x \geq 0)$ cut off by the line $y = x$.

9. Find the area of the segment of the curve $y = x^2 - 2x + 2$ cut off by the line $y = 5$.

10. Find the area of the curve $y = x(x - 2)$ cut off by the line $y = x$.

Revision Paper 1

1. Given that the equation
$$x^2 - (3 + 2k)x + 2k + 11 = 0$$
has real roots, show that
$$4k^2 + 4k - 35 \geq 0.$$
Given further that the roots are equal, find the possible values of k, and the associated values of x.

2. (a) Sketch the graph of $y = \cos x$ for values of x between $0°$ and $360°$.
   (b) Find the values of x between $0°$ and $360°$ satisfying
$$4 \sin^2 x + 8 \cos x - 7 = 0.$$

3. The third term of a geometric series is $\dfrac{1}{4}$ and the fifth term is $\dfrac{1}{16}$.

   (a) Find the possible values of the common ratio.
   (b) Find the sum to infinity of the series with the positive common ratio.

4. A is the point (1, 3), C is the point (3, 7) and D is the midpoint of AC. Show that the line through D perpendicular to AC is given by
$$2y + x - 12 = 0.$$
The line meets the x-axis at B. Find the area of triangle ABC.

5.

   Two points A and B are located on a circle of centre O and radius r such that $A\hat{O}B = \theta$, as shown.
   Given that the shaded area is one third of the area of the circle, show that
$$3\theta - 3 \sin \theta - 2\pi = 0.$$

   By drawing sketches of the graphs $y = \theta - \dfrac{2\pi}{3}, y = \sin \theta$, show

   that θ lies between $\dfrac{\pi}{2}$ and π.

6. The curve $y = x^2 + 6$ and the line $y = 5x$ intersect at the points A and B, where the x-coordinate of A is less than the x – coordinate of B.

   (a) Sketch the curve and the line.

   (b) Find the coordinates of A and B.

   (c) The line through B parallel to the y-axis meets the x-axis at C, and O is the origin. Find the area enclosed by the line OA, the arc AB, the line BC and the x-axis.

7. An open rectangular tank is 2 metres wide, x metres long and y metres in height. Write down in terms of x and y the area A in square metres of thin sheet metal to be used in its construction.
   The volume of the tank is 6 cubic metres.

   (a) Show that $A = 2x + \dfrac{12}{x} + 6.$

   (b) Find the length and depth of the tank if the least area of sheet metal is to be used.

Revision Paper 2

1   A, B, C are the points (1, 3), (–1, 5), (3, 7), respectively. The midpoints of AB and BC are E and F respectively.

(a) Find the coordinates of E and F.

(b) Show that EF is parallel to AC.

(c) Show that $EF = \dfrac{1}{2}AC$.

2 (a) State the set of values of y between $0°$ and $360°$ for which $\sin y < 0$.

   (b) Find the pairs of values of x and y between $0°$ and $360°$ satisfying

$$2\cos x + 3\sin y = -\frac{1}{6}$$

$$3\cos x - 2\sin y = \frac{5}{6}.$$

3   Find $\displaystyle\int \frac{(1+2x)^2}{\sqrt{x}}\, dx$.

4 (a) Find and determine the nature of the stationary values of the function given by
$$f(x) = x^3 - 12x + 15.$$

   (b) Sketch the graph of $y = x^3 - 12x + 15$ and deduce the number of real roots of the equation
$$x^3 - 12x + 15 = 0.$$

5   The first term of an arithmetic series is a and the common ratio is d. Show that the sum of the first n terms is given by

$$S_n = \frac{n}{2}\big[2a + (n-1)d\big]$$

The first term of an arithmetic series is 4 and the common difference is –2. The sum of the first n terms is –1116. Find n.

6 (a) Sketch the curve $y = x^2 - 4x + 3$.

   (b) Find the area enclosed by the x-axis, the curve $y = x^2 - 4x + 3$ and the lines $x = 0$ and $x = 2$.

7

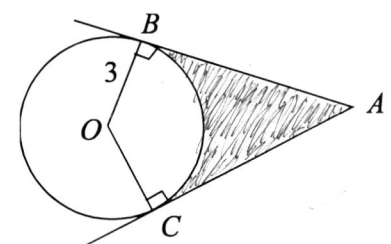

A circle of centre O is of radius 3 cm. The tangents to the circle from a point A meets the circle at points B and C as shown. The length of OA is 5 cm. Find the shaded area correct to two decimal places.

Revision Paper 3

1. Simplify $\left(\dfrac{\sqrt{5}+2}{\sqrt{5}-1}\right)$.

2. Express $1-x-x^2$ in the form $b-(x+a)^2$ and find the maximum value of the expression. Sketch the graph of $y = 1 - x - x^2$.

3. The vertices of a quadrilateral ABCD are A(4,0), B(14,11), C(0,6), and D (–10, –5). Show
   (a) that AC and BD are perpendicular,
   (b) the midpoints of AC and BD coincide,
   (c) BD = 4AC.

4. A cylinder is such that the sum of its diameter and height is 18 cm.
   (a) Express the volume of the cylinder in terms of r, the base radius of the cylinder measured in centimetres.
   (b) Find the greatest possible volume of the cylinder.

5. Given that $y = 3\sqrt{x} + \dfrac{5}{x^{\frac{3}{2}}} - \dfrac{6}{x^2} + 4,$ find the value of $\dfrac{dy}{dx}$ when $x = 4$.

6. The curve C given by $y = x(2 - x)$ intersects the x-axis at the origin O and another point A.
   (a) Sketch the curve C.
   (b) The straight line $y = x$ intersects C at O and at another point B. Find the area enclosed by the line OB, the arc BA and the x-axis.

7. A chord AB of length 4cm divides a circle of radius 4cm into two segments. Find the area of each segment.

Revision Paper 4

1 (a) Sketch the graph of $y = \tan x$ for values of x between $0°$ and $360°$.
   (b) Using your sketch, or otherwise, find all values of x satisfying
         $$8 \tan^2 x + 10 \tan x - 3 = 0.$$

2 Given that $f(x) = 3x^2 - 4x + 7$, find the value of $f(x + h) - f(x)$.
   Deduce that
   $$f'(x) = 6x - 4.$$

3 The vertices of a triangle are $A(2, 4)$, $B(-8, 2)$ and $C(4, -6)$. The points P and Q are the mid points of AB and AC respectively. The line through P perpendicular to AB meets the line through Q perpendicular to AC at R.
   (a) Show that the equation of PR is $y + 5x + 12 = 0$ and find the equation of QR.
   (b) Find the coordinates of R.
   (c) Show that $BR = CR$.

4 A girl sits her GCSE examinations in nine subjects. An enthusiastic, possibly unthinking parent suggests that he will reward the girl for examination success as follows :-

   the first pass will gain 10 p,
   the second pass will gain 20 p,
   the third pass will gain 40 p,

   up until the ninth pass, the reward for every pass being twice as much as that for the previous pass.
   Given that the girl passed in the nine subjects, find
   (a) the reward gained for the ninth pass,
   (b) the total reward gained by the girl, expressing your answer in pounds and pence.

5 Find and determine the nature of the stationary values of the function f given by
   $$f(x) = \frac{3x^5}{5} - \frac{3x^4}{4} - 2x^3 + 2.$$

   Sketch the curve $y = \dfrac{3x^5}{5} - \dfrac{3x^4}{4} - 2x^3 + 2$.

6 Given that real values of x and y exist that satisfy the equations
   $$y = mx + 5,$$
   $$x^2 + y^2 - 4x - 2y + 3 = 0,$$
   show that
   $$m^2 + 8m + 7 \geq 0.$$

7 Sketch the curve $y = -x^2 + 3x$ between the origin 0 and the point A, where $x = 3$. The line $y = 2$ cuts the curve in points B and C, where the x – coordinate of B is less than that of C. Find the area of OBCA.

Revision Paper 5

1   The first term of a geometric series is $\sqrt{3}$ and the common ratio is $-\dfrac{1}{\sqrt{3}}$. Find the sum to infinity of the series in the form $a + b\sqrt{c}$, where a, b and c are rational numbers.

2   Find all values of x between $0°$ and $360°$ satisfying $12\cos^2 x - 5\sin x - 10 = 0$.

3   A is the point (3,5), C is the point (5, 1), and D is the midpoint of AC. The line through D perpendicular to AC intersects the y-axis at B.
  (a) Find the equation of BD.
  (b) Show that the line through D parallel to AB passes through the midpoint of BC.

4   Find the value of $k(k \neq 1)$ such that the quadratic function
$$k(x+1)^2 - (x-2)(x-3)$$
is equal to zero for only one value of x.

5

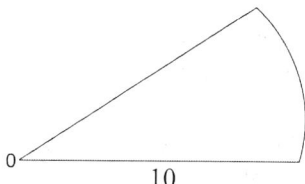

Given that the perimeter of a sector of a circle of centre 0 and radius 10cm is 25cm, find the area of the sector.

6

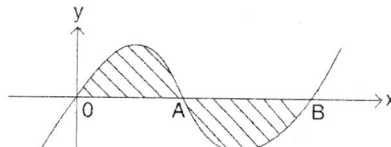

The curve $y = x^3 - 3x^2 + 2x$ intersects the x-axis at the origin 0 and two other points A and B. Evaluate the total shaded area.

7   A farmer wishes to enclose a rectangular area within a large field. A straight hedge on one side of the field acts as one boundary, the remaining three boundaries being constructed from fencing. The length of fencing available is 100 metres. A length x metres of the hedge is used.
  (a) Show that the area enclosed, Am^2, is given by
$$A = 50x - \frac{x^2}{2}.$$
  (b) Find the maximum value of A.

Revision Paper 6

1   A triangle ABC has A at the point (7,9), B at (3,5), C at (5,1); E and F are the midpoints of AB and AC, respectively.
  (a)   Show that EF is parallel to BC.
  (b)   EF meets the x and y axes at the points P and Q respectively. Find the area of triangle OPQ, where 0 is the origin.

2 (a)   Find all values of x between $0°$ and $360°$ satisfying
$$3(\sin^2 x - \cos^2 x) = 1 + \cos x.$$
  (b)   Find all values of θ between $0°$ and $180°$ satisfying
$$\tan 4\theta = \sqrt{3}.$$

3   The first term of an arithmetic series is -2, and the eleventh term is equal to four times the fourth term.
  (a)   Find the common difference.
  (b)   The product of the nth term and the $(n+1)$st term is 3190. Find n.

4   Given that
$$\int_0^a \frac{6\sqrt{x}}{a} + \frac{2a^{\frac{3}{2}}}{x^2}\, dx = 6,$$
find the value of a.

5   Given that
$$f(x) = \frac{4x^3}{3} - 6x^2 + 15x + 3,$$
find $f'(x)$.
By completing the square, or otherwise, for $f'(x)$ deduce that f is an increasing function.

6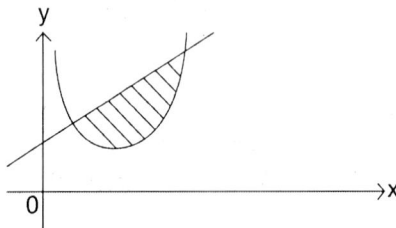

The diagram shows the curve $y = x^2 - 3x + 8$ and the line $y = x + 5$. Evaluate the shaded area.

7   The total cost of running a ship per hour (in thousands of pounds) is given by
$$C = 8 + \frac{s^3}{2000},$$
where s is the speed in kilometres/hour.
  (a)   Write down the time for a voyage of 2000 km assuming the ship travels at a constant speed of s kilometres/hour.
  (b)   Write down the cost of a 2000 km voyage in terms of s.
  (c)   Find the value of s which minimises the cost of a 2000 km voyage.

ANSWERS

Chapter 1
Exercises 1.1

1.   (i) $\dfrac{1}{a^2}$ (ii) $\dfrac{1}{x^{\frac{1}{2}}}$ (iii) $\dfrac{1}{b^6}$ (iv) a (v) b^2

2.   (i) a (ii) b^8 (iii) $\dfrac{1}{x}$ or x^{-1} (iv) $4a^2b^3$ (v) $\dfrac{1}{2}x^2y^7$

    (vi) 4 (vii) $\dfrac{1}{2}$ (viii) $\dfrac{9}{25}$ (ix) $\dfrac{64}{27}$

3.   (i) $7ab^3$ (ii) $4x^3y^2$ **4.** $\dfrac{1}{128}$

Exercises 1.2

  (i) $\dfrac{1}{\left(x^2+1\right)^{\frac{3}{2}}}$ (ii) $\dfrac{2a+3}{a+1}$ (iii) $\dfrac{b^2-b+2}{b(b^2+2)^2}$

  (iv) $\dfrac{\left(x^2-y^2\right)^{\frac{1}{2}}-1}{\left(x^2-y^2-1\right)(x-y)^{\frac{1}{2}}}$ (v) $\dfrac{1}{x}$ (vi) $\dfrac{3}{2x^2+3}$

Exercises 1.3
    See Text

Exercises 1.4

1.   (i) $2\sqrt{5}$ (ii) $3\sqrt{2}$ (iii) $6\sqrt{2}$ (iv) $6\sqrt{5}$ (v) $5\sqrt{10}$
2.   (i) $2\sqrt{3}-3$ (ii) $5\sqrt{2}-4$ (iii) 1 (iv) $2\sqrt{3}+14$
    (v) $58-12\sqrt{6}$ (vi) $x-x^2$ or $x(1-x)$
3.   (i) $\dfrac{\sqrt{5}}{5}$ (ii) $\dfrac{\sqrt{2}}{6}$ (iii) $\dfrac{\sqrt{6}}{6}$ (iv) $\dfrac{1}{2}(\sqrt{3}-1)$

    (v) $\sqrt{2}+1$ (vi) $5(\sqrt{5}+2)$ (vii) $\dfrac{1}{2}(\sqrt{5}+\sqrt{3})$ (viii) $\sqrt{3}$

Exercises 1.5

  (i) x^2-16 (ii) $2x^2+5x+2$ (iii) $2x^3+3x^2-5x-6$
  (iv) $x^4+x^3-5x^2-35x-18$ (v) $9x^2+3xy-20y^2$ (vi) x^2+4x+4
  (vii) $9x^2-12x+4$ (viii) $x^3+9x^2+27x+27$ (ix) x^3-3x+2

Exercises 1.6

1.   (i) $(x+1)(x+4)$ (ii) $(x-1)(x-4)$ (iii) $(x+1)(x-4)$
  (iv) $(x+5)(x+18)$ (v) $(x-5)(x-18)$ (vi) $(x-5)(x+18)$
  (vii) $(l-2)(l+3)$ (viii) $(l+2)(l-3)$ (ix) $(p-7)(p+9)$
  (x) $(x+4)(x-7)$
2.   (i) $(x+1)(2x+1)$ (ii) $(3t+4)(t+1)$ (iii) $(x-4)(4x+1)$
  (iv) $(x-2)(4x+1)$ (v) $(x-5)(4x+5)$ (vi) $(3x-2)(2x+1)$
  (vii) $(y-2)(3y+1)$ (viii) $(2y-7)(4y-1)$ (ix) $(2x-3)(5x+3)$
  (x) $(x+3)(7x-4)$

Chapter 2
Exercises 2.1
(i) identity   (ii) equation   (iii) equation   (iv) identity   (v) identity
(vi) equation   (vii) equation   (viii) identity

Exercises 2.2
1.   (i) $y = 22$ (ii) $a = -35$ (iii) $x = 21$
2.   15525 m^2 **3.** 15   **4.** 70 at £5.50, 50 at £2.50
5.   5 km   **6.** £12   **7.** 23

Exercises 2.3
1.   (i) $-1, 7$ (ii) $1, 12$ (iii) $\frac{1}{2}, 8$ (iv) $-4, -5$ (v) $-\frac{5}{3}, 4$ (vi) $-\frac{2}{5}, -6$

2.   (i) $3.56, -0.56$ (ii) $-4.56, -0.44$ (iii) $2.85, -0.35$
     (iv) 0.67 (twice)   (v) 0.60 (twice)   (vi) no real solutions

3.   (a) (i)   (b) (iii)   (c) (i)   (d) (i)   (e) (i)   (f) (ii)

4. $a = 1, x = 1$ (twice)   **6.** 32

Exercises 2.4
(i)   -2, 3 (minimum)   (ii)   -2,11 (maximum)

(iii) $-\frac{3}{2}, \frac{13}{4}$ (maximum)   (iv) $-\frac{3}{4}, -\frac{45}{4}$ (minimum)

(v) $-\frac{1}{4}, \frac{55}{8}$ (minimum)   (vi) $\frac{3}{8}, \frac{25}{16}$ (maximum)

(vii) $\frac{1}{2}, \frac{37}{4}$ (maximum)   (viii)   1, 1 (maximum)

(ix)   0, 4 (minimum)   (x)   0, 9 (maximum)

Exercises 2.5
1.   (i) $x = 3, y = 1$ (ii) $x = 2, y = -2$ (iii) $a = 8, b = 3$

2. $a = 6, b = 4$ **3.** 12, 20   **4.** $\frac{5}{2}, -\frac{7}{2}$ **5.** $-\frac{19}{3}, \frac{59}{3}$ **6,** $-\frac{1}{2}, -\frac{5}{4}$

7. $-\frac{232}{3}, -\frac{104}{3}$ **8.** $\frac{17}{5}, -\frac{16}{5}$

Exercises 2.6
1.   (i) $x = 6, y = -4$ or $x = -5, y = 7$ (ii) $a = 5, b = -2$ or $a = -26, b = -33$

     (iii) $x = 2, y = 26$ or $x = 13, y = 4$ (iv) $a = 2, b = -1$ or $a = -\frac{7}{11}, b = -\frac{69}{11}$

     (v) $x = 4, y = -3$ or $x = -\frac{15}{14}, y = \frac{171}{14}$ (vi) $x = -4, y = -6$ or $x = \frac{116}{13}, y = \frac{6}{13}$

     (vii) $x = -4, y = -2$ or $x = \frac{6}{9}, y = -\frac{4}{9}$

2.   (i) $\frac{1}{2}$ (ii) -17 (iii) $9, -1$

3.   (i) No   (ii) No   (iii) Yes

Chapter 3
Exercise 3.1
15
Exercises 3.2

1. 5, 8, n ; divergent   **2.** $\dfrac{1}{32}, \dfrac{1}{2^{n-1}}$; convergent, limit = 0

3. 4^n, No   **4.** No, convergent, limit = 0   **5.** Oscillatory
6. Yes   **7.** Divergent   **8.** No   **9.** Oscillatory
10. x^n (i) Convergent, limit = 0 (ii) Convergent, limit = 0 (iii) Divergent
    (iv) Oscillatory (v) Convergent, limit = 0
11. 1, Yes

Exercises 3.3
1. (i) 0   (ii) 1   (iii) 0   (iv) 1   (v) 0
   (vi) no limit (vii) 0   (viii) no limit   (ix) 1
2. (a) Yes, limit = 0   (b) Yes, limit = 1   (c) No   (d) Yes, limit = 1
   (e) Yes, limit = 0   (f) Yes, limit = 1   (g) No   (h) Yes, limit = 1

Exercises 3.4

1. $\displaystyle\sum_{r=1}^{\infty} \frac{1}{r^2}$ **2.** $\displaystyle\sum_{r=1}^{\infty} \frac{(-1)^{r+1}}{r}$ **3.** $\displaystyle\sum_{r=1}^{\infty} \frac{1}{2^{r-1}}$ **4.** $\displaystyle\sum_{r=1}^{7} 2^r$

5. $\displaystyle\sum_{r=1}^{20} (2r-1)$ **6.** $\displaystyle\sum_{r=1}^{\infty} \left(r + \frac{1}{r+1} \right)$

Exercises 3.5
1. No   **2.** Yes   **3.** Divergent   **4.** Yes

7. $\dfrac{r+2}{r(r+1)(r+3)}$; $\displaystyle\sum_{r=1}^{\infty} \dfrac{r+2}{r(r+1)(r+3)}$; $\dfrac{29}{30}$; Yes   **8.** $\dfrac{1}{n(n+1)}$; 0

9. $2n+1$; neither converge   **10.** $\dfrac{2}{3} \left(\dfrac{1}{3} \right)^{n-1}$; both converge

Exercises 3.6
1. 22   **2.** $a-3b$; $a-5b$; $a-7b$ **3.** 27   **4.** 12th
5. 2500   **6.** 2; $2n-6$ **7.** $8n-7$ **8.** 15
9. £2010 ; £102000   **10.** £1665   **11.** No   **12.** 14; 4
13. $3\dfrac{1}{2} ; \dfrac{1}{10} ; 148\dfrac{1}{2}$ **14.** 8; −3, −410   **15.** 3525

Exercises 3.7

1. (a) 54; 162   (b) $\dfrac{1}{5} ; \dfrac{1}{25}$ (c) − 40.5 ; 60.75   (d) 0.0002 ; 0.00002

2. 64   **3.** $-\dfrac{64}{81}$ **4.** 2.48832   **5.** 2.737152

6. £8857.81 to nearest penny   **7.** £2146835.06, to nearest penny   **8.** 1 ; 4

9. $\pm 3; \pm \dfrac{2}{3}$ **10.** 6; $13\dfrac{1}{2}$ **11.** $\sqrt{2}-1; 5\sqrt{2}-7$

Exercises 3.8

1.   (i) $3^n - 1$ (ii) $31.25\left[1 - \left(\dfrac{1}{5}\right)^n\right]$ (iii) $4.8\left[1 - (-1.5)^n\right]$ (iv) $\dfrac{2}{9}\left[1 - (0.1)^n\right]$

2.   (ii) 31.25 (iv) $\dfrac{2}{9}$ **3.** (i) $\dfrac{3}{2}$ (ii) $\dfrac{2}{3}$ (iii) $\dfrac{2}{33}$

4. 17.531 (3 dec. places)   **5.** (i) $\dfrac{x^n - 1}{x - 1}$ (ii) $\dfrac{\left[1 - (-x)^n\right]}{1 + x}$

   (iii) $\dfrac{a^2}{1 - a}\left[\left(\dfrac{1}{a}\right)^n - 1\right]$ (iv) $\dfrac{2b}{(b - 2)}\left[\left(\dfrac{b}{2}\right)^n - 1\right]$ **6.** 15.77 (2 dec. places)

7. 45 **8.** (i) $\dfrac{4}{9}$ (ii) $\dfrac{42}{99}$ (iii) $\dfrac{419}{990}$ (iv) $\dfrac{335}{1998}$ **10.** £1000000

11. $-\dfrac{1}{4}, \dfrac{1}{3}; \ 13\dfrac{1}{2}$ **12.** $\pm\dfrac{1}{2}$

Chapter 4
Exercises 4.1

1.   (a) $\sqrt{5}$ (b) $\sqrt{5}$ (c) $\sqrt{5}$ (d) 5 (e) $2\sqrt{2}$
3.   (i) $\sqrt{41}$ (ii) 5 (iii) $\sqrt{34}$

Exercises 4.2

1.   (a) $\left(\dfrac{3}{2}, 3\right)$ (b) $\left(0, \dfrac{5}{2}\right)$ (c) $\left(1, \dfrac{3}{2}\right)$ (d) $\left(-\dfrac{3}{2}, -2\right)$ (e) $(-3, -4)$

2. $(5, 8)$; 14 **3.** $(-5, -1)$ **4.** $(2, 6)$; $\sqrt{5}$ **6.** 10 **7.** 8

Exercises 4.3

1.   (i) 2 (ii) $\dfrac{1}{2}$ (iii) $\dfrac{1}{4}$ (iv) -1 (v) $-\dfrac{11}{5}$

Exercises 4.4

1.   (a) Parallel   (b) Perpendicular   (c) Perpendicular   (d) Parallel
2. $a = 1, b = 0$ **3.** 8 **4.** -2 ; 30 **5.** 32 **7.** 1

Exercises 4.5

1.   All except (c) and (e) represent straight lines.

Exercises 4.6

1.   (a) $2 ; 0$ (b) $-1 ; 1$ (c) $-2 ; 3$ (d) $\dfrac{1}{2} ; -\dfrac{5}{2}$ (e) $\dfrac{3}{4} ; -\dfrac{7}{4}$

2.   (a) $y = 2x$ (b) $y = -5x$ (c) $y = \dfrac{7}{2}x$ (d) $y = -\dfrac{1}{3}x$ (e) $y = 0$

3.   (a) $2y = x + 3$ (b) $y = 3x + 5$ (c) $y = 4x + 1$ (d) $2y + x + 2 = 0$
4.   (a) $y - x - 1 = 0$ (b) $y = 3$ (c) $2y + x - 2 = 0$ (d) $y - 3x - 5 = 0$
5.   (a) $y = 3x + 6$ (b) $y = -\dfrac{1}{2}x + 2$ (c) $2y = x + 8$ (d) $3y - 2x - 18 = 0$

6.   (a) $y = -x + 2$ (b) $y = 2x + 1$ (c) $4y = 3x + 6$
   (d) $5y - 3x - 7 = 0$ (e) $7y - 4x = 0$ **7.** $(2, 3)$; $y = x + 1$
8. $y = -x + 3$; $y = -x + 4$ **9.** $3y - 5x - 6 = 0$; $3y - x - 14 = 0$

Exercises 4.7

1.　　(a), (c), (e) and (f)　　3. (a) Yes　(b) No　(c) Yes　(d) Yes　(e) No

4.　　(a) -6　(b) 1　(c) $\dfrac{5}{2}$　(d) 18　(e) $-\dfrac{1}{10}$　　　5. $2, -3$; ± 3

Exercises 4.8

1.　　(a) $\left(\dfrac{11}{5}, \dfrac{2}{5}\right)$　　(b) $\left(-\dfrac{17}{8}, \dfrac{19}{8}\right)$　　(c) $(-1, 1); (-6, -9)$　(d) $\left(-\dfrac{1}{3}, \dfrac{7}{9}\right)$

　　　(e) $(0, 0)$; $\left(-\dfrac{1}{2}, -\dfrac{3}{4}\right)$　　　　　3. $(0, 0)$; $(1, 3)$

4.　　$\left(0, -\dfrac{5}{3}\right)$; $(0, 2)$; $\left(\dfrac{22}{5}, -\dfrac{23}{5}\right)$　　5. $a = -2, b = \dfrac{9}{2}$; $\dfrac{5}{3}$

6.　　$A(11, -7)$; $B(5, -1)$; $C(7, 1)$; $D(6, 0)$　　7. $y - 2x + 3 = 0$, $4y + x - 21 = 0$

8. $3y + x - 5 = 0$; $\dfrac{3\sqrt{10}}{10}$

Chapter 5
Exercise 5.1

1.　　(i) $45°$; $\dfrac{\pi}{4}$　(ii) $60°$; $\dfrac{\pi}{3}$　(iii) $40°$; $\dfrac{2\pi}{9}$　　　(iv) $30°$; $\dfrac{\pi}{6}$

　　　(v) $90°$; $\dfrac{\pi}{2}$　(vi) $48°$; $\dfrac{4\pi}{15}$

In Questions 2 and 3 answers are given correct to two decimal places.

2.　　(i) $0.63 \left(\dfrac{\pi}{5}\right)$　(ii) $0.94 \left(\dfrac{3\pi}{10}\right)$　　(iii) $2.73 \left(\dfrac{13\pi}{15}\right)$　(iv) $3.35 \left(\dfrac{16\pi}{15}\right)$

　　　(v) $5.03 \left(\dfrac{8\pi}{5}\right)$　(vi) 2.09

3.　　(i) $67.5°$　　(ii) $25.71°$　(iii) $57.30°$　(iv) $42.97°$

Exercises 5.2

1.　　(i) $\dfrac{\pi}{4}$　　　(ii) $\dfrac{4\pi}{3}$　　(iii) $\dfrac{3\pi}{2}$　　(iv) $\dfrac{5\pi}{3}$

2.　　(i) $\dfrac{\pi}{2}$　　　(ii) $\dfrac{9\pi}{4}$　　(iii) $\dfrac{\pi}{3}$　　(iv) $\dfrac{13\pi}{3}$　　3.　　$\dfrac{50}{\pi} cm^2$

4.　　28.5cm　　　5.　　8, 1.5　　　6.　　25

Exercises 5.3

1.　　(i) $\dfrac{1}{2}$; $\dfrac{12}{13}$; $\dfrac{3}{5}$　　(ii) $\dfrac{7}{25}$; $\dfrac{3}{5}$; $\dfrac{\sqrt{8}}{3} = \dfrac{2\sqrt{2}}{3}$

2.　　(i) $\dfrac{1}{\sqrt{3}}$; $\dfrac{12}{5}$; $\dfrac{3}{4}$　　(ii) $\dfrac{24}{7}$; $\dfrac{4}{3}$; $\dfrac{1}{\sqrt{8}} = \dfrac{\sqrt{8}}{8}$

Answers in Questons 3, 4 and 5 are given correct to four decimal places.

3.　　(i) 0.5922　(ii) 0.8948　(iii) 0.2795　(iv) 0.7314　(v) 0.6540

4.　　(i) $44.9995°$; 0.7854　(ii) $63.4349°$; 1.1071　(iii) $23.6376°$; 0.4126

5.　　(i) $54.4623°$　(ii) $36.8699°$　(iii) $69.6359°$

Exercises 5.4

1. 20° 2. 15° 3. 45° 4. $\dfrac{\pi}{6}$ 5. $\dfrac{7\pi}{48}$

6. 2.25° 7. $\dfrac{\pi}{20}$ 8. 5.5°

Chapter 6
Exercises 6.1

1. (i) positive (ii) negative (iii) positive (iv) positive (v) positive
    (vi) negative (vii) positive (viii) negative (ix) negative (x) positive
2. (i) $-\cos 76°$ (ii) $\sin 66°$ (iii) $-\sin 10°$ (iv) $\tan 3°6'$ (v) $-\sin 15°$
    (vi) $-\cos 68°$ (vii) $-\tan 86.9°$ (viii) $-\cos 45°$ (ix) $\tan 80°$
3. 1 ; 0 ; undefined ; 0 ; -1 ; 0 ; -1 ; 0 ; undefined ; 0 ; 1 ; 0
4. (i) second (ii) third **5.** $-\tan\theta$ **6.** $\tan\theta$ **7.** $-\tan\theta$

Exercises 6.2
Where necessary answers are given correct to four decimal places.

1 (a) 9 (b) 30 (c) 6.5 (d) $\sqrt{3} \approx 1.7321$ (e) 3.8567
   (f) 16.0869 (g) 3.4641
2. 1.9603 3. (a) 8 (b) 5 (c) 35.6710 (d) 7.5175 (e) 10
3. (a) 8 (b) 5 (c) 35.6710 (d) 7.5175 (e) 10
4. $\dfrac{9}{2}(2\sin\theta - \theta)$ 5. $\dfrac{1}{2}r^2(\theta - \sin\theta)$

Exercises 6.3

1. (a) 45°; 135° (b) 60°; 300° (c) 30°; 210° (d) 30°; 330° (e) 0°; 360°
    (f) 0°; 180°; 360° (g) 240°; 300° (h) 180° (i) 135°; 315°
2. $\dfrac{\pi}{8}; \dfrac{3\pi}{8}$ **3.** (i) 0 (ii) 0 (iii) $\sqrt{3}$ (iv) $\sqrt{3}$ (v) $-\dfrac{1}{2}$

    (vi) $\dfrac{1}{2}$ (vii) $\dfrac{\sqrt{3}}{2}$ (viii) $-\dfrac{\sqrt{3}}{2}$

4. $\dfrac{\pi}{18}; \dfrac{7\pi}{18}; \dfrac{13\pi}{18}$

5. (i) 90° (ii) 15° ; 75° (iii) 75°
6. (a) 30°, 150°, 210°, 330° (b) 30°, 150°, 210°, 330°

    (c) 90°, 210°, 330° (d) 30°, 150°, 210°, 330°

    (e) 0°, 135°, 180°, 315°, 360° (f) 60°, 90°, 270°, 300°

    (g) 0°, 180°, 199.47°, 340.53°, 360° (correct to two decimal places)

    (h) 60°, 90°, 120°, 240°, 270°, 300° (i) 0°, 60°, 180°, 300°, 360°

Exercises 6.4
Answers are given correct to two decimal places, wherever necessary.

1. (i) 270° (ii) 30°,90°,150° (iii) 0°,90°,180°,360°
    (iv) 46.67°,313.33°

2. (i) $\dfrac{\sqrt{3}}{2}$ (ii) $-\sqrt{3}$ **3.** (i) $-\dfrac{1}{2}$ (ii) $\sqrt{3}$

4. $\dfrac{1}{\sqrt{2}}$ **5.**   (i) $a\cos\theta$ (ii) $\tan\theta$

6.   (i) $b\sin\theta$ (ii) $\tan\theta$

Chapter 7
Exercises 7.1

1.   (i) 56   (ii) $-\dfrac{10}{11}$ (iii) 0   (iv) -6 (v) $\dfrac{1}{1000}$ (vi) $\dfrac{1}{3}$ (vii) $-\dfrac{3}{7}$

Exercises 7.2

1.   12.61 **2.** $12+3h$, 12   **3.**   24   **4.** $4x+3$ **5.** $14x-3$

6. $3x^2-2x$ **7.**   (i) $9x^2$ (ii) $4x$ (iii)   6

(iv) $9x^2+4x+6$ (iv)   = (i) + (ii) + (iii)

Exercises 7.3

2. $3x^2$ **3.**   1   **4.**   0   **6.** $15x^2+6x+2$

7.   (i)   6   (ii) $4x$ (iii) $9x^2$ (iv) $9x^2+4x+6$

(iv) = (iii) + (ii) + (i)

Exercises 7.4

1.   (i) $90x^9$ (ii) $-\dfrac{12}{x^5}$ (iii) 0   (iv) $3\sqrt{x}$ (v) $-\dfrac{6}{x^{\frac{5}{3}}}$ (vi) $4x-9$

(vii) $9x^2+18x$ (viii) $2x-1$ (ix) $1-\dfrac{4}{x^2}$ (x) $2x+2=2(x+1)$

(xi) $\dfrac{3}{2}\sqrt{x}+2x-\dfrac{1}{2\sqrt{x}}-1$ (xii) $-\dfrac{2}{x^2}-\dfrac{4}{x^3}-\dfrac{12}{x^4}$

2.   (i) 6   (ii) 9   (iii) $-\dfrac{1}{4}$ (iv) -14 (v) $-\dfrac{1}{2}$ (vi) 6

3.   (i) $(-4, 20)$ (ii) $(0, 2)$ (iii) $(2, 12)$ (iv) $(-11, 80)$

(v) $\left(\dfrac{1}{2},3\right);\left(-\dfrac{1}{2},-3\right)$ (vi) $\left(\dfrac{\sqrt{3}}{3},-3\sqrt{3}\right);\left(-\dfrac{\sqrt{3}}{3},3\sqrt{3}\right)$

(vii) $\left(\dfrac{4}{3},\dfrac{256}{27}\right);(-2,-2)$

4. -1 **5.**   3   **6.** $-4, 4$ **7.** $0, 2$; $\dfrac{1}{2}$ **8.** $(0, 6), (2, 2)$

Chapter 8
Exercises 8.1

1.   (i)   (a) $x>\dfrac{3}{2}$ (b) $x<\dfrac{3}{2}$ (ii) (a) $x>1$ or $x<-2$ (b) $-2<x<1$

(iii) (a) $x>1$ (b) $0<x<1$ (iv) (a) $x<-\dfrac{3}{2}$ (b) $x>-\dfrac{3}{2}$

(v) (a) $x>\sqrt[3]{2}$ (b) $x<\sqrt[3]{2}$ (vi) (a) $x>3$ or $x<-3$ (b) $-3<x<3$

2.   (i) $\dfrac{3}{2}$ (ii) $-2, 1$ (iii) 1   (iv) $-\dfrac{3}{2}$ (v) $\sqrt[3]{2}$ (vi) $0, \pm3$

Exercises 8.2
1.   (i)   B minimum, D maximum
     (ii) F, J minimum; G, L maximum; H stationary point of inflexion
     (iii) O, S stationary points of inflexion; Q minimum

Exercises 8.3
1.   (1,2) minimum
2.   (3,18) maximum
3.   (-4,-107) minimum; (1,18) maximum
4.   (0,0) stationary point of inflexion; (3,-27) minimum
5.   (0,2) stationary point of inflexion; (1,1) maximum
6.   (0,0) stationary point of inflexion; $(\frac{3}{2},-\frac{27}{16})$ minimum
7.   (0,0) minimum
8.   (0,0) stationary point of inflexion
9.   (0,0)   maximum

Exercises 8.5
1. $\left(-1,\frac{16}{3}\right)$ maximum ; $\left(3,-\frac{16}{3}\right)$ minimum
2. $\left(-1,\frac{23}{6}\right)$ maximum ; $\left(-4,-\frac{2}{3}\right)$ minimum
3.   (0, 0) maximum ; (− 2, − 16) minimum ; (2, − 16) minimum
4.   (− 1, − 4) minimum ; (1, 4) maximum
5.   (0, 0) minimum ; (− 4, 32) maximum
6.   (− 1, 2) minimum ; (1, 6) maximum
7. $\left(-\sqrt{3},6\right)$ minimum ; $\left(\sqrt{3},6\right)$ minimum
8.   (2, 8) minimum ; (− 2, − 8) maximum

Exercises 8.6

1
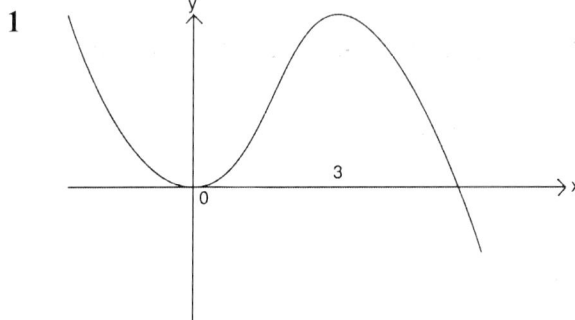

2
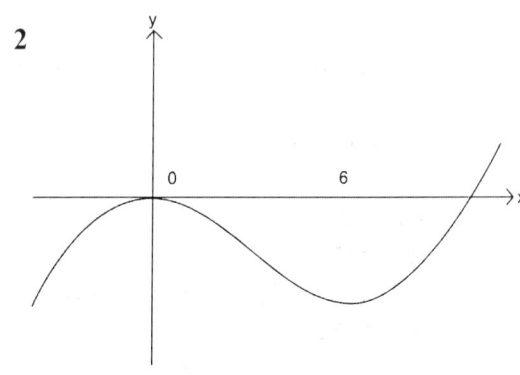

3

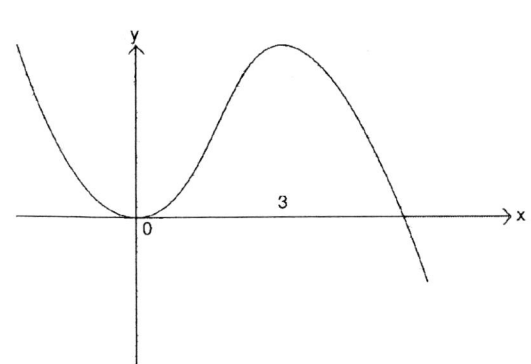

4

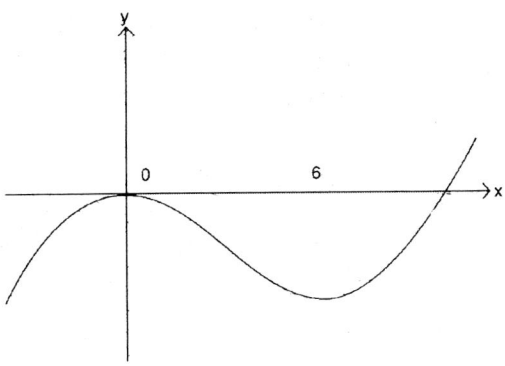

5

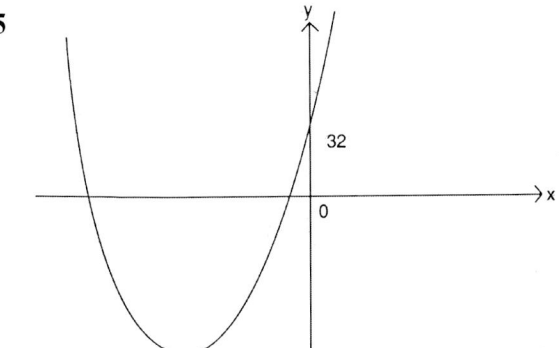

6

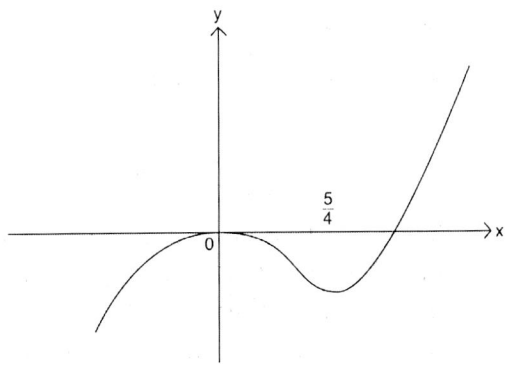

Exercises 8.7

1. 24m   **2.** 4.62cm; 4.62cm (2 decimal places)

3. 1024cm^3 **4.** Depth = 61.24cm, breadth = 43.30cm (2 decimal places)

7. 4000cm^3 **8.** 1.12m^2 (2 decimal places)

Chapter 9

Exercises 9.1

(i) x^3 (ii) x^4 (iii) $x^5 + x^6$

Exercises 9.2

(i) $\dfrac{x^9}{9}$ (ii) $\dfrac{3}{5}x^{\frac{5}{3}}$ (iii) $-6x$ (iv) $-\dfrac{3}{2x^2}$ (v) $\dfrac{2}{3}x^{\frac{3}{2}}$

(vi) $\dfrac{-1}{9x^9}$ (vii) $\dfrac{9}{4x^4}$ (viii) $2\sqrt{x}$ (ix) $\dfrac{-2}{5y^{\frac{5}{2}}}$ (x) $4x - 3x^2 - \dfrac{x^4}{4}$

(xi) $\dfrac{x^2}{2} - \dfrac{1}{x}$ (xii) $\dfrac{1}{3}x^{\frac{3}{2}} + \sqrt{x}$ (xiii) $\dfrac{x^3}{3} + \dfrac{x^2}{2}$ (xiv) $\dfrac{y^5}{5} + 2y - \dfrac{1}{3y^3}$

163

(xv) $x + 2\sqrt{x}$ (xvi) $\dfrac{3x^2}{2} + \dfrac{2x^{\frac{3}{2}}}{3}$ (xvii) $\dfrac{-1}{3x^3} + \dfrac{8}{5}x^{\frac{5}{4}} + 4x^{\frac{3}{4}}$

(xviii) $y^2 - \dfrac{2}{3}y^{\frac{3}{2}} - 6y$ (xix) $\dfrac{2}{7}x^{\frac{7}{2}} + \dfrac{4}{5}x^{\frac{5}{2}} - 2x^{\frac{3}{2}}$ (xx) $y - \dfrac{1}{y}$

(xxi) $\dfrac{y^{n+1}}{n+1}$

Chapter 10
Exercises 10.1

1. $y = \dfrac{x^4}{4} - 1$ 2. $y = x^3 + x^2 + x - 14$

3. $f(x) = x^2 - \dfrac{1}{x}$ 4. $y = 2x^{\frac{3}{2}} - \dfrac{1}{x} + 2x + 3$

Exercises 10.2

1. $4\dfrac{1}{2}$ 2. $10\dfrac{2}{3}$ 3. $2\dfrac{2}{3}$ 6. $\dfrac{8}{15}$ 7. $10\dfrac{2}{3}$

8. $2\dfrac{2}{3}$ 9. $10\dfrac{2}{3}$ 10. $4\dfrac{1}{2}$

INDEX